Thinking and Feeling with the Churches

Proceedings of the
23rd International Congress of Jesuit Ecumenists

Vienna, Austria, 13–19 July 2015

Edited by
Robert J. Daly, S.J. and Patrick Howell, S.J.

Institute for Advanced Jesuit Studies
Boston College
2017

ISBN 978-0-9973167-2-8

Table of Contents

Preface

The 23rd International Congress of Jesuit Ecumenists met from July 13–19 at the Kardinal-König-Haus in Vienna, Austria. Under the leadership of Markus Schmidt, S.J., Jesuits from nineteen provinces gathered to engage the thought-provoking theme: "Thinking and Feeling with the Churches."

Our first evening on Monday, July 13, was devoted to establishing or re-establishing familiarity with each other's work before getting down to the actual work of the congress the next morning. Ten of the wide-ranging presentations and discussions of the next few days were designated for inclusion in these Proceedings. We arrange them here in more or less thematic order.

Edward Farrugia, S.J.'s "St. Ignatius of Loyola, Theology of the Heart and Theological Discord" brought us directly to the heart of the matter: the challenging task of purifying memory in order to move beyond mere particulars to the underlying fundamental issues. To do this, and to help us recognize that our ecumenical malaise is more a dissonance in the Church's heart rather than in its mind, Farrugia suggests that we look to St. Ignatius's theology of the heart as adumbrated, for example, in Annotation 2 of the *Exercises* and helpfully developed by some contemporary Jesuit theologians.

Paolo Gamberini, S.J.'s "The Principle and Foundation of the *sentire cum ecclesiis*" delves directly into the recently much-discussed and much argued question: Where does/do the Church/Churches actually subsist/exist? Gamberini suggests that the apparent inconsistencies in interpretations of the *"subsistit in/*subsists in" of *Lumen gentium* 8 can be at least softened by distinguishing between an *ontological* dimension (the fullness—i.e., without degrees and differentiation) of the Church of Christ (only in the Catholic Church) and a *phenomenological* dimension (participation in a graded way in the presence of Christ—in the other churches). This enables us to think and speak of *sentire* not only in and with the Church but also in and with the churches.

Markus Schmidt, S.J.'s "Sentire in Ecclesia: Its Contribution to the Ecumenical Endeavor" finds resources for a contemporary and authentically ecumenical "Thinking and Feeling with the Churches" in the very text of Ignatius's *Spiritual Exercises*, and specifically in a deep understanding of the much-misunderstood Rules for Thinking with the Church (*SE* 352–370) with which Ignatius brings the *Exercises* to a close.

In his "Thinking with the Church: From Msgr. Oscar Romero to Pope Francis," *Thomas P. Rausch, S.J.* begins by highlighting the ecclesiological similarities in the visions of Church exemplified by two of the most stunningly charismatic Catholic Church leaders of the past few decades. He then points out resonances of this vision in recent position papers of the World Council of Churches, before going on to remind us that it is not in the traditional Western and Northern centers of Christianity but rather in the churches of Asia, Africa, and Latin America that most of the ecclesial potential is to be found.

Next, *Patrick Howell,S.J.*, in "A Theology of Brokenness as a Source for Ecumenical Unity: Collaborative Efforts to Support People with Mental Illness and Their Families" invites us to enter into what he calls the "ecumenism of mental illness," and to become aware that "a Theology of the Cross, a sharing of our life in Christ through our brokenness, sinfulness, healing, and redemption, can be the source of profound ecumenical unity." Howell goes on to detail some of the ways in which this is already being done in some of the Christian Churches.

Jocelyn Rabeson, S.J., in his "Ecumenism and Inculturation or, Thinking and Feeling with the Churches in an African Context" focuses on the vast but still largely unrealized ecumenical potential of the churches in Africa. "The Christianity that came to Africa," he points out, "was and continues to be a divided Christianity." For it is a fact that the impressive and sometimes heroic African efforts at ecumenical rapprochement have, generally, neither reached down to the grass roots level nor been supported by sufficient theological reflection. Ecumenism has not yet become a priority in most African communities. But, on the positive side, suggests Rabeson, the African concept of *Ubuntu*—stressing the interpersonal rather than the ontological aspects of being human—may be the key to the African ecumenicity that we seek.

Moving now back a few centuries to Kerala in Southwest India, *Antony Mecherry, S.J.* in *"Sentir con la iglesia* and Ecumenical Rapprochements of the Sixteenth Century: An Indian Reality" recounts the remarkable situation in which the Jesuits in Rome, even as early as Ignatius and the first decades of Jesuit history were, vis-à-vis the Malabar Christians, discovering and trying to implement what we now recognize as a truer "intra-Catholic" ecumenical policy than were the Jesuit missionaries actually on the local scene.

And sadly, as in our own day we look to Gujarat in Northwest India, we find that interreligious and ecumenical tensions remain part of the Indian religious scene. *Cedric Prakash, S.J.,* in his "Responding Together to an Anti-Christian Climate: The Gujarat United Christian Forum for Human Rights (GUCFHR)" recounts how the need for common self-defense seems to be the primary motive for Christian ecumenical cooperation in that part of India. Whether intended, or not, Prakash's account strongly suggests that, however necessary in particular instances, self-defense alone is not an adequate motive for authentic, lasting Christian unity.

In our penultimate chapter, Dorian Llywelyn, S.J.'s "Both Thinking and Feeling with the Churches: Catholic-Orthodox Ecumenism and Christian Spirituality" challenges us to recognize that, over the past thousand years, as Patriarch Bartholomew put it, "the manner in which we exist has become ontologically different." Therefore, we need an approach that breaks down a wall between cultural anthropology and theology; an approach that begins, for example, not with *theologia secunda*—as is so common in the West—but with an approach rooted in prayerful, doxological *theologia prima*. This would mean a *sentire cum ecclesiis* by beginning with "understanding others not primarily by what they say or think, but rather how they act and feel."

In our final chapter, *Patrick J. Ryan, S.J.*, in his "Thinking and Feeling with the Churches about Islam: Changes from the Early 20th Century to the Early 21st Century" poses the question: "How much can we Jesuits do to help the Catholic Church to think and feel about Islam?" After reverently naming the six deceased Jesuits and humbly invoking the support and blessing of the many still-living Jesuits who have been helping him to begin to answer this question, Ryan, in an attempt to portray the magnitude and complexity of this task, presents the outline of what could be three different major works: *first*, "Catholic Attitudes towards Islam, 1915–2015"; *then*, "Byzantine Orthodox Attitudes towards Islam, 1915–2015"; *and finally*, "Protestant Attitudes towards Islam, 1915–2015."

As we go to press, preparations are already under way for the next meeting of the Jesuit Ecumenists from July 10–15, 2017 at the Centro ad Gentes in Nemi in the Roman Hills. The main theme, under the guidance of Edward Farrugia, S.J., will be "Ignatian Insights for Crises and Councils."

Robert J. Daly, S.J. and Patrick Howell, S.J.
Editors

St. Ignatius of Loyola, Theology of the Heart and Theological Discord

Edward G. Farrugia, S.J.

Heresy, properly understood, is not primarily a matter of propositions. Rather, it is dissonance at the Church's heart, understood with the East as inclusive of the mind. What heals it forms part of that theologia cordis *also present in Ignatius, especially in Annotation 2 of the Exercises. Concord and discord are categories which may help us to understand better the relation between truth and heresy.*

One of the more urgent tasks facing Churches not yet sharing the same communion is to purify memory. A stumbling block towards that goal is that saints revered in one Church are still reviled as sinners in another. The problem is critical. The breakup of communion usually entails not only refusing sacramental hospitality to those not in communion with the Church celebrating, but also not recognizing saints on both sides: that is to say, refusing not only the communion of sinners in the Church on earth, but also the communion of the saints in heaven.[1] Although some Churches are quietly dropping anathemas, it goes much more against the grain to venerate those vilified a short while ago.

As all Catholics should know from the catechism, the Church is infallible when it teaches dogma and morals. Does this infallibility cover the condemnation of heretics? In our times alone Antonio

---

[1] John Zizioulas, "Ecclesiological Issues Inherent in the Relations between Eastern Chalcedonian and Oriental Non-Chalcedonian Churches," *Does Chalcedon Divide or Unite? Towards Convergence in Orthodox Christology*, Paulos Gregorios, William Henry Lazareth and Nikos A. Nissiotis, eds. (Geneva: World Council of Churches, 1981) 138–56 at 140–53.

Rosmini-Serbati[2] (1798–1855), censured in 1887 for a number of his views (DH 3201–3241), has been rehabilitated to the point of being declared Blessed, whereas Honorius (pope, 625–638), in spite of St. Maximus the Confessor's spirited defence of his orthodoxy, was condemned as a heretic at the ecumenical Council of Constantinople III (680–681)—thus not merely for negligence in repressing heresy, as the pro-infallibility lobby at Vatican I claimed, but for downright heresy! However, the respected Jaroslav Pelikan (1923–2006), an Orthodox convert in later life, says: Honorius was only verbally, that is, nominally, a heretic.[3] The rehabilitation of those condemned as heretics renders the question only more poignant—what then is a heretic?

To come straight to the point we must turn to the underlying fundamental issues, rather than the particular cases, and ask: what is then ultimately disruptive in the Church, and, on the other side of the spectrum, what helps heal wounds and restore communion? To compound matters, while the Catholic Church has abandoned, through *Dei verbum*, an exclusively or even a predominantly propositional approach[4] to revelation, many have not kept step with

---

[2] Exonerated in 1855 from charges of unorthodoxy, Rosmini-Serbati was again censured after his death in 1888 when 40 of his propositions were indexed as hardly reconcilable with Catholic truth: *"catholicae veritati haud consonae"* (*DH* 3201–41). In John Paul II's encyclical *Fides et ratio* (1998) no. 74, Antonio Rosmini-Serbati is extolled for promoting a fecund dialogue between the Word of God and philosophy; cf. *Enchiridion delle Encicliche 8: Giovanni Paolo I e Giovanni Paolo II (1978-1998)* (Bologna: Dehoniane, 1998) 1940. Rosmini-Serbati was beatified in 2007 by Benedict XVI.

[3] Jaroslav Pelikan, *The Spirit of Eastern Christendom* (London: University of Chicago Press, 1977) 150–53. The idea of being merely a "nominal heretic" and therefore deep down no heretic at all is an idea espoused by J. Lebon in his treatment of Severian monophysitism; cf. J. Lebon, "La christologie du monophysisme syrien," *Das Konzil von Chalkedon 1. Der Glaube von Chalkedon,* ed. Alois Grillmeier and Herbert Bacht (Würzburg: Echter, 1951) 425–580 at 576–80.

[4] "By divine revelation, God wished to manifest and communicate both himself and the eternal decrees of his will concerning the salvation of humankind" (*Dei verbum* 6), *The Documents of Vatican II,* gen. ed. Austin Flannery, O.P. (Northport, New York: Costello Publishing) 99; Karl Rahner and Herbert Vorgrimler, *Kleines Konzilskompendium* (Freiburg i.Br.: Herder, 1981) 362: "Im I. Kapitel, das von der Offenbarung Gottes selbst handelt, wird manches verdeutlicht, was das

Vatican II and still talk primarily of the infallibility of propositions rather than the indefectibility of the Church, and speak more of heresy than of theological discord. Yet the very word discord gives us a hint: we would come closer to the truth if we saw the malaise as being a dissonance at the Church's heart rather than locate it in its mind, understanding by heart the more comprehensive of the two.

Here we explore whether we can bypass difficulties inherent in a purely propositional approach to truth. Indispensable though it is, the verbal articulation of a truth is not the sole moment. The Church does not teach that the Son is only the Father's Word (Logos), but that he is also his (non-verbal) image as well as "God's Wisdom" (1 Cor 1:24), the Word ultimately pinning down truth to concrete formulations, the image illustrating it in the hues of life and art, and Wisdom raising the issue of the insight dogma affords as well as the opportuneness of certain dogmas without questioning their truth. By taking up just one point from Ignatius as to the heart and its integrative facilities we may then fathom its viability as a sounding board in ecumenical dialogue, and finally draw conclusions on theological currency today and the possibility of its being re-minted.

1. Ignatius and the Theology of the Heart

One will look in vain for a systematic theology of the heart in Ignatius. A perusal of the Indexes of the Exercises show that the

---

Konzil von Trient und das 1. Vatikanische Konzil in einer gewissen Einseitigkeit gesagt hatten, und so wird, wie das Vorwort ankündigte, die Lehre dieser Konzilien wohl nicht revidiert, aber weitergeführt. Dazu gehört, dass Offenbarung als Selbstmitteilung Gottes verstanden wird und darum hinfort nicht mehr intellektualistisch als bloße Mitteilung von Sätzen "über" Gott und seine Heilsabsichten missverstanden werden darf. Sie ist überhaupt nicht nur im Wort und in der Lehre zu sehen, sondern als Einheit von Tat- und Wortoffenbarung, als ereignishaftes Handeln Gottes am Menschen, zu dem das dem Glauben gesagte Wort als ein inneres Wesensmoment gehört." Cf. Joseph Ratzinger, „Revelation Itself," *Commentary on the Documents of Vatican II, vol. 3*, Herbert Vorgrimler, ed. (New York: Herder and Herder, 1969) 170–180 at 170–72.

word *corazón* is not frequent.[5] Though he had earned his theological stirrups at no less a place than the Sorbonne, Ignatius's stature as recognized by posterity was due to his being conversant with God; or, as one would have said in times prior to our own, his knowledge of

---

[5] Dominique Bertrand et al., *Exercices Spirituels* (Paris, 1985) 263. In *San Ignacio de Loyola: Obras Completas*, ed. Ignacio Iparraguirre and Cándido de Dalmases (Madrid: Biblioteca de autores cristianos, 1963) the term *corazón* does not even appear in the indexes. In an inspiring introduction to the fundamental words of St Ignatius's spirituality, *Aus Liebe zur Wirklichkeit: Grundeworte ignatianischer Spiritualität* (Mainz: Matthias-Grünewald Verlag, 1991), Willi Lambert has no special section, not to say chapter, which is dedicated to the heart. One need only shed a glance, for example, at what Lambert says on "Ich Selbst" (i.e. Myself, ibid., 76–77) to convince oneself that the heart is taken into account. Indeed, in the case of a term such as "theology of the heart," much nearer to us than to Ignatius, we have to go beyond the categories used and search for equivalents. For example, when Roland Barthes, in his Preface to the *Spiritual Exercises*, compares the *Exercises* to a cybernetic machine meant to attain equilibrium among the elements of choice (Saint Ignace de Loyola, *Exercices spirituels*, trans. Jean Ristat [Paris: Union générale d'éd, 1972] 29–30, those familiar with Karl Rahner's "'Coeur de Jésus' chez Origène?" *RAM* 14 (1934) 171–74 may recall the German theologian's use of the Greek term *hēgemonikon* for heart. The *hēgemonikon* or the leading or controlling element in man (cf. *A Patristic Greek Lexicon*, ed. G. W. H. Lampe [Oxford: Clarendon Press, 1995] 599–601) would correspond, over and above Rahner, to "cybernetic," deriving from the Greek *kyvernō*: command, control. David M. Stanley, *A Modern Scriptural Approach to the Exercises* (St. Louis, MO: Institute of Jesuit Sources, 1973) 32, comments: "If the time of retreat is a time of listening, as, indeed, my whole life is, I can only listen in the silence of the heart. And by the term 'heart' I mean that innermost part of myself, as the Bible uses the term; that part of me which is unique, that part of me which is most authentic. I must listen with my whole personality, I must worship, I must pray with everything that is most truly myself." And commenting on the prayer, *Shema, Israel* (Deut 6:4–5), on loving God "with all your heart, and with all your soul," Stanley (ibid. 221) further explains: "In the Bible the heart does not symbolize, as among occidental peoples, the emotional affective side of man, but rather that part of man which is most truly himself. Thus it includes his intellectual activity, which is the reason for the strange sounding phrase of the psalmist, employed in the Introit of the Mass of the Sacred Heart, 'the thoughts of his heart. P5 33 (32) 11.'" Of course, it includes also that affective part of the human person which is most genuine. The German translation of A. Deissler, *Die Psalmen*, [Dusseldorf: Patmos, 1964] 135: "die Pläne seines Herzens," or, in English, the scheming of his heart," bring us much closer to the point of coincidence between Hebrew thought and modern parlance.

the matter was "*de arriba*" (from above), an infused knowledge.[6] This divine wisdom tailored so as to be at the reach of the common run may be found in some of his spiritual insights. This creative tension between the long-range divine breakthrough into the world and the human brake of those still lingering[7] in immediate satisfaction finds a resolution, in Ignatius, in what he has to say about the heart.

1.1. *Annotation 2 of the Exercises and the Affections of the Heart*

Although Ignatius did not share our immediate concerns in developing an existential theology of the heart, central places in his writings speak, directly or indirectly, of the heart in a biblical-patristic sense that calls for a wholehearted engagement. His *Contemplatio ad obtinendem amorem* (nos. 230 ff.), the *Suscipe*[8] and the prayer often printed at the beginning of the *Exercises*, *Anima Christi*, may be said to reflect such an integrative aspect.[9] In describing the role of our

---

[6] Hugo Rahner, *Ignatius the Theologian*, trans. M. Barry (New York: Herder and Herder, 1968) 3. This tension of a spiritual gift descending on everyone may be resumed in Luis Gonçales da Camara's quip: "He was affable with all and familiar with none" (ibid. 30).

[7] "A lingering-out swéet skíll" is the way Hopkins describes the long maturation that was needed for the Augustine of the "give me chastity, but not right away" (Gerard M. Hopkins, *The Wreck of the Deutschland*, strophe 10: "Whether at once, as once, at a crash Paul, / Or as Austin, a lingering-out sweet skíll") to become St. Augustine. They represent two of the three times noted by Ignatius for decision-making.

[8] Annotation 5.1 of the *Exercises* (Édouard Gueydan et al., trans., *Ignace de Loyola: Exercices Spirituels* [Paris: Desclée de Brouwer/Montréal:Bellarmin, 1986]) speaks, with reference to the *Suscipe*, of entering the Exercises with a big heart (cf. Annotation 234.2), synonym of generosity, the other references being simply biblical quotations. This translation places references pertinent to a theology of the heart under affections (ibid. p. 260). With regards to the *Suscipe* itself, the adage that one should pray as if everything depended on God and work as if everything depended on oneself is not from Ignatius, but from a Hungarian Jesuit of the 18th century, G. Hevenesi; see Edward G. Farrugia, "Im Banne des Ostens: Werdegang und Zukunftsorientierung des hl. Ignatius von Loyola," in: Andreas Falkner and Paul Imhof, eds. (*Ignatius von Loyola*, Würzburg, Echter, 1990) 406–408, note 27.

[9] One of the reasons for a certain prudence in evoking the thoughts concerned with the heart can be seen in a recent controversy. When Tomáš (later cardinal) Špidlík first wanted to publish his book on Theophan the Recluse, *La doctrine*

faculties in the *Spiritual Exercises*, he touches the cords of the human heart. In the second explanatory note as to how to give and do the *Exercises*, he says:

> This [brief or summary explanation of a point of salvation history] brings more spiritual relish and spiritual fruit than if the one giving the Exercises had lengthily explained and amplified the meaning of the history. For what fills and satisfies the soul consists, not in knowing much, but in our understanding the realities profoundly and in savouring them interiorly (*"porque no es el mucho saber harta y satisfice al anima, mas el sentir y gustar de las cosas internamente"*).[10]

In its literal import, this short annotation makes a contrast between the detailed knowledge one might accrue about a Gospel passage and the sheer delight in tasting the spiritual fruit tendered to us for contemplation in even just one word, during the course of the *Exercises*, or some pertinent comment, capable of galvanizing the attention for long, even in repeated sessions, ultimately able to help us reorder our life priorities. Tarrying on this point may seem like focusing on an insignificant detail, which recalls the hemorrhaging woman touching the hem of Christ's attire (Luke 5:25–34). Why, did Christ perchance not know who had touched him—or is it not rather that Christ, fully aware of what was going on, wanted to haul the woman from the periphery of the assembly's attention to the centre of the happening and so heal her? The points often indicated as stumbling blocks on the way to establishing communion can be trifles

---

spirituelle de Théophane le Recluse: Le Coeur et l'Esprit (Roma: Pontificio Instituto Orientale, 1965), practically all his Jesuit colleagues were against its publication, and it was saved only through the then delegate, René Arnou, S.J., but only at the price of making the title with the heart into a subtitle. Only 39 years later—in 2004—could the work appear with its original title, *Il cuore e lo Spirito: la dottrina spirituale di Teofane il Recluso* (Città del Vaticano, 2004). For the whole controversy, see Edward G. Farrugia, "Un cuore per lo Spirito," in Tomáš Špidlík, "*Lezioni sulla Divinoumanità* (Roma: Lipa, 1995) 30–31.

[10] George E. Ganss, S.J., *The Spiritual Exercises of Saint Ignatius: A Translation and a Commentary* (St Louis, MO: Institute of Jesuit Sources, 1992) 21–22; Ignacio de Loyola, *Ejercicios Espirituales: Introducción, texto, notas y vocabulario por Candido de Dalmases, S.I.* (Santander: Sal Terrae, 1987) 43–44.

which, blown out of all proportion, blur the vision; but reduced to their right dimension, help restore it, by revealing the hidden malaise at the heart of the matter. This resetting of the coordinates is usually called *hierarchia veritatum* (*Unitatis redintegratio* 11), a hierarchy of truths to be established in terms of the relationship of a particular truth to the foundations of faith, from the margin to the center.

1.2. Adolf Haas's Interpretation of This Passage in Its Capacity to Help Develop a Theology of the Heart

Annotation 2,[11] for Haas, is a veritable theology of the heart in a nutshell (*theologia cordis*). On bumping into something new but anchored in the narration—the subjective aspect must go hand in hand with the objective aspect,[12] God's Word. The one doing the Exercises opens as it were a little door leading to an inner vision of the mystery; just as, for instance, Gothic windows are opaque if you look at them from the market place, but illuminate the cathedral if you look at them from within.[13] Ignatius describes in this way the process of acquiring an insight into things, an insider's view of how spiritual things function. Nobody can reckon with an intellectual insight on command, but one may very well receive an inner flash that illumines the gloomy landscape of one's inner world. To reach this point, the scriptural truth must be driven home without apocryphal amalgams. Whereas, on the part of the one doing the

[11] *Ignatius von Loyola, Geistliche Übungen: Übertragung aus dem spanischen Ur-text, Erklärung der 20 Anweisungen von Adolf Haas* (Freiburg i.Br.: Herder, 1967) 130–40. The importance of this Annotation lies in that it shows where the action is in the *Exercises*: i.e., not in the work of the one who gives the *Exercises*, but in the one who "does" them, the activities of the one who does the retreat, forcing the spiritual director into the background.

[12] Erich Przywara, in *Deus semper maior*, vol. 1 (Freiburg i.Br.: Herder, 1938) 20–21, comments on annotation 2 so: the one giving the Exercises has not only the objective order of the matters he offers for consideration in his hand, but also the way of considering this material, the subjective order. This, however, is in part contradicted by Adolf Haas, insofar as the real director of the Exercises is concerned: it is the one doing them, for he stops where he feels struck.

[13] *Ignatius von Loyola, Geistliche Übungen* 131. The image of the Gothic windows derives from Johann Wolfgang v. Goethe (1749–1832).

Exercises, one must let go the desire to rationally restructure what one hears and, in letting go, to let God speak.[14] Again, reaching the boiling point presupposes that God is at work at the other end of the line. Yet, since God is sovereignly free in vouchsafing grace, the one doing the Exercises may only prepare oneself negatively, by removing hindrances.[15] The new discovery must be personal if it is to work: one must be existentially touched if the novelty is to strike home.[16] It is this state of affairs that creates the condition of the possibility of savoring the insight[17] into one's own inner reality;[18] indeed, God loves the cheerful giver (Sir 35:11; 2 Cor 9:6–7).[19] At this point, Ignatius reveals himself to be a connoisseur of the heart, in the sense at least that he knew how to make his own experiences palatable for the

---

[14] *Ignatius von Loyola, Geistliche Übungen* 134.

[15] Relying on the Scholastic adage: "facienti quod est in se Deus non denegat gratiam," i.e. God does not deny grace to one who does his best.

[16] *Ignatius von Loyola, Geistliche Übungen* 141.

[17] "Insight," says Lonergan, "occurs in all human knowledge, in mathematics, natural science, common sense, philosophy, human science, history, theology. It occurs (1) in response to inquiry, (2) with respect to sensible presentations or representations including words and symbols of all kinds. It consists in a grasp of intelligible unity or relation in the data or image or symbol. It is the active ground whence proceed conception, definition, hypothesis, theory, system. This proceeding, which is not merely intelligible but intelligent, provided the human model for Thomist and Augustinian Trinitarian theory"; Bernard Lonergan, *Method in Theology* (New York: Herder and Herder, 1971) 212–13. The importance of insight for the *Exercises* with its prop in the examination of conscience may be brought out as follows: "Thus, insight into insight brings to light the cumulative process of progress"; Bernard Lonergan, *Insight: A Study of Human Understanding,* 5th ed. (Toronto, University of Toronto, 1992) 8.

[18] Willi Lambert, *Aus Liebe zur Wirklichkeit: Grundworte ignatianischer Spiritualität,* 2nd ed. (Mainz: Matthias Grünewald, 1993) 20–21: "Realismus, Wirklichkeitssinn sind keine Haltungen, die man spontan mit Frömmigkeit verbindet. Bei Ignatius kann und muß man das tun. Er kann als Realist unter den Heiligen bezeichnet werden, auch wenn am Anfang seines Weges, pubertäre und skuril wirkenden Großtaten standen. Zumeist ist Ignatius wortkarg und 'läßt Taten sprechen,' doch zeigt auch seine Sprache seine Nähe zur Wirklichkeit: Erfahrung, Werke, Wirklichkeit, Ziel und Mittel, 'Gott in allen Dingen' sind wichtige Begriffe für ihn. Vor allem seine Sicht von Christus als dem 'Herrn und Schöpfer aller Dinge' verweist auf einen 'Glauben, der die Erde liebt' (Karl Rahner)."

[19] *Ignatius von Loyola, Geistliche Übungen* 142.

benefit of others.[20] Ignatius thus had two open books before him: the open Bible and one's open heart. The heart, in the Bible (Lev 9:18; Deut 6:5; Matt 22:34–40), is understood as the personal core of the human, the hub whence all our energies radiate, whether they find expression in our religious and moral acts or in our psychological striving.[21] The heart is not only the midpoint where decisions are taken (Sir 35:11), especially the more they involve the whole person,[22] the fundamental option,[23] but also the seat of memory: "Do not let loyalty and faithfulness forsake you; bind them around your neck, write them on the tablet of your heart!" (Prov 3:3).

1.3. A Short Note on the Theology of the Heart in Contemporary Jesuit Theologians

The publication of Pius XII's *Haurietis aquas* (1956) to mark the first centenary of the extension of the feast of the Sacred Heart to the whole Church served as an occasion for many Jesuits to write on the heart in the context of the Sacred Heart. One need only remember how much space both Hugo and Karl Rahner dedicated to the theme.[24] However, we should not see theological questions relative

---

[20] "Was Ignatius in den Exerzitien vorlegt, erweist ihn weniger als Meister theoretischen Wissens, sondern als Lehrmeister einer Theologie des Herzens"; *Ignatius von Loyola, Geistliche Übungen* 143.

[21] *Ignatius von Loyola: Geistliche Übungen* 142–43.

[22] "Im Herzen fällt die Entscheidung," Anton Dosenberger, Alois Frank, Karl Stelzer, *Die Zehn Gebote: Gesetze des Lebens* (Augsburg: Palotti, 1979) 205.

[23] In his poem "Madrigal," Shakespeare has his own way of distinguishing between central and peripheral decisions, and of the perennial struggle between the mind and the heart for primacy over one another: "Tell me where is Fancy bred, / Or in the heart, or in the head? / How begot, how nourishéd? / Reply. Reply. // It is engender'd in the eyes,/ With gazing fed, and Fancy dies /In the cradle where it lies: / Let us all ring Fancy's knell; /I'll begin it,—Ding, dong, bell./—Ding, dong, bell"; Francis Turner Palgrave and John Press, eds. *The Golden Treasury* (London/New York: Oxford University, 1964) 30–31

[24] One of the publications in Rome was divided into two volumes, one theological and the other historical, both edited by Augustin Bea, Hugo Rahner, Henri Rondet, and Friedrich Schwendimann: *Cor Iesu: Commentationes in Litteras Encyclicas Pii XII "Haurietis Aquas"* 2 vols. (Roma: Herder, 1959). Among the contributors we may list Anibale Bugnini, Charles Boyer, Carlo Colombo,

to the heart as coterminous with those relating to the Sacred Heart, and especially not in the East.[25] We start with Eastern spirituality, where the heart functions like the receptionist of all undertakings, from the prayer of the heart to the divine presence in the heart.[26] The very all-inclusiveness of the concept seemed too much for the speculative Greeks, who translated the Hebrew *lev* into Greek *nous*, or mind.[27] A reaction was bound to set in, and this was to find a record in the Russian Theophan the Recluse's theology of the heart,[28] which takes the heart simply for a synonym of my I.[29] As Hugo Rahner put it, his brother's "Theologie des Symbols" is a synthesis of all his theology.[30] Hugo's doctoral dissertation (1931), *Fons Vitae*, was on John 7:37–38, water gushing in streams from the side (Christ's? the thirsty believer's), and Karl's (1936), *E latere Christi* on John 19:34.[31] Both works are important, because they do the necessary spadework for the subsequent elaboration of *Realsymbol*, which

Salvatore Garofalo, Franz Lakner, Karl Rahner, Antonio Piolanti, David M. Stanley, and Sebastian Tromp.

[25] Mauricio Gordillo, "La devoción oriental al Sagrado Corazón de Jesús y la encíclica 'Haurietis aquas'," *Cor Jesu* 2.265–90. With more reserve Tomáš Špidlík, in "Il cuore nella spiritualità russa," in R. Faricy, E. Malatesta, eds., *Cuore di Cristo: cuore dell'uomo* (Neapoli: Dehoniane, 1982) 49–73 indicates Boris P. Vyšeslavcev as one who could see the continuity between the Eastern and the Western sense of the heart, including the Sacred Heart.

[26] Tomáš Špidlík, *The Spirituality of the Christian East*, trans. Anthony P. Gythiel (Kalamazoo, MI: Cistercian Publications, 1986) 103.

[27] Špidlík, *Spirituality* 104. This is at the root of many misunderstandings in reading the Greek Fathers; that is, the Logos-Nous Christology is often taken *tout court* as an intellectualistic reduction of the heart.

[28] Špidlík, *The Spirituality* 105.

[29] Theophan the Recluse puts it this way: "The function of the heart consists in feeling everything that touches our being. Consequently, the heart always feels the condition of body and soul as well [as] the multiform impressions created by concrete activity, whether spiritual or physical, the things that surround us or cross our path and, in general, the course of life"; quoted in Špidlík, *Spirituality* 105.

[30] Hugo Rahner, "Eucharisticon Fraternitatis," in Johann Baptist Metz, Walter Kern, S.J. et al. eds., *Gott in Welt*, 2 vols. (Freiburg i.Br.: Herder, 1964) 2.895–99 at 896.

[31] Andreas R. Batlogg, "Editionsbericht," *Karl Rahner, Sämtliche Werke*, vol. 3 (Freiburg i.Br.: Herder, 1999) xvii-xliii.

may be rendered as that non-conventional type of symbol capable of rendering what it promises on account of its ontological connection, of which sacraments are by no means the only example. Hugo's study, "Flumina de ventre Christi," pleads, with the Antiochene tradition, for interpreting the *koilia*, belly, or better still, the heart, in question (John 7:38) as Christ's.[32] In his *Theologie des Symbols* K. Rahner starts out by saying that the heart of Jesus is the symbol of his love, a *Realsymbol*[33] (*STh*[34] IV, 279), around which all the themes of dogmatic theology gravitate (*STh* IV, 29 1ff). The ontology underpinning theology would go awry without such a *Realsymbol* (*STh* IV, 276, 291). The theology of the Logos is the most profound theology of the Symbol, therefore of the Trinity—the Word as the perfect reflection of the Father and consequently of the Trinity (*STh* IV, 291–93), and accordingly of Christology also, where the humanity of Christ is the real symbol of the Logos (*STh* IV, 293–99), again reflected in the theology of the sacraments, which deliver what they promise (*STh* IV, 299–301). It is this symbol, by no means a conventional one, but a direct reflection of the real, for the East the quintessence of all religions,[35] in the West

[32] Hugo Rahner, "Flumina de ventre Christi: Die patristische Auslegung von Joh 7:37–38," *Symbole der Kirche: Die Ekklesiologie der Väter* (Salzburg: Müller, 1964) 175–235 at 233–35.

[33] The term *Realsymbol*, suggested by Hugo Rahner through his work with the Byzantinologist, the Catholic priest Franz Dölger (See Karl H. Neufeld, *Die Brüder Rahner: Eine Biographie* (Freiburg i.Br.: Herder, 2004) 26, 92, 196–207 and 237, was meant to be a safeguard against the riotous use of symbols in the comparative religions school. On the other hand, the term is completely at home in Catholic theology; Charles de Journel uses instead "ontological symbol"; Charles Journet, *Primauté de Pierre dans la perspective protestante et dans la perspective catholique* (Paris: Alsatia, 1953), in his answer to Oscar Cullmann on the symbol in *Pierre: disciple, apôtre, martyr: histoire, et théologie* (Neuchatel: Delachaux & Niestlé, 1952). As a concept, real symbol is contradistinguished from a conventional symbol, precisely because the symbol and the symbolized in real symbol have an intrinsic link tying them together. Obviously, this intrinsic link goes beyond the intrinsic link at the physical level between smoke and fire, the link of real symbol being theological or spiritual by nature.

[34] Karl Rahner, "Zur Theologie des Symbols," *Schriften zur Theologie*, IV (Einsiedeln: Benziger, 1967) 275–311.

[35] „La nozione del cuore . . . occupa il posto centrale nella mistica, nella religione e nella poesia di tutti i popoli" (P. Vyeslavcev, quoted in Špidlík, "Il cuore

increasingly upgraded as an antidote against a sterile rationalism and in the ongoing dialogue with the East; it is this symbol that is at stake in our considerations here.

An important symbolical relation that Karl Rahner fails to mention here is the relation between dogma and spirituality, which is not simply devotion associated with dogma but lived-out dogma. He will mention it later on in the *Grundkurs* and elsewhere as essential to the all-embracing horizon within which all theology must be done, especially in relation to faith and experience, the cross, and the reflection on the unity of theology, and in terms of the unity of theology and philosophy, theory and praxis, dogmatic theology and fundamental theology, and the unity of dogma and spirituality.[36]

2. The Breaking of the Heart: Concord and Discord

Indeed, it is this all-comprehensive heart, with solid roots in the Bible, the Fathers, and theology, that is broken when schism is proclaimed or heresy taught. It is this all-integrating heart that we celebrate in the third Mass of Christmas, the three Masses being for the three births of the Logos—the eternal generation from the bosom of the Father, the temporal birth from the womb of Mary, and the mystical birth from the heart of the faithful.[37] And if we are tempted to think that this is all too vague, that would augur ill for building bridges with the Orthodox, for whom the liturgy plays roughly the same role in their theology that philosophy does in Western dogmatic theology, nay, more, because it is covered by the *lex orandi, lex credendi*

nella spiritualità russa" in Faricy and Malatesta, eds., *Cuore di Cristo* 49–73 at 49).

[36] Karl Rahner, *Foundations of Christian Faith*, trans. William V. Dych (New York: Seabury, 1978) 1–23; see Edward G. Farrugia, *Aussage und Zusage: zur Indirektheit der Methode Karl Rahners veranschaulicht an seiner Christologie* (Rome: Pontificia Universita Gregoriana, 1985) 118–26.

[37] See Hugo Rahner, "Die Gottesgeburt: Die Lehre der Kirchenväter von der Geburt Christi aus dem Herzen der Kirche und der Gläubigen," *Symbole der Kirche: Die Ekklesiologie der Väter* (Salzburg: Müller, 1964) 79. The interpretation goes back to Pope Innocent III (pope 1198–1216).

axiom.[38] The thought, however, of the heart into which Christ is born as being the heart of the Church and the faithful has penetrated even popular piety: If Christ were born a thousand times in Bethlehem, but not within you, he would have been born in vain.[39]

2.1. The Hardening of the Categories

It is in this context that the question comes up: what then is heresy? Heresy has generally been defined in terms of propositions or dogmas rejected. Yet Vatican II has abandoned the idea of revelation which may be reduced to a series of propositions (*Dei verbum* 2), it must thus be more inclusive, indeed, it must be all-inclusive as summing up all that may be said of God disclosing himself to the world and, in its all-inclusiveness, it can only be grasped by that integrative organ that is the heart. Heresy is, further, distinguished from apostasy which, on the one hand, rejects the whole structure of faith, and schism which, on the other hand, only goes against Church order. This distinction, though classic, needs to be supplemented by being seen primarily from the wider context of the theology of the symbol as the theology of the heart so as to render its use more supple in the purification of memory.

How then should we define heresy? We have to take into account various aspects. Eastern canon law, here re-echoing the Latin code, defines a heretic as a baptized "person who denies some truth that must be believed by divine and Catholic faith, or calls it into doubt" (*CCEO* 1436.1). Among the progress achieved is that now only relapsed Catholics, in effect, may be considered to be heretics,[40] not, however,

---

[38] The maxim is ascribed to St. Prosper of Aquitaine (ca. 390–ca. 463) (*DH* 246).

[39] Angelus Silesius is the name the German mystical poet Johannes Scheffler (1624–1677) assumed on becoming a Catholic.

[40] In the PIO-Benedictine Code of 1917 (c. 1325.2, we read as follows: "*Post receptum baptismum si quis, nomen retinens christianum, pertinaciter aliquam ex veritatibus fide divina et catholica credenda denegat aut de ea dubitat, haereticus; si a fide christiana totaliter recedit, apostata; si denique subesse renuit Summo Pontefici aut cum membris Ecclesiae ei subiectis communicare recusat, schismaticus est.*" Therefore, in the Code of 1917, the category of heretic applied within the

those born into a separation: "However, one cannot impute the sin of separation to those who at present are born into these Communities and are instilled therein with Christ's faith" (*UR* 3).[41] Yet we have failed to make capital of such a switch in ecclesiological mood and to ask such questions as: could we not adopt a similar distinction when it comes to a *bona fide* agent who really wanted the good of the Church, sought to implement it and was even ready to suffer and die for his convictions? Would there be alternative categories capable of doing justice to the changed situation and to the particular case of those in difficulties? And, dealing with non-heretics, formally considered, does this give us means to burn the bridges and rush to conclusions?

Real yet good-intentioned heretics are few, and one can understand why.[42] The traditional distinction between *material* (unwittingly holding heretical positions, condemned by the Church) and *formal* (whoever clings pertinaciously to error) heretics shows how unlikely it is that people willing to die for their religious convictions also do so in order to explicitly contradict God's authority.[43] Basically, the heretic is one who lacks the suppleness to resonate with the trends of the times, lacking a *hierarchia veritatum*. The moment of truth he exaggerates is due to the fact that he loses sight of the relation of his important insight of reform to the fundamentals of faith. Though rare, however, especially when an age has as its priority dialogue and understanding, heresy makes the whole edifice rickety, for it attacks the heart of the Church. It destroys the concord of the Church. Heretics sow the seeds of discord; the Christian theologian propagates the truth that will make us free, the presupposition of concord.

category of whoever was baptized.

[41] *The Documents of Vatican II*, Walter M. Abbott, gen. ed. (Baltimore, 1966) 345. For a commentary on *UR* 3 see Johannes Feiner, "Commentary on the Decree", *Commentary on the Documents of Vatican II*, 5 vols., Herbert Vorgrimler, gen. ed. (New York: Herder and Herder, 1968) 2.57–164 at 71: the sense can only be that of being in *bona fide* in the continued separation.

[42] For the problematic nature of the category of heresy nowadays see Wolfgang Huber, "Häresie III. Systematisch-Theologisch," *TRE* 14 (1985) 341–48.

[43] Christopher O'Donnell, *Ecclesia: A Theological Encylopedia of the Church* (Collegeville, MN: Liturgical Press, 1996) 192.

2.2. Concord and Discord

In this sense, the words concord and discord portray very well that both truth and its opposite depend on the heart. If we want to see how little platitudinous this thesis is, we need only look at current praxis among theologians. Right from the start one may object that although Catholics and Orthodox have the *Realsymbol* in common—call it ontological symbol, iconic relation, real symbol or the heart—nonetheless the same does not hold true of the Protestants.[44] For this one may offer the answer that the winning card in the dialogue with Protestants would be the image of God as found in the Rhenish mystics such as Meister Eckhart[45] (1260–1328), Jan van Ruysbroeck (1293–1381) and John Tauler (ca. 1300–1361) and, a tradition held in common between Protestants and Catholics, ultimately is a throwback to the *Realsymbol*.[46] In his "Theology of the Image" Vladimir Lossky remarks that the Old Testament's image of God in the human person especially regarding Gen 1:26–27 would be insufficient to ground a religious anthropology on the notion of the image of God on the

---

[44] A personal note may here help to underline this truth. On visiting Karl Rahner as a doctoral student and passing on to him Prof. Eberhard Jüngel's greetings, Rahner explained, spontaneously, that the difference between himself and Jüngel was—the real symbol!

[45] Adolf Haas, in his "Meister Eckhart," in Gerhard Ruhbach, Josef Sudbrack, eds., *Grosse Mystiker: Leben und Wirken* (München: C. H. Bock, 1984) 166, remarks: "Der 'Adel der Seele' besteht nun genau in der Abgeschiedenheit, darin der 'innere Mensch,' der 'Geist,' das 'Bild Gottes in der Seele' zu sein, Leben und Seligkeit der Schau Gottes durchbricht." This image of God in the human person, also called the divine spark, is what enables us to be divinized: when humans divest themselves of all earthly attachment, then they can be divinized. Since Luther was greatly influenced through this *theologia deutsch*, it represents hope that one day we can bridge the gap between many concepts which seem too far-fetched to the Protestants, but very close to the Orthodox; Rudolf Haubst, "Theologia deutsch," LThK² 10 (1965) 61–62; Gerhard Ruhbach, "Theologia Deutsch," *LThK³* (2000) 1434; Christian Peeters, "Theologia deutsch," *TRE* 33 (2002) 258–62. See also Bernard McGinn, "Meister Eckhart: Mystical Teacher and Preacher," *The Harvest of Mysticism in Medieval Germany (1300–1500)* (New York: Crossrsoad, 2005) 94–194.

[46] Vladimir Lossky, "The Theology of the Image," *In the Image and Likeness of God*, John H. Erickson and Thomas E. Bird, eds. (Crestwood, NY: St. Vladimir's Seminary Press, 1974) 125–39.

basis of the Hebrew text, since the Hebrew text is concerned with the transcendental gap between God and his creatures, not with any intrinsic link or continuity between them.[47] It is quite different if we turn to the New Testament and seek the real symbolical valence in the Son as the Logos and image of the Father (Col 1:14; 2 Cor 4:4), for through his incarnation and redemptive work, Christ has bridged the gap between the uncreated Creator and created reality.[48]

Like all extremes the heresy of the sincere thinker and the truth of the uncompromising believer have much in common, just as sickness may deliver the best lesson on health, as many know who learn what they should have done and what they have avoided only when the doctor's verdict is brought home to them. Yet as with the problem of good and evil it is not evil itself which is a problem, for evil itself cannot survive on its own but only as a parasite of the good, and at any rate, good is philosophically speaking no less of a problem for how can there be anything rather than nothing at all? Certainly, Bergson retorted that the question presupposes an already existing being and is thus an issue that begs the question.[49] The problem is rather the *coexistence* of good and evil in the same person, in the same community, to which the parable of the tares is a telling example. In theology, however, the question is infinitely better than quibbling over philosophical issues. In this sense, the history of theology, with its mysticism and heresies, with its insights and cul-de-sacs, resembles the larger history of the human kind, struggling for recognition and survival, with so many victories and defeats, but also drawing closer to the finish line. The very history of heresy reveals the human desire for God and the human search for salvation, especially the truth about all this.[50]

---

[47] Lossky, "The Theology of the Image" 129.

[48] Lossky, "The Theology of the Image" 133–39.

[49] Henri Bergson, *Oeuvres, édition de centenaire* (Paris: Presses univ. de France, 1961).

[50] To which, see Goethe's famous line in the Prologue to *Faust* I: "Es irrt der Mench so lang er lebt / Wer immer wieder sich bestrebt, den können wir er-retten": "Man errs so long as he lives—but if he keeps trying he can be saved."

2.3. Reformer's Blessed Rage for Order

The term is borrowed from David Tracy's work, *Blessed Rage for Order.*[51] Surprisingly, he nowhere discusses the feverish desire of the reformers to bring what they consider to be their corrupt Church into line. One such reformer is surely Jan Hus, who was burnt at the stake 602 years ago in 1415. If one wants to realize in a few words how difficult it is for us mortals to discern between rival factions and theories, one need only remember what Philip Hughes says in his history of the Council of Constance:

> There are three really remarkable councils in the fifteenth century,— councils of a new kind altogether—that took place all within forty years: Pisa, where two rival popes were declared no pope at all (on their refusal to resign) and a third was elected, a council never reckoned as a General Council; Constance, which deposed the pope who summoned it (the Pisan pope), accepted the resignation of one of those "deposed" at Pisa, deposed the third of the rivals, and finally elected a pope whom the whole Church acknowledged as pope; Basel, a council lawfully called, dissolved, then revived, then dissolved again on its refusal to accept its translation to Ferrara, and finally—as a kind of rival to the Ferrara Council—condemned anew, to be for all time henceforth (and especially for the sixty years that followed) the very symbol of the theory that popes are subject to general councils, and to make the very word council ominous in papal ears.[52]

What does error mean at a time when everybody seemed to be in error, when even saints found it hard to decide which pope to obey, with St. Catherine of Siena (ca. 1347—1380) siding with the Roman Pope Urban VI (pope 1378–1389) while St. Vincent Ferrer (1350–1419) sided at least for a long time, with the Spanish pope Pedro de Luna (pope 1394–1417)? Or at least, can we blame almost anyone for

---

[51] David Tracy, *Blessed Rage for Order* (New York, Seabury, 1976). It is remarkable that this original work nowhere discusses heresy and the reformers' unconditional desire to reform what they consider to be a corrupt Church, but remains indebted to the attempt to sedate pluralism and enable all theologians to agree.

[52] Philip Hughes, *The Church in Crisis: A History of the Twenty Great Councils* (London: Burns & Oates, 1961) 228.

feeling confused? Need one wonder that in the urgency of reform many councils see nothing else? Are not many good-intentioned heretics characterized by an invincible ignorance?

3. *Concordia dissonantium*

Here we can only draw some tentative conclusions:

(a) First, by eliminating Hus in such an unfair way, Constance started with a goal of its own and finished with a stalemate. Norman Tanner, S.J. commented:

> In my opinion the Council of Constance should be considered a general council of the western church and its three major decrees be taken as authentic. There remains the problem of how to reconcile them with other statements of the Church's magisterium, especially the decrees of Vatican I on the papal office. But it is more correct to leave the various statements alongside each other, in a certain healthy tension, than to seek a consistency that does not exist.[53]

The three decrees in question can be interpreted as an exception for which by its very unusual nature it is hard to legislate in advance. It need not, and should not be interpreted as a concession to conciliarism.[54]

(b) Had Dante known Russian he could have created for impatient reformers a special accommodation close to purgatory and invented a category not of *strastoterpzij*, those who patiently bore their sufferings, used for Sts. Boris and Gleb, (d. 1015 and 1019), but *neterpzostrastnjie* (impatient sufferers).

(c) The very idea of heresy should be revised to bring it in line with Vatican II. Our traditional idea of heresy is too tied down to the intellectualist idea of denying truths recognized officially as such by the Church, but, as we have seen, already *Dei verbum* has relativized

---

[53] Norman P. Tanner, *The Councils of the Church: A Short History* (New York: Crossroad, 2001) 70.

[54] Conciliarism as the heresy of the superiority of an ecumenical council over the pope was definitely condemned at Lateran V in 1516 (*DH* 1445).

the propositional theory of truth. So instead of defining the heretic as going against the mind of the Church, we could better understand him as going against the heart of the Church, heart meant as the highest principle of integration of Church life and thought. And if heart is a symbol and the Sacred Heart is the highest symbol, then the heretic is one who disrupts the correspondence between the symbol and the symbolized, and is left with a pottery shard broken in two for future generations to try to put together again. Without such an integrative symbol, orthodoxy is unduly emphasized at the expense of orthopraxis. Does this mean that propositions defined by the magisterium are useless? Of course not. They are an indispensable element as object of the assent of faith, indispensable but not sufficient. Indeed, a person who does not understand the exact meaning of what the Churches proposes for our assent is not thereby a heretic if he accepts whatever the Church proposes for our assent, whereas someone who understands but does not give his assent, is. What the common run perhaps understands of the more demanding dogmas like the Trinity is a caricature, but they are saved because, to paraphrase St. Ignatius of Antioch and St. Irenaeus of Lyons, they follow their bishop.[55] At the same time, can we consider someone who is ready to die for his convictions to be a heretic—or not rather an "orthodox of desire," on the model of baptism of desire? When his executioners set the stake on fire, Jan Hus sang thrice in a loud voice: "Christ, Son of the living God, have mercy on me."[56]

---

[55] By all the differentiated message in St. Ignatius of Antioch's authentic letters, the insistence on the obligatory reference to the bishop as guarantee of Church unity is meant to sidetrack the arbitrariness of the Docetists' or Judaizers' criterion of knowledge, succumbing to appearances and plausibility; Mikael Isacson, *To Each Their Own Letter: Structure, Themes and Rhetorical Strategies in the Letters of Ignatius of Antioch* (Stockholm: Almqvist & Wiksell, 2004) 186–92. The same holds true of St. Irenaeus, who against the Gnostics' pretentious appeal to private revelations, appealed to the public criterion of the Scriptures and their public valence (St. Irenaeus, *Adversus haereses* 3.1–3).

[56] Ernst Werner, *Jan Hus: Welt und Umwelt eines Prager Frühreformators* (Weimar: Böhlaus, 1991) 214. One is struck by the fact that the prayer is very close indeed to the Jesus Prayer of the East.

And Jerome of Prague, his follower, died at the stake the following year (1416) in prayerful recollection[57]—in stark contradistinction to the Grand Master of the Templars, who, dying at the stake, called out both Philip the Fair for having intrigued during the Council of Vienne (1311–1312) to expropriate the Knight Templars, and Pope Clement V before the throne of God (both died within a year).

3.2. Beyond the Heresy-Truth Defile

With all the insistence on the assent of faith and obedience to the pastors of the Church, we may forget to do something for dissenters in the Church, those who though they love the Church dearly in their heart of hearts do not feel understood or even welcome. Theology can progress only if we steer abreast of both error (including heresy) and intolerance.

According to linguistic analysis, disagreement is not a bad thing in itself; it is the vehicle through which the genuine position is reached. A typical example: strikers will agree to return to work not if one agrees with the principles underlying the conflict, but if the employers agree to raise the pay. From this they draw the conclusion that it is not agreement on the facts that ultimately clinches the deal but the attitudes, or, if you like, not the ontology, but the psychology. We can thus take a more positive look at disagreement itself, though we may still frown on discord. Why? Discord, as the very word structure betrays, is a sort of verbal heart attack, a failure of nerves. The Church can thrive on disagreement, but not on discord.

Discord is the opposite of concord, but both can combine in seemingly contradictory formulations, as in Gratian's masterpiece, *Concordia discordantium canonum* (1140–1142).[58] Discord is not just disagreement, but that kind of disagreement that disrupts the throbbing heart of the Church. Thus, disagreement is certainly

---

[57] E. Amann, "Jérôme de Prague," *DThC VIII* 986–995 at 994: "Il mourut avec un courage héroïque, en donnant jusqu'au but les margues de la plus grande pieté et de la plus absolue confiance en Dieu."

[58] Known more commonly as the *Decretum Gratiani*, it served as the basic text for the study of canon law in the West until replaced in 1918 by the *Codex Iuris Canonici*.

not obnoxious when people agree to disagree. The Church should encourage in all things that are not essential (*"in dubiis libertas"*), given that most disagreements would seem to be minutiae,[59] although a fraction of an error in mathematics can cause an airplane crash. But discord and concord do have something in common—the heart and its cords. Indeed, while there is a disagreement that is insidious of society, society is also built on disagreement. A person's attitude to one's wife should be different from all other people's attitude.

3.3. Better to Prevent Than to Heal

Trying to purify memory means first of all trying to do something about those who were condemned unjustly or even without a fair trial, especially when their credentials for sincerity and an upright life come from both friend and foe, as with Hus.[60] On 29 September 1965 Cardinal Beran of Prague issued an apology, perhaps the first of the kind that have been issued in recent times, offering his excuses for the way the Church had dealt with the Hus question.[61] With some important dialogues outstanding, one could wish that the names of Nestorius and of Theodore of Mopsuestia may emerge cleared of the charges which have hung over their heads for centuries, a decision which should be left to the highest Church authorities, especially since a pertinent dialogue is under way. But to purify memory means

---

[59] Constantine's initial reaction to the Arian crisis, perhaps the most famous heresy in Byzantine history, was to dismiss it as a trifle.

[60] Werner says in lapidary fashion that Bishop Jacob of Lodi (who preached at the Hus trial) did not even allow for his universally praised moral uprightness; see Ernst Werner, *Jan Hus: Welt und Umwelt eines Prager Frühreformators* (Weimar: Böhlaus, 1991) 213.

[61] Winfried Ehrhard, "Hus, Hussiten," *LThK³* 5, 340–43 at 341. As a matter of fact, John Paul II, addressing an international Symposium on Jan Hus held in December of 1999, expressed his apologies for the death inflicted on Hus and the consequent divisions created among the Bohemian faithful; see the informative (as yet unpublished) paper of Zdzisław J. Kijas, O.F.M.Conv., "Eretico o Santo? La figura di Jan Hus dal punto di vista teologico e ecclesiale." Member of the Congregation for the Cause of Saints, Fr. Kijas reaches the conclusion that Hus was not a heretic, for he basically moved on the moral level rather than the dogmatic level (9), arguing at the same time that his canonization is neither necessary nor opportune (12). See, on this point, Werner, *Jan Hus* 214–15.

at the same time so to promote a living theology as to prevent similar repetitions of the same. So here are some suggestions.

a) In a truly ecumenical council where non-Catholics may sit not only as observers but as partners, one may hope for a general revision of so many condemnations in the past. After a millennium and a half of reproaches, all dialogues between Chalcedonians and non-Chalcedonians have established full convergence in that issue which triggered one of the worst schisms of all times.[62] The popes and the heads of Churches concerned signed common declarations to this tune, thanks to the pioneering work of *Pro Oriente*. While the Church, given her mission, cannot overlook false teaching, it should clear the names of those who prove to be innocent.

b) Many theologies are not false, but just unbalanced, and they are unbalanced because they have a tenuous connection to Scripture or because they fail to distinguish between traditions which may be regional and Tradition which is a vehicle of the Word of God. From a Western perspective, light-heartedness with the Word of God makes a theology superficial, even superfluous, but from an Eastern perspective, balance is attained through an iconic dimension. "In effect, the loss of an iconic consciousness in the West has rendered dogma cerebral, morality voluntaristic, and liturgy ritualistic. Without beauty, truth is less true and truth is less good."[63] Both perspectives are necessary.

---

[62] Harding Meyer, Paulos Gregorios, William Henry Lazareth, Nikos A. Nēssiōtēs, eds., *Dokumente wachsender Übereinstimmung* (Geneva: World Council of Churches, 1981) 3–16.

[63] Sante Babolin, "La teologia orientale dell'icona," in: *Credere oggi* (1986) 76; quoted in Edward G. Farrugia, *Introduzione alla teologia orientale: sussidio per la scuola* (Roma: Ed. Pisani, 1997) 82: "L'importanza della teologia iconica scaturisce da un presupposto antropologico e ontologico: le linee portanti dell'antropologia sono la logica (intelligenza), la morale (volontà e libertà) e l'estetica (sensibilità), inoltre la sintesi dei trascendentali dell'essere, della verità e della bontà, è la bellezza . . . Infatti la perdita dell'icona, nell'Occidente, ha reso cerebrale la dogmatica, voluntaristica la morale, ritualistica la liturgia. Senza la bellezza, la verità è meno vera, la bontà è meno buona. La presenza dell'icona, accolta e compresa, trasforma la dogmatica in preghiera, la morale in amore, la liturgia in rito vivo di identificazione simbolica con la Chiesa orante, nel coinvolgimento di tutta la persona, anima e corpo, mediante dei divini misteri."

c) We note the presence of such unbalances very much with us. The Latin Code that goes by the name of the Code of Canon Law, is really the *Code of Latin Canon Law*, whereas the Eastern Code—itself, for all its deficiencies, a giant step forward—is known as *The Code of Canons of the Eastern Churches*.

d) We usually speak of Church History when what we actually mean is Western Church history, whereby the Eastern Churches are given a step-fatherly treatment. In this way, prejudice and unbalance is ingrained from the start.

Conclusion

After so much talk of heresy and heretics, concord and discord, I'd like to finish in the same tone in which I started: that self-searching which sees the sectarian in ourselves[64] before ever pointing a finger against others, that spiritual tone which measures criticism of others on the model of self-criticism, and reflecting how much ecumenism stands to gain from such a dialogical attitude towards ourselves. So I quote Thomas J. Green, S.J.:

> I have reached the conclusion that the greatest obstacle against genuine discernment (and against true growth in prayer) is not the ineffable nature of God but . . . the fact that we do not know ourselves sufficiently, nor do we even want to know ourselves for what we really are. Almost all of us hide behind a mask, not only in front of others, but also when we look in front of the mirror.[65]

How true, how bitterly true of failure in ecumenism! If only we had managed to spot the sectarian in ourselves, instead of being ever ready to condemn rather than to condone, if only we had not failed to see that ecumenism starts at home, then we would have

---

[64] Edward G. Farrugia, "The Sectarian in Us," *Tradition in Transition: The Vitality of the Christian East* (Rome: Mar Thoma Yogam, 1966) 205–34.

[65] My English translation of Green as quoted by Laura Bonanni, *Desiderio di equilibrio: L'Analisi Transazionale in dialogo con gli Esercizi Spirituali Ignaziani* (Bologna: Pardes, 2006) 15.

come a long way toward helping the Church to come to grips with real heresy wherever necessary. For this, however, the awe before the ineffable mystery of truth should go hand in hand with the humble admission of our own limitations, a wedding possible only in the marriage chamber of the heart (in the language of the mystics) to which only God possesses the key.

Edward G. Farrugia, S.J. teaches dogma and Eastern patristics at the Pontifical Oriental Institute, Rome. One of his favorite themes is the relationship between dogma and spirituality.

The Principle and Foundation of the *sentire cum ecclesiis*

PAOLO GAMBERINI, S.J.

The sacramental dimension of the Church of Christ[1] is the principle and foundation of the common sentire cum ecclesiis. This has been well expressed in Vatican II's subsistit in in Lumen gentium 8. Much "dissent" (dissentire) rather than "consent" (sentire) happened in the post-conciliar theological and ecumenical debate. A renewed appraisal of the sacramental reality of the Church of Christ may lead us to a fulfilled sentire cum ecclesiis.

During the time of the most hostile confrontation between the Church of Rome and the Church of England in the 16th and 17th centuries the book of the *Spiritual Exercises* of Saint Ignatius did not loose its appreciation among Anglicans.[2] The *Spiritual Exercises* had been given and received by Protestants even during those turbulent years. Some specific Roman Catholic doctrinal elements, however, were dropped off and changed into a much more Calvinist approach. The practice of addressing Mary in the meditation on the Two

---

[1] Throughout this article, the phrase "the Church of Christ" refers *not* to those Protestant denominations called "The Church of Christ: or "The Churches of Christ" but to the transcendently universal meaning that it has in *Lumen gentium* 8.

[2] Michael C. Questier, "'Like Locusts over all the World': Conversion, Indoctrination and the Society of Jesus in late Elisabethan and Jacobean England," in Thomas M. McCoog, ed., *The Reckoned Expense: Edmund Campion and the early English Jesuits* (Woodbridge: Boydell, 1996) 346. See Victor Houliston, *Catholic Resistance in Elisabethan England. Robert Person's Jesuit Polemic 1580-1610* (Burlington: Ashgate, 2007); Ernest Edwin Reynolds, *Campion and Parsons: The Jesuit Mission of 1580-1* (London: Sheed and Ward, 1980); Francesca Bugliani Knox, *The Eye of the Eagle: John Donne and the Legacy of Ignatius Loyola* (Oxford: Peter Lang, 2011).

Standards was either set apart or substituted by mentioning the Holy Spirit (instead of Mary); the word "confession" was interpreted in a broader sense and not merely as ritual or sacramental; for instance, "doing penance" was changed to "being repentant"; words like merit and purgatory were avoided. The rules for thinking with the Church (*sentire cum ecclesia*) were mitigated and adapted to the Anglican ethos. The Anglican understanding of "obedience" does not eliminate "discretion" and does not mean or imply "blind obedience."

According to John Donne and later commentaries on the book of the *Exercises*, the recognition of the authority of the Church must always be reconciled with personal discretion. John Donne suggested that "the wings of obedience should have eyes to discern, namely that we know whom and what we are obeying."[3] According to John Donne, we should not obey things that are neither essential articles of faith nor authentic laws or decrees of the Catholic Church. Extending such *theological* and *ecclesiological* obedience to issues regarding the temporal jurisdiction of the Pope over princes and subjects would mean stepping on the blood of the martyrs' faith.

William Hawks Longridge, a member of the Anglican religious Society of Saint John, published in 1919 a translation, with commentary, on the *Exercises* from the Spanish Autograph, which had many editions up to 1950. Then in 1931 he wrote *A Month's Retreat for Religious,* a popular publication used for the revival of spiritual life within the Church of England.[4] In his comment on the 13th of the *Rules for Thinking with the Church,* where it states that "we ought to be ready to believe that what seems to us white is black, if the hierarchical church so defines it: believing that between Christ our Lord the Bridegroom and the church His Bride there is one and the Same Spirit," Longridge notes that "this is not to be taken too literally. What St. Ignatius means is that we should be very distrustful

---

[3] Francesca Bugliani Knox, *The Eye of the Eagle* 238.

[4] William Hawks Longridge, *Retreats for Priests: According to the Method and Plan of the Spiritual Exercises of St. Ignatius* (London: SPCK, [2]1962); *A Month's Retreat for Religious* (Oxford: SSJE Mission House, 1931).

of our own judgment, which indeed we have often found to be utterly mistaken, and should be ready to yield to the authority of the church when duly and clearly expressed."[5] We find here a first ecumenical reception of the Ignatian *sentire cum ecclesia.* Such an interpretation of the Ignatian rules, "not to be taken too literally," has inspired this presentation and has guided me in researching the ecclesiological foundation for the *sentire cum ecclesia.*

It is interesting that in this 13th rule Ignatius puts in parallel the hierarchical church with the spiritual dimension of the church: "Christ our Lord the Bridegroom and the church His Bride shares one and the same Spirit." The same spirit we have mention of here is an indirect reference to Phil 2:1–2 "τὸ αὐτὸ φρονῆτε, τὴν αὐτὴν ἀγάπην ἔχοντες, σύμψυχοι, τὸ ἓν φρονοῦντες—be of the same mind, having the same love, being in full accord and of one mind."

This kind of parallel is clearly present in *Lumen gentium* no. 8 which reads:

> [T]he society structured with hierarchical organs and the Mystical Body of Christ, are not to be considered as two realities, nor are the visible assembly and the spiritual community, nor the earthly church and the church enriched with heavenly things; rather they form one complex reality which coalesces from a divine and a human element. For this reason, by no weak analogy, it is compared to the mystery of the incarnate Word. As the assumed nature inseparably united to Him, serves the divine Word as a living organ of salvation, so, in a similar way, does the visible social structure of the Church serve the Spirit of Christ, who vivifies it, in the building up of the body.[6]

The conciliar texts goes further and clarifies that the "one complex reality," made up of a social and visible dimension (*phenomenological*) and a pneumatological dimension (*ontological*), is composite in its differentiation and articulation.

---

[5] William Hawks Longdridge, *The Spiritual Exercises of Ignatius of Loyola Translated from the Spanish with a Commentary and a Translation of the Directorium in exercitia* (London: Robert Scott, ²1922) 199–200.

[6] All references to conciliar and official church documents are to the official English versions available on the Vatican website: http://www.vatican.va.

This Church constituted and organized in the world as a society, subsists in the Catholic Church, which is governed by the successor of Peter and by the Bishops in communion with him, although many elements of sanctification and of truth are found *(inveniantur)* outside of its visible structure. These elements, as gifts belonging to the Church of Christ, are forces impelling toward catholic unity. (LG 8)

Lumen gentium 8 guides us in interpreting the Ignatian *sentire cum ecclesia* in a broader ecclesiological mindset and context *(unam realitatem complexam)* as *sentire cum ecclesiis*. By this reformulation of the Ignatian lemma we may catch a glimpse into the "common mind" of the conciliar fathers. It is an ecumenical development of the Ignatian *sentire*.

My paper will deal with the principle and foundation of this developed *sentire cum ecclesiis*. What are the possibilities for this "common mind"? I will proceed by three theses. (1) The sacramental dimension of the Church of Christ (*Lumen gentium* no. 8) is the principle and foundation of *sentire cum ecclesiis*. The sacramental dimension of the Church of Christ is well expressed in the Vatican II ecclesiological key words of *subsistit in* which have been much discussed in the aftermath of the council and has been the reason for much "dissent" (*dissentire*) rather than "consent" (*sentire*) in the ecumenical debate. (2) The official Catholic interpretation of the *subsistit in* has been influenced by the controversial distinction between churches and ecclesial communities. Such interpretation has raised disagreement among ecclesial communities and is constructed upon an inconsistency expressed in the church documents of the post-conciliar era. (3) Churches and ecclesial communities have a common mind because they realize differently and by degrees the presence of the Church of Christ. By acknowledging the two different and essential dimensions of the Church of Christ: an *ontological* dimension pointing to the *presence* of the Church of Christ, without degrees and differentiation, and a *phenomenological* dimension where *subsistence* expresses the *full* presence or actualization of the Church of Christ in the Catholic Church, we may find an ecclesiological rationale for the *sentire cum ecclesiis*.

The Sacramental Dimension of the Church in Ecumenical Dialogue

The Second Vatican Council irrevocably opened the Catholic Church to the grace of the Ecumenical Movement, which promotes the restoration of the unity of all Christians. The most significant ecumenical documents of the council and the post-conciliar period are: the Dogmatic Constitution on the Church *Lumen gentium,* the Decree on Ecumenism *Unitatis redintegratio,* the Ecumenical Directory of 1993 and John Paul II's 1995 Encyclical *Ut unum sint.*

This irreversible stand of the Catholic Church on Ecumenism is well expressed in the documents of the bilateral dialogues that the Catholic Church has had with various Christian churches and ecclesial communities over the past forty years. First came the dialogues with Lutheran, Anglican, and Orthodox churches separated from Rome.[7] The fundamental ecclesiological idea, expressed in these ecumenical documents, is that the Church is a sign and instrument of Christ's presence in the world. The Church is sacrament of the Kingdom of God.[8] Catholics, Lutherans and Anglicans all recognize that the Church embodies the communion that humanity has with God and with every human being.[9]

The Dogmatic Constitution *Lumen gentium* I declares "the church is in Christ like a sacrament or as a sign and instrument both of a very closely knit union with God and of the unity of the whole human race." The Catholic sacramental vision of the Church understands the Church of Christ as a concrete and permanent institutional structure in which the episcopal ministry, collegiality and the Petrine primacy are essential elements. The Church is a society of communion, whose innermost reality is the union between

---

[7] Walter Kasper, *Harvesting the Fruits: Basic Aspects of Christian Faith in Ecumenical Dialogue* (New York: Continuum, 2009).

[8] *Church and Justification. Common Statement by the Lutheran-Roman Catholic Joint Commission* 1994.

[9] International Lutheran-Roman Catholic Dialogue: *Church and Justification* (1993); Anglican-Roman Catholic International Commission, *The Church as Communion* (1991).

God and humanity and is well expressed in its institutional visibility. Each local church "re-*presents*" the One, Holy, Catholic and Apostolic Church. Both the Orthodox churches, separated from Rome, and the churches of the Reformation, ecumenically share a similar understanding of the local church. The fundamental problem in ecumenical dialogue is how to understand the relationship between the local church and the universal church; the particular church and the One, Holy, Catholic and Apostolic Church.

For Protestants, generally speaking, the Church is fully and effectively present in each local community. Here the word of God is preached and the sacraments are duly administered, as is affirmed in the *Augsburg Confession* art. VII. These two elements are sufficient (*satis est*) in order to identify the Church of Christ. For the Orthodox churches, the local church (diocese) by celebrating the Eucharist *fully* represents the Universal Church.[10] For Catholics, however, the Church of Christ is fully but not completely realized in the local church. By declaring that the Church of Christ *subsists in* the Catholic Church, the Catholic vision is that the local church is concretely, fully, permanently and effectively realized only when it is in communion with the successor of Peter. The unity and communion between the local churches and the Church of Rome is not an external but an internal element for the sacramental understanding of the unity and essence of the local church. "The evidence of this truth can be seen in the mention of the name of the diocesan bishop and the bishop of Rome in the Eucharistic Prayer *in memento Ecclesiae*."[11] According to the CDF, the Petrine primacy is not a mere ecclesiological addition to the local church or an external and legal decoration. The celebration of the Eucharist is a sign of communion and is validly celebrated when such sacramental visibility of union between the local church, the communion of churches, and the Church of Rome, is expressed. "In fact, the unity of the church is also rooted in the unity of the

[10] Kurt Koch, "A che punto è il cammino," *Il Regno-documenti* 56 (2011) 23–42 at 27.
[11] Koch, "A che punto è il cammino" 27.

Episcopate. [. . .] The unity of the Episcopate involves the existence of a Bishop who is Head of the Body or College of Bishops, namely the Roman Pontiff (12)."[12]

The individual bishop is rooted in the apostolic succession only when he is incorporated in the episcopal collegiality; the college of bishops is in apostolic succession, but never without the bishop of the *prima sedes.* No local church can isolate itself from the one and only Church; every church is the presence of the *catholica ecclesia* when it is in communion with the other local churches and the see of Rome. Whether by the "One Church" is to be understood immediately the Church of Rome or rather the Universal Church has been the focus of debate between Ratzinger and Kasper.[13] According to Ratzinger there is an ontological and temporal priority of the Universal Church over the particular churches; whereas according to Kasper the two aspects of the Church of Christ, universal and particular, should be seen in reciprocal and simultaneous relationship. Such debate reveals the truth of what *Lumen gentium* states at no. 8, that the Church "forms one complex reality" made up of a divine and human element; an external visible structure (order) and its hidden spiritual reality (grace); a particular and universal aspect.

Churches and Ecclesial Communities

The Decree on Ecumenism *Unitatis redintegratio* 3 declares that

the separated churches and communities as such, though we believe them to be deficient in some respects, have been by no means deprived of significance and importance in the mystery of salvation. For the Spirit of Christ has not refrained from using them as means of salvation which derive their efficacy from the very fullness of grace and truth entrusted to the church.

---

[12] CDF, *Letter to the Bishops of the Catholic Church on some aspects of the Church understood as Communion* (1992).

[13] Walter Kasper, *The Catholic Church: Nature, Reality and Mission* (New York: Bloomsbury/T & T Clark, 2015) 274. See Killian McDonnell, "The Ratzinger/Kasper Debate: The Universal Church and Local Churches," *Theological Studies* 63 (2002) 227–50.

In the churches and ecclesial communities separated from Rome, the Church of Christ is present and active, and Christ uses these ecclesial realities as means of salvation. It is good to remember that the distinction between "churches" and "ecclesial communities" was introduced during the council with the primary intent of respecting the self-consciousness of those Christian bodies, which did not wish to be called "churches."[14] During the 70th session of the council Card. Franz König explicitly proposed to define these Christian bodies not merely as "communities" but "ecclesial communities" because they are not simply sociological entities, but essentially defined by their being "church."[15] Only later was the term "churches" used to mean those bodies that have more of the essential elements of the Catholic Church (apostolic succession, ordained ministry and Eucharist) and the term "ecclesial communities" those bodies with fewer elements.[16] The Catholic Church formally recognizes as "churches" of a nature similar to its own particular churches the Orthodox Churches separated from full communion with Rome, and some Western churches not in communion with Rome. The Old Catholic Churches and the Anglican Communion fall into this category.[17] Paul VI described the latter as "our beloved sister church," during the visit of the Archbishop of Canterbury, Dr. Michael Ramsey, to Rome in 1966.

The ecclesiological shift which occurred in Vatican II, dealing with the ecclesial realities outside the visible boundaries of the Catholic Church, has brought a different understanding of the presence of the Church of Christ: from the fullness in the Catholic Church to the gradual presence in the other churches and ecclesial communities. The Catholic Church differs from the Orthodox Churches because,

---

[14] See Johannes Feiner, "Kommentar. Dekret über den Ökumenismus," in *Lexikon für Theologie und Kirche. Das Zweite Vatikanische Konzil. Teil II* (Herder: Freiburg, 1967) 40–126 at 55–56.

[15] David Neuhold, *Franz Kardinal König–Religion und Freiheit: Versuch eines theologischen und politischen Profils* (Stuttgart: Kohlhammer, 2008) 101.

[16] See Walter M. Abbott, S.J., *Unitatis Redintegratio*, in *The Documents of Vatican II* (Piscataway, NJ: America Press, 1962) 355[45].

[17] See Feiner, "Kommentar. Dekret über den Ökumenismus" 55.

although the latter possess both apostolic succession and collegiality, they lack communion with the Bishop of Rome and Successor of Peter. Even greater is the difference between the Catholic Church and the ecclesial communities born with the Reformation because they lack not only the Petrine ministry but also apostolic succession and collegiality. Therefore they have no valid Eucharist. Both documents of the CDF, *Letter to the Bishops of the Catholic Church on Some Aspects of the Church Understood as Communion* and *Responses to Some Questions Regarding Certain Aspects of the Doctrine on the Church*, restate that not only episcopal succession and collegiality are essential and constitutive factors for a church to be fully considered Church, but communion with the Bishop of Rome is also required.

> The communion with the universal church, represented by Peter's Successor, is not an external complement to the particular church, but one of its internal constituents; the situation of those venerable Christian communities also means that their existence as particular churches is *wounded*. The wound is even deeper in those ecclesial communities which have not retained the apostolic succession and a valid Eucharist.[18]

If all these three elements (Petrine ministry, apostolic succession and episcopal collegiality) are intrinsically and essentially related one to the other, and necessary in order to have what we properly call "Church," the lack of one or more of these makes it impossible for an ecclesial reality to be recognized as "Church." If the mutual interiority between Universal Church and a particular church defines the nature of an ecclesial reality, and this mutual interiority is not some external complement to a particular church but rather one of its internal constitutive principles, then how can we still consider and recognize the Orthodox Churches as "churches," when they are separated from the Roman See? How can the declaration of the CDF *Dominus Iesus* declare that these Orthodox Churches "are explicitly true particular churches"? How can the fourth answer given by the

---

[18] CDF, *Letter to the Bishops of the Catholic Church on Some Aspects of the Church Understood as Communion*, no. 17.

CDF to *Some Aspects Regarding the Doctrine on the Church* call them "particular churches" and "sister churches of the particular Catholic Churches," if they lack one of the essential attributes of the "esse ecclesiae"?[19] "If the ministry of Peter belongs to the essence of the particular church, how do the Orthodox Churches hold the rank of sister churches if they lack such an essential trait?"[20]

One might say that such inconsistency could be overcome if we keep in mind that the episcopacy is "one and indivisible." The lack of an *explicit* recognition of the head of the *collegium* does not deny an "implicit" link with the Successor of Peter as its head. However, if they lack full communion with the Roman Pontiff, these churches are more than diminished in their visible and sacramental expression, since the Petrine ministry ensures the unity of the episcopate, which is essential for a valid Eucharist. "The Episcopate is *one*, just as the Eucharist is *one*: the one Sacrifice of the one Christ, dead and risen. The liturgy expresses this reality in various ways, showing, for example, that every celebration of the Eucharist is performed in union not only with the proper bishop, but also with the Pope, with the episcopal order, with all the clergy, and with the entire people. Every valid celebration of the Eucharist expresses this universal communion *with Peter* and with the whole church, or *objectively* calls for it, as in the case of the Christian churches separated from Rome."[21] Invoking the unity and indivisibility of the episcopate, therefore, does not solve the question of ecclesiology for Orthodox Churches. Stating that these churches do not want to deny explicitly the head of the episcopate, that is the bishop of Rome, but only reject those prerogatives that the Catholic Church has defined during the second millennium, it remains true that the episcopate of these Orthodox Churches, separated from Rome, is deficient and these churches cannot be recognized as particular churches.

---

[19] Ibid., loc. cit.

[20] Gerard Remy, "L'Église du Christ et les Églises," 605.

[21] CDF, *Letter to the Bishops of the Catholic Church on Some Aspects of the Church Understood as Communion*, no. 14.

Such inconsistency is even more evident when we look at the Assyrian Church of the East, with which John Paul II signed a Common Christological Declaration in 1994 in which the Catholic and Assyrian churches can recognize each other as sister Churches.[22] We should keep in mind that the Assyrian Church of the East does not have the same canon of Scripture nor the same seven sacraments. Most importantly until 2001 their Eucharist was considered dubious because of a *defectus formae* in the Anaphora *Addai and Mari*. According to the analysis of Hervé Legrand "this church must be considered in a situation similar to the churches born with the Reformation."[23] Yet these deficiencies do not deprive the Assyrian church of true sacraments, since they enjoy a valid apostolic succession, although lacking the Petrine ministry. However, if the Petrine ministry is constitutive and essential in order that a particular church may be inserted into the universal church, can we consider such deficiency (*defectus*) only as a "wound," or it is more an "absence" (*privatio*)? The ecclesiological structure of the *college of bishops* and the *Petrine ministry* are not purely external, historically or socially useful, but express the mutual interiority between the *Universal Church* (the Church of Christ) and the *particular church*.

The lack of just one of the necessary and essential elements for the "esse ecclesiae" does alter, and not only simply wound the ecclesial status of a church. The document of the CDF, *Letter to the Bishops of the Catholic Church on Some Aspects of the Church Understood as Communion*, no. 13 states that the church is "fully" church, when there is the "presence of the universal Church with all its essential elements." The same position is found in *Dominus Iesus* no. 17 and in *Ut unum sint* no. 14. Both documents declare that "the elements of this already-given church exist, found in their fullness in the Catholic Church and, without this fullness, in the other Communities." In the

---

[22] Catholic Church—Assyrian Church of the East, *Common Christological Declaration* (1994).

[23] Hervé Legrand, "Consensus différencié sur la doctrine de la Justification (Augsbourg 1999)," *Nouvelle Revue Théologique* 30–56 at 45 n. 31.

Orthodox churches separated from Rome there is no such fullness of means of salvation. Certainly they possess a greater presence of them (apostolic succession and episcopal collegiality) than the churches of the Reformation, since these latter have none of these elements. For this very reason the Orthodox churches can be called "churches," whereas the communities of the Reformation cannot be called "church" in the proper sense.[24] If they lack the Petrine ministry, however, which is "an internal and constitutive principle," an element belonging from within (and not from without) to the essence of each particular church, how can these churches still be called "churches"? How can such inconsistency be overcome? We may have a solution, by saying that the Petrine ministry is essential to the fullness (*plene esse*) and not to the essence (*esse*) of the church. In that sense only the Orthodox churches separated from Rome can be recognized as churches, even if not fully, since they are in an imperfect union with the Catholic Church.

What we affirm of the Petrine ministry can also be applied to the other essential and constitutive elements of the Church: apostolic succession and episcopal collegiality. The lack of these elements in the ecclesial communities of the Reformation does not alter their being-church (*esse ecclesiae*). The documents already mentioned from the CDF are right to say that the lack of these elements deeply wound these ecclesial communities in their communion with the Catholic Church, but it cannot be said that they are not "churches." Kasper pointed out that these ecclesial communities, because in them the Church of Christ is active and present, must be defined as "true and real churches."[25] They are "churches" in an analogical sense.[26] But if we keep on saying, as Kasper also does, that these are "churches of another type, which lack from the Catholic standpoint of view essential elements of the Church," the same can be said also of the

---

[24] CDF, *Dominus Iesus*, no. 17.

[25] Walter Kasper, "L'unica Chiesa di Cristo. Situazione e futuro dell'Ecumenismo," *Il Regno-attualità* 46 (2001) 132.

[26] Walter Kasper, "Il lungo cammino da compiere," *L'Osservatore Romano* (June 2, 2001) 1.

Orthodox churches which lack the Petrine ministry which is essential for any particular church.

Ontological *and* Phenomenological *Dimension of the Church of Christ*

An ecclesiology of the elements of the Church must pay attention to the gradual realization of the Church of Christ. The first stage of realization is the communication of the faith: the event of the *communicatio evangelii*.[27] The *kerygma* is the nexus between God's self-communication and the historical and communal experience of the Risen Lord (*ecclesiogenesis*). If the church-event depends on the communication of faith, there may be different forms by which this event is realized. The Church of Christ is actively present in the preaching of the Good News, although in an implicit and embryonic form. Whenever and wherever the Gospel is preached, the Church of Christ is present: "the communicative act of faith is theologically first, since it is the event by which the Church is built up and by which is realized the relation of the Church with others."[28]

The beginnings of the Catholic Church in Korea provide a clear example of this gradual realization of the Church of Christ. A layperson Yi Seung-hun, baptized by a Jesuit missionary, built up a Catholic community in the mid-1780s. For more than fifty years this community lived as a church, even though no ordained ministry and hierarchical bond was established. Only after the killing of more than 300 people of this community (among them Yi Seung-hun) was the Catholic hierarchy established with the ordination to the priesthood of Kim Tae-gon Andrew, from a family of Catholics that had suffered in the persecutions.[29]

---

[27] *Confessio Augustana* no. 7: "The Church is the assembly of saints where the Gospel is preached in purity and the sacraments are administered in the right way."

[28] Severino Dianich, "Questioni di metodo in ecclesiologia," in: *Sui problemi in ecclesiologia. In dialogo con Severino Dianich,* ed. Antonio Barruffo (Cinisello Balsamo [Milano]: San Paolo, 2003) 21–54 at 50.

[29] Jai-Keun Choi, *The Origin of the Roman Catholic Church in Korea: An*

If the communication of faith constitutes the Church and its hallmark is the sacrament of baptism, we may say that the beginning of the institutional dimension of the Church of Christ *is* baptism. "Baptism makes possible a communion (although imperfect), that unites churches among themselves in a fundamental reality (the baptized members as Body of Christ). There is already a communion grounded in baptism, which does not represent a full ecclesial communion, but signifies a real participation in the Body of Christ."[30] The Decree on Ecumenism no. 3 declares that the ecclesial communities are a means of salvation. That is, they are "sign and instrument of the intimate union with God for all humanity" (cf. *Lumen gentium* no. 1).

The communication of the faith, however, is only *causa fiendi* of the Church, not its *causa essendi.*

> It is the church that celebrates the baptism and when she does that, the faith of the whole church is expressed, and not the faith of just that person who is baptized. The church is not generated by the fact that people gather to form a church. We do not enter into the church through baptism; rather we are welcomed into the church as a pre-existing reality of salvation.[31]

Baptism does not generate the Church of Christ, but incorporates us into it. Through the other sacraments, especially the Eucharist, a greater participation in the Church of Christ is realized. The fullness of the *elementa ecclesiae* (baptism, Eucharist, ordained ministry, apostolic succession, collegiality and Petrine ministry) is to be found in the Catholic Church. Furthermore, in such hierarchical understanding of the means of salvation, the fullness can be realized only once. Therefore, if the Catholic Church has been endowed with all means of grace, it follows that the Church of Christ *subsists in* the

Examination of Popular and Governmental Responses to Catholic Missions in the Late Chosn Dynasty (Cheltenham, PA: Hermit Kingdom Press, 2006).

[30] Silvia Hell, "Auf der Suche nach sichtbarer Einheit," *Zeitschrift für Katholische Theologie* 125 (2003) 18–46 at 28.

[31] Walter Kasper, "Ecclesiological and Ecumenical Implications of Baptism," *Ecumenical Studies* 52 (2000) 526–41 at 530.

Catholic Church, because in it the Church of Christ is *fully* present, although the Church of Christ is present *by degrees* in other churches. "The Catholic church is convinced that in it the fullness of all means of salvation is present. Only in it the church of Jesus Christ subsists in a lasting way."[32]

An essential distinction must be made, therefore, between the *ontological* and the *phenomenological* dimension of the Church. From the *ontological perspective*, there is no gradual differentiation of the Church of Christ. Wherever the Church of Christ is present and active, the Spirit of Christ is effective at work and uses Christian communities as a means of salvation. Nevertheless from the *phenomenological perspective,* there are degrees of realization of the Church of Christ: from a *full* presence (*subsistence*) to a greater or lesser realization of the active presence of the Church of Christ. Only when we consider the Church of Christ from the *phenomenological* perspective, can we appreciate the different stages of its realization.

> The church of Christ, without ceasing to be incarnate and historical in its social existence, transcends the Catholic church so that we may not only speak of non-Catholic Christians as in some way belonging to it, but are also justified in regarding non Catholic Christian communities as being imperfect or defective realizations of it. The teaching of the constitution on the church, therefore, leaves theological grace for other churches. The church of Christ that constitutes one single complex reality with the Catholic church is present in other Christian churches, even though according to Catholic faith these are institutionally imperfect or inadequate realizations of Christ's church.[33]

In order to clarify that in which the distinction between the *ontological* and *phenomenological* dimension of the Church consists, a Christological reference may help. In God's self-communication (grace), what is really communicated, is God's own being. In one particular and unique man, Jesus of Nazareth, there fully abides

---

[32] Kasper, *The Catholic Church* 160.
[33] Gregory Baum, "The Ecclesial Reality of the Other Churches," *Concilium* 4 (New York: Paulist Press, 1965) 62–86 at 71–72.

the Word of God (Col 1:19). In Jesus lives "bodily all the fullness of God" (Col 2:9). Since the Word of God *fully* abides in Jesus, we identify in him the *subsistence* of the Word of God. Jesus is *totus deus*; however, Jesus' divine nature exceeds the visible boundaries of Jesus' humanity. Jesus is *totus deus* but not *totum dei*. We also participate in the divine nature through and by means of the humanity of Jesus. In confessing that Jesus is *the Christ,* we claim that his humanity has *fully* realized God's self-communication and that is why it is in Jesus alone that the Word of God subsists. Karl Rahner repeatedly stresses that the hypostatic union is "an intrinsic moment within the whole process by which grace is bestowed upon all spiritual creatures."[34] The fulfillment and unique event of the hypostatic union does not differ in its nature from the other spiritual subjects. In Jesus the human reception of the Word of God reached its full climax. "The Incarnation of God is the unique and highest instance of the actualization of the essence of human reality."[35] On our part, such reception is only by degrees and partial (Col 2:10). However, we too are filled with the fullness of God (cf. Eph 3:19), because God will be all in all (1 Cor 15:28).

In God's self-communication (grace), God's own being is always and everywhere *fully* given and *fully* efficacious, but *not* always and everywhere fully accepted by human freedom. The Word of God as such (*verbum dei qua deus*) cannot be present partially or by degrees. God gives His own being always and everywhere, fully and totally. But the Word of God as incarnate (*verbum dei qua homo*) is particularly, temporally and gradually actualized. Here, not there; now, not tomorrow; more or less; fully, or partially. The human (individual and institutional) reception of God's self-communication is realized by degrees.

An analogous understanding may apply to the Church of Christ and its fulfilled actualization in the Catholic Church. Between the

---

[34] Karl Rahner, *Foundations of Christian Faith* (New York: Crossroads, 1978) 200–201.

[35] Rahner, *Foundations of Christian Faith* 218.

Catholic Church and the Church of Christ there is a *formal* identity (*ecclesia catholica est tota ecclesia*), but if there are *elementa ecclesiae* beyond and outside the Catholic Church, we must acknowledge that *ecclesia catholica non est totum ecclesiae*. That's why the conciliar fathers introduced the *subsistit* and avoided *est*. They wanted to avoid an exclusive identification of the Catholic Church with the Church of Christ. Only if we give up such an exclusive claim, may we then acknowledge that there are ecclesial elements outside the Catholic Church. Therefore, the term "church" can be applied not only to the Orthodox churches but also to the ecclesial communities.[36] The council realized that outside the fullness of the Catholic Church (*tota ecclesia*) there is a much more fundamental reality: the Church of Christ (*totum ecclesiae*).

> This fundamental opening showed the way for the postconciliar reception process, which communicated the insight that the Catholic Church, while she is "of course *the* institutionally perfect realization" of the church of Jesus Christ, does not completely exhaust the latter, so that "many elements of sanctification and of truth [. . .] can be found outside the Catholic church as gifts belonging to the church of Christ" that impel believers toward Catholic unity.[37]

We identify in the Catholic Church the subsistence of the Church of Christ, because here visibly abides the fullness of the Church of Christ. Therefore, the CDF declares "the full identity of the church of Christ with the Catholic church."[38] The adjective "full" does not point to an *exclusive* identity (*tota ecclesia = totum ecclesiae*) but rather to the *fullness* of ecclesial elements.[39] There is full identity of

---

[36] See Peter Lüning, "Das ekklesiologische Problem der *subsistit in* (LG 8) im heutigen ökumenischen Gespräch," *Catholica* 52 (1998) 1–23 at 6.

[37] Maximilian Heinrich Heim, *Joseph Ratzinger: Life in the Church and Living Theology* (San Francisco: Ignatius Press, 2007) 75.

[38] CDF, *Response to Some Questions Regarding Certain Aspects of the Doctrine of the Church*.

[39] Karim Schelkens, "Lumen gentium 'subsistit in' Revisited: The Catholic Church and Christian Unity after Vatican II," *Theological Studies* 69 (2008) 875–93 at 876.

the Church of Christ with the Catholic Church (*tota ecclesia*) from the *phenomenological* perspective. However, the Church of Christ exceeds and is present beyond the visible boundaries of the Catholic Church. The Catholic Church does not exhaust the *totum ecclesiae*. Thus, from the *ontological* perspective, the Church of Christ always is present and active everywhere, without measure and degrees; but from the *phenomenological* perspective, the Church of Christ has many degrees of realization, from less to more, until its fullness is realized and can be found in the Catholic Church. Kasper states, "the council thus advocates a graded concept of church according to which the non-Catholic churches and ecclesial communities participate in a graded way in the unity and catholicity of the Catholic church."[40]

By replacing *est* with *subsistit in* two different dimensions of the Church are taken into account: an *ontological* dimension where the *presence* of the Church of Christ, without degrees and differentiation, is acknowledged; but also a *phenomenological* dimension where *subsistence* expresses the *full* presence or actualization of the Church of Christ. The *ontological* dimension has a priority over the phenomenological dimension, but it cannot be revealed without the phenomenological. Therefore, the *universal* aspect of the Church is prior to all its local realizations, but the *particular* realization has a temporal priority over the universal aspect of the Church. The CDF says as much:

> From the Church, which in its origins and its first manifestation is universal, have arisen the different local Churches, as particular expressions of the one unique church of Jesus Christ. Arising within and out of the universal church, they have their ecclesiality in it and from it. Hence the formula of the Second Vatican council: *The church in and formed out of the churches (ecclesia in et ex ecclesiis)*, is inseparable from this other formula: *The churches in and formed out of the churches (ecclesiae in et ex ecclesiis)*.[41]

The distinction between the presence (*totum ecclesiae*) and

---

[40] Kasper, *The Catholic Church* 160.
[41] CDF, *On Some Aspects of the Church as Communion*, no. 9.

subsistence (*tota ecclesia*) prevents us from saying that there are *degrees of subsistence,* or that the Church of Christ *subsists* equally in many other churches. The subsistence is attributed only to that Church to which the fullness of the means of salvation has been entrusted and received. The Church of Christ is not divided into many parts, as if each one were a totality. It would be contradictory to affirm many totalities. Rather a fulfilled totality can be only "one." For this reason the declaration *Dominus Iesus* no. 16 explicitly added "only" while speaking of the Church of Christ subsisting fully in the Catholic Church. The declaration wanted to underline that *only one* Church can be considered the *full* realization of the Church of Christ, whereas *many* can be the degrees of such fulfillment.

Consistently the Catholic Church affirms that therefore there are no *partial* or *many* subsistences of the Church of Christ, but only one subsistence, just as from the Christological perspective there is just one single subsistence of the Word of God in Jesus Christ.[42] The Catholic Church understands herself as *formally* identical (*ecclesia catholica est "tota" ecclesia*) with the Church of Christ, since in her there is the fullness of the means of salvation.

> To say that the Church of Christ continues to exist fully only in the Catholic Church means that the Catholic Church alone has preserved everything that belongs to the Church's integrity, such as the unity that is preserved through the communion of all its bishops with the pope, along with the fullness of the means of grace.[43]

Nonetheless, the visible boundaries of the Catholic Church are not *materially* identical with the Church of Christ: *ecclesia catholica non est "totum" ecclesiae.* "Outside her visible confines there are not only individual Christians but ecclesial elements or, as in the case of the churches of the East, even genuine particular churches."[44]

---

[42] Joseph Ratzinger, "L'ecclesiologia della costituzione 'Lumen Gentium'," *Il Concilio Vaticano II. Recezione e attualità alla luce del Giubileo,* ed. Rino Fisichella (Cinisello Balsamo [Milano]: San Paolo, 2000) 66–81 at 79.

[43] Sullivan, "The Meaning of *subsistit in*" 119.

[44] Walter Kasper, *That They May All Be One: The Call to Unity Today* (London:

An ecumenical ecclesiology, grounded on the distinction of the ontological and phenomenological dimension of the Church, gives a rationale to the vision of the conciliar fathers who were aware of the difference between *totum ecclesiae* and *tota ecclesia*. The Church of Christ is present by degrees in the churches and ecclesial communities, and they are endowed with the same grace and truth that has been fully entrusted to the Catholic Church. The ontological presence of the Church of Christ is principle and foundation of the *sentire cum ecclesiis*.

Paolo Gamberini, S.J., associate professor at the University of San Francisco, formerly full professor at the Pontifical Theological Faculty of Southern Italy (Naples), has also served as visiting professor at Loyola University (Chicago), College of the Holy Cross (Worcester, MA), Boston College's STM, and The Jesuit School of Theology (Berkeley, CA).

Burns & Oates, 2004) 65.

Sentire in Ecclesia:
Its Contribution to the Ecumenical Endeavor

Markus Schmidt, S.J.

Ignatius of Loyola gives guidelines for feeling with and thinking in the Church. Though Church means here the confessional church, that is, the Roman Catholic Church, this paper will open towards a perspective to the Universal Church. Feeling with and thinking in the Church leads to the fullness of Church and this is nothing else than Catholicity. This is the ecumenical realm.

1. Introduction

The theme of our congress is "Thinking and Feeling with the Churches."[1] The *Spiritual Exercises* of St Ignatius of Loyola[2] come to mind as a valuable resource for ecumenism in our day, especially the guidelines for *sentire in ecclesia* which can be found at numbers 352 to 370 of the *Spiritual Exercises*.

Ignatius of Loyola lived in the 16th century. It was a time of turmoil and confusion. Martin Luther and other reformers published

---

[1] This talk was given at the *23rd International Congress of Jesuit Ecumenists*, held at Vienna, July 13–19, 2015.

[2] Iosephus Calveras. S.J. and Candidus de Dalmases, S.J., eds., *Sancti Ignatii de Loyola Exercitia Spiritualia: textum antiquissimorum nova editio; lexicon textus hispani.* Nova Editio, Monumenta Historica Societatis Iesu a patribus eiusdem societatis edita 100: Monumenta Ignatiana: Series Secunda: Exercitia Spiritualia S. Ignatii de Loyola et eorum Directoria Tomus I (Roma: Insitutum Historicum Societatis Iesu, 1969). David L. Fleming, S.J., *Draw Me Into Your Friendship: A Literal Translation and A Contemporary Reading of The Spiritual Exercises.* Number 17 in Series IV: Studies on Jesuit Topics (Saint Louis: The Institute of Jesuit Sources, ³2002). The abbreviation for the numbersof the *Spiritual Exercises* used in this article is "*SE*."

their theological thoughts and worked on reforming the Church or on breaking with the Church in separating their own congregations from the whole of the Church. People certainly got confused about their faith. Moreover, political interests were involved as well, making the time even more confusing and unstable. It is not difficult to recognize similarities to our own time.

Ignatius's statement and reflections were meant for his own time of the 16th century. Yet, they still are valuable for us today to support our growth as members of the Church. His guidelines for *sentire in ecclesia*, as David Fleming, S.J. writes, "are meant to be helpful in developing a true and loving sensitivity to the ways of thinking, feeling, and acting as a Catholic in our present-day church."[3]

The founder of the Jesuits was convinced that people who made the Spiritual Exercises would be more active in the Church because they would follow Jesus Christ more wholeheartedly. They would be more deeply concerned with the Church's mission. Ignatius, however, also "knew the difficulty of maintaining a mature balance, a clear-headed judgment, and a loving reverence for both tradition and change."[4] This challenge made him write the guidelines for *sentire in ecclesia*. They are meant to be taken into the heart like the guidelines regarding eating or the guidelines for the discernment of spirits. The hope is that with the support of these guidelines people could better arrive at appropriate judgments and responsible decisions. This is true of inner-denominational as well as of inter-denominational matters, that is to say, of the ecumenical realm.

The first step of our discussion will be to clarify the obvious difference between the two "translations" of *SE* 352: *"sentire in*

---

[3] Fleming, *Into Your Friendship* 281. Cf. also Calveras and Dalmases, *Exercitia Spiritualia* 4: *"Regulae duodeviginti de vero sensu in Ecclesia militante tenendo [352–370] diriguntur ad rectum criterium sibi efformandum et obsequium praeceptis et dogmatibus Ecclesiae catholicae exhibendum, in modo oboediendi superioribus ecclesiasticis, in recta doctrina tenenda in rebus theologicis, additis monitis de modo loquendi in quaestionibus de gratia et praedestinatione, deque Dei timore una cum amore fovendo."*

[4] Fleming, *Into Your Friendship* 281.

ecclesia" and *"sentire cum ecclesia."* We will then proceed to the text of the guidelines and their meaning and widen the horizon to the *sentire in ecclesia universali.* Finally, we shall apply the findings to the ecumenical endeavor.

2. *Sentire cum ecclesia* vs. *sentire in ecclesia*

We turn now to the first step of our discussion to clarify the obvious difference between the two "translations" of *SE* 352: *sentire in ecclesia* and *sentire cum ecclesia,* of which the latter is more common. It might seem that this is not a big deal. Generally speaking that is true. The difference should not be overstated. The critical edition confirms this in its conclusion about the *Versio Vulgata* as well.[5] I will argue that both *in* and *cum* are mutually inclusive. But this should not be neglected because it paves the way to fruitful ecumenism.

In the Spanish autograph Ignatius writes: "Para en sentido verdadero que en la Yglesia militante debemos tener, se guarden las reglas siguientes" (*SE* 352).[6] Ignatius clearly does not speak of "con la Yglesia" (*sentire cum ecclesia*), but speaks of "en la Yglesia" (*sentire in ecclesia*). So where does the *"cum"* come from?

There are two Spanish texts that differ in that particular place (*SE* 352) from the autograph as well. Both *Codex ARSI, Exerc. 3* (= E) and *Codex Domenici* (=D) read "a la" instead of "en la Yglesia." This, however, does not indicate a transformation to *"cum."* It simply does not signify "con" (*cum*).

We are now left with the two *Versiones primae.* Both the *Versio prima A. 1541* (= P1) and the *Versio prima A. 1547* (= P2) do not reflect the *"cum"* in their text of *SE* 352: *"Ad certe et vere sentiendum in Ecclesia*

---

[5] Cf. Calveras and Dalmases, *Exercitia Spiritualia* 135: *"Differentiae, si quae sunt, minime tribuendae sunt interpretis intentioni tenuiorem reddendi asceticam doctrinam textus hispani."*

[6] Calveras and Dalmases, *Exercitia Spiritualia* 404. Here the autograph has the *siglum* "Autographum (= A)." Cf. also Ignacio de Loyola, *Obras Completas de San Ignacio de Loyola: Edición manuale,* Ignacio Iparraguirre, S.J., ed., Biblioteca de autores cristianos (Madrid: La Editorial Catolica, 1952) 235.

militanti, sicut tenemur, serventur regulae sequentes."[7] It is only the *Versio Vulgata (= V)* which translates into Latin with *"cum"*: *"Regulae aliquot servandae, ut cum orthodoxa ecclesia vere sentiamus."*[8] It seems reasonable therefore to suggest that the *"cum"* entered the phrase with the *Versio Vulgata.*

However, there is an overwhelming witness for the *sentire in ecclesia.* Jesús Corella, S.J. interprets the *"in"* as accentuating the belonging ("identificación," "pertenencia"), the *"cum"* as accentuating the agreement ("acuerdo"). Both terms describe the relationship with the Church.[9] The point I would like to make is that, if I feel and think in the Church, I do not have to think and feel with the Church. I still can do my own thing, although I am in the Church. A person who is outside of the Church can think and feel with the Church, although this person is outside. Only if I think and feel *with* the Church *in* the Church, will I put into practice what is meant by *sentire in ecclesia* and *sentire cum ecclesia.*[10] The point is that we need both. It is therefore apt to say "feeling and thinking *within* the Church."

3. The Text of the Guidelines

3.1. Structure

The text consists of 18 rules in regard to thinking and feeling within the church. The rules are appended at the end of the *Spiritual Exercises* and belong to the Fourth Week.[11] The rules can be roughly ordered into the following groups:[12]

---

[7] Calveras and Dalmases, *Exercitia Spiritualia* 405.

[8] Calveras and Dalmases, *Exercitia Spiritualia* 404.

[9] Cf. Jesús Corella, S.J., *Sentir la Iglesia: Comentario a las reglas ignacianas para el sentido verdadero de Iglesia.* Colección Manresa 15 (Bilbao: Ediciones Mensajero, 1996) 106.

[10] Cf. also Santiago Arzubialde, S.J., *Ejercicios Espirituales de S. Ignacio: Historia y Análisis.* Colección Manresa 1 (Bilbao: Ediciones Mensajero, 1991) 809 n. 2.

[11] Cf. Arzubialde, *Ejercicios Espirituales* 809.

[12] Cf. Arzubialde, *Ejercicios Espirituales* 812–813. Corella, *Sentir la Iglesia* 108–09, recognizes three groups: *SE* 353–61, *SE* 362–65, *SE* 366–70. Alex Lefrank,

- *SE* 353: A general call to obedience to the Church as Christ's spouse.
- *SE* 354–55: Praise liturgy and prayers.
- *SE* 356–57: Praise religious orders, religious vows etc.
- *SE* 358–60: Praise what belongs to veneration and devotion.
- *SE* 361–64: Praise and be prompt to precepts, constitutions, and recommendations of Church and superiors.
- *SE* 365: Believe the Church and her dogma.
- *SE* 366–69: Regarding how one should speak about predestination, faith, and grace.
- *SE* 370: Serving God much out of pure love is to be esteemed above all. Yet, we ought to praise filial fear of God, too, because filial fear is at one with divine love.

Three numbers are in a certain sense special: *SE* 353, 365, and 370.[13] They stand out because of the fundamental character of their content. These three rules coin the perspective in which the guidelines should be understood.

3.2. Content

Ignatius articulates as a first rule (*SE* 353) to be always ready to obey the hierarchical Church ("la nuestra sancta madre Yglesia hierárchica") because she is the spouse of Christ. If this is right, then to obey cannot be just technical obedience, but must be an expression of relationship, that is a matter of heart. Everything belonging to Christ's spouse will be something to praise. This might clarify why Ignatius has all the rules of praise included, even some we might not include today.

Umwandlung in Christus: Die Dynamik des Exerzitien-Prozesses (Würzburg: Echter, 2009) 410, orders the rules differently. He recognizes two main groups: one group concerning the fundamental relationship of the individual with the church (*SE* 353; 365), the other group concerning ecclesiastical life and church dogma (*SE* 354–64; 366–70).

[13] For an exact analysis of the structure of these three rules see Arzubialde, *Ejercicios Espirituales* 814–19, 833–36.

The first rule is about obedience. It will be fully understood only if it is considered together with the last rule (*SE* 370). In this rule Ignatius states clearly that "serving God our Lord much out of pure love is to be esteemed above all."[14] In this context Ignatius also emphasizes that filial fear, even servile fear, of the Lord is good as well. This fear helps to acknowledge God as God and is about supporting us in not offending the Father who cares for and loves us.[15] Santiago Arzubialde, S.J. calls the last number of the guidelines (*SE* 370) "concluding words" regarding the purification of intentions and the transition from fear to service of love for God.[16]

We can conclude that obedience is essential for Ignatius in his guidelines for thinking and feeling within the Church; but serving God out of pure love is important above all. And the two cannot be separated. They belong together. Obedience, then, seems to be the habit of living this pure love.

4. The Meaning of the Guidelines

The guidelines for thinking and feeling within the Church are like an epilogue of the *Exercises* and are meant, as Ignacio Iparraguirre, S.J. suggests, to widen the horizon to support the application of everything new that can be offered.[17] Peter Knauer, S.J. considers the 18 rules to be an application of the *Praesupponendum* (*SE* 22) to institutions. The guidelines are about solidarity that is appropriate to the essence of the Church. This solidarity needs visible behavior because of the visible institution of the Church.[18] This sounds similar

---

[14] Fleming, *Into Your Friendship* 290.

[15] Cf. Fleming, *Into Your Friendship* 291.

[16] Cf. Arzubialde, *Ejercicios Espirituales* 813 (emphasis in original): "Cierran todo el Libro unas palabras de *conclusión* sobre la purificación de las motivaciones y la transición del temor al servicio por amor a Dios nuestro Señor."

[17] Cf. Ignacio de Loyola, *Obras Completas* 235, n. 149 (*SE* 352): "Son estas reglas como un epílogo de los ejercicios. [. . .] Pero como siempre, el Santo amplía el horizonte, y da principios de aplicación segura para todas las novedades que se puedan ofrecer."

[18] Cf. Ignatius von Loyola, *Gründungstexte der Gesellschaft Jesu*, Peter Knauer,

to Arzubialde's conclusion. Ignatius's key points can be adapted at all times: (1) to defend the incarnation of spiritual ecclesial life, (2) to always have a positive attitude to authority, and (3) to defend sound theology which can never be derived from a denial of free will or from an incorrect response to salvation.[19]

A tension obviously exists between the guidelines and our modern feeling. Ignatius lived in the 16th century, we live in the 21st century. The intention, however, may be the same: the inner renewal of the Church. According to Jesús Corella, S.J., three considerations are of fundamental significance to grasp the meaning of the guidelines despite the tension for us today: (1) the rules are rooted in Ignatius's life itself; (2) the rules are part of the *Spiritual Exercises* and their dynamics; (3) the rules contain an ecclesiological perspective.[20] Santiago Arzubialde, S.J. suggests that the key to understand the tension seems to be found in the dialectic between sound humanism, which criticizes the shortcomings of the institution, and the mystery of the Church. Obedience is the indispensable bond of unity.[21]

However we try to deal with the tension, the guidelines of *sentire in ecclesia* challenge us. They need a certain relationship with the Church to be understood and, at the same time, they want to foster this very relationship with the Church. Jesús Corella, S.J. calls to mind that three habitual attitudes are necessary for us to be enlightened by the guidelines: (1) we are sinners in a sinful Church, (2) we need the Church, and (3) we desire to love the Church.[22] These three habitual attitudes form the background from which the guidelines may be fruitfully applied.

S.J., ed., Deutsche Werkausgabe 2 (Würzburg: Echter, 1998) 262 n. 83 (*SE* 352; emphasis in original): "Die Regeln über das 'Gespür in der Kirche' sind eine Anwendung des *Praesupponendum* (no. 22) auf Institutionen. Mit dem *Gespür in der Kirche* ist die dem Wesen der Kirche gemäße Solidarität mit ihr gemeint, die aufgrund der sichtbaren Institutionalität der Kirche auch sichtbarer Verhaltensweisen bedarf."

[19] Cf. Arzubialde, *Ejercicios Espirituales* 836.
[20] Cf. Corella, *Sentir la Iglesia* 17–18.
[21] Cf. Arzubialde, *Ejercicios Espirituales* 834–35.
[22] Cf. Corella, *Sentir la Iglesia* 16–17.

5. Sentire in Ecclesia Universale

Ignatius calls his guidelines "Para en sentido verdadero que en la Yglesia militante debemos tener, se guarden las reglas siguientes" (*SE* 352). It is not easy to translate "sentido." Santiago Arzubialde, S.J. interprets it as equivalent to a criterion of discernment which arises from an intimate knowledge in faith of the mystery of the Church. The *koinonia* of love, so Arzubialde, is the origin of knowledge that is able to discern.[23]

This seems to be in concord with Javier Melloni, S.J. who writes that Ignatius presents with his guidelines a new criterion for the discernment of spirits. If the personal experience fosters unity, it is the good spirit that works behind the scene, because it communicates the inner trinitarian life; if the experience is one of division, then the bad spirit is at work, because it is characteristic of the bad spirit to cause division.[24] The discernment of spirits as Ignatius understands it is always personal and ecclesial, although it is true that we usually recognize both dynamics as one.[25]

5.1. *Presupposition (SE 22)*

The fruit of the good spirit is without doubt the strengthening of relationships. The *Praesupponendum* (*SE* 22) is an excellent tool for that aim. It seems to be a small detail but, in fact, though challenging,

---

[23] Cf. Arzubialde, *Ejercicios Espirituales* 805 n. to *SE* 352: "Equivale al criterio de discernimiento que emana del conocimiento cordial en fe (la sintonía del Amor) del misterio de la Iglesia, esposa de Cristo. La koinonía de amor es el origen de un conocimiento que discierne."

[24] Cf. Javier Melloni, S.J., *La Mistagogía de los Ejercicios*. Colección Manresa 24 (Bilbao: Ediciones Mensajero, 2001) 268: "Sin que lo explicite, San Ignacio aporta con estas reglas un nuevo criterio de discernimiento de espíritus: la experiencia personal que tiende a la comunión es del Buen Espíritu, mientras que la que lleva a la separación es del Mal Espíritu, porque lo propio del Mal Espíritu es separar. El Buen Espíritu comunica la vida intratrinitaria, donde el máximo de personalización se da en un máximo de comunión, mientras que el Mal Espíritu trata de fomentar la contradicción entre lo personal y lo comunitario."

[25] Cf. Corella, *Sentir la Iglesia* 58–60.

it supports much of what Ignatius says a good Christian has to do: "every good Christian is to be more ready to save his neighbor's proposition than to condemn it" (*SE* 22).[26]

Jesús Corella, S.J. calls it "a model of relationship."[27] It is about greater readiness to save one's proposition than to condemn it. This attitude has its origin not so much in education, but, as Corella says, in an "act of being a good Christian."[28] It is a life-style, one could say, that is, a style of relating to others in trust and freedom. It is also an ecclesial relationship. Corella calls it a "catechetical relationship" and therefore a trustworthy one.[29]

It might be easier now to understand why Peter Knauer, S.J. interprets the guidelines of *Sentire in ecclesia* as an application of the *Praesupponendum* (see above, n. 18). The guidelines need to be approached on the basis of a trustworthy relationship with the Church. If the relationship is full of suspicion, it will more often foster opposition to the Church than trust in the Church; the guidelines would then become unbearable, which seems to me to be a logical consequence of such suspicion. If the relationship, however, is based on trust, then the way is open to be led into deeper relationship with the Church by the guidelines. This does not mean that I am less critical, but that I am more ready to save the proposition of the Church. Such a stance opens us for a growing relationship with the church and with others. When I say others I also include other churches and ecclesial communities.

It is easy to see how fundamental the attitude is that is articulated in the "Presupposition" of the *Spiritual Exercises*, not only for individual relationships but also for the ecumenical endeavor. We will now turn to the three main numbers *SE* 353, 365, and 370 to see how they can be applied to the ecumenical endeavor. The hope is that

---

[26] Fleming, *Into Your Friendship* 22. Calveras and Dalmases, *Exercitia Spiritualia* 164: "todo buen xpriano a de ser más prompto a salbar la proposición del próximo, que a condenarla."

[27] Corella, *Sentir la Iglesia* 60: "modelo de relación."

[28] Corella, *Sentir la Iglesia* 60: "hecho de ser buen Cristiano."

[29] Cf. Corella, *Sentir la Iglesia* 61: "relación catequética, y por lo tanto, confiada."

one's *sentire in ecclesia* will support a vision of *ecclesia universalis* and that it will strengthen the ecumenical perspective and the longing for church unity.

5.2. Obey the Church, the True Spouse of Christ (SE 353)

"*First rule.* The first: all judgment laid aside, we ought to have our mind ready and prompt to obey, in all, the true spouse of Christ our Lord, which is our holy mother the Church hierarchical."[30]

Alex Lefrank considers both rule 1 (*SE* 353) and rule 13 (*SE* 365) as of great significance because they deal with the Christ-relationship of the individual and his/her relationship with the Church.[31] Ignatius characterizes the Church as "our holy mother" and as hierarchical. The saint calls the Church, first, holy mother and only then hierarchical. A mother is usually someone whom we can trust. She is also someone who teaches us (as children), but this will only work out, if we obey her, that is, if we are ready and prompt to listen to her. This is the maternal aspect of the Church. On the side of the believer it has a kenotic aspect regarding one's own will. One will understand only if the whole relationship is a relationship of love with the Church.[32]

The Church, however, is not only our mother. Ignatius calls her also "the true spouse of Christ," which highlights the nuptial aspect of the Church. Javier Melloni, S.J. recognizes this when he talks about the "aspecto nupcial y maternal de la Iglesia."[33]

With both aspects, the maternal and the nuptial, we touch the demand of the first rule, that is, obedience. If the church is the spouse

---

[30] Fleming, *Into Your Friendship* 280 (*SE* 353; emphasis in original). Calveras and Dalmases, *Exercitia Spiritualia* 404 (emphasis in original): "1ª *regla.* La primera. Depuesto todo juyzio deuemos tener ánimo aparejado y prompto para obedescer en todo a la vera sposa de Xpo nuestro Señor, que es la nuestra sancta madre Yglesia hierárchica."

[31] Cf. Lefrank, *Umwandlung in Christus* 410.

[32] Cf. Melloni, *Ejercicios* 268 (emphasis in original): "En la *primera Regla* [353] se expone de pleno, desde el comienzo, el aspecto kenótico de la propia voluntad y del propio juicio por amor a la Iglesia."

[33] Melloni, *Ejercicios* 269.

of Christ, then she is very close to the Lord and the Lord to her. This reality provokes and affirms our trust in her. To trust in her also means to listen to her and to value what she says. It will include to think critically about her statements and decisions and to take them seriously. One will be able to obey wholeheartedly only if one thinks through what the Church teaches because one trusts in her. Ignatius, therefore, does not demand that one stop one's own thinking, but that one put aside one's own judgment. Jesús Corella, S.J. puts it this way: "No es lo mismo 'deponer el juicio' que 'no pensar,' e Ignacio no nos pide lo segundo, sino lo primero."[34]

Ignatius demands obedience, but it is obedience "en todo" ("in all")—radical obedience. With "en todo" Ignatius does not mean something quantitative but qualitative, as Jesús Corella, S.J. concludes. It simply does not suffice to just do (externally) what is demanded. Obedience "en todo" involves the whole (internal) person. What Ignatius means is true experience of the mystery of faith and love. Ignatius is, so to say, in love with the spouse of Christ, who is the Church.[35] This loving relationship seems to be the key to understand Ignatius's demand for obedience.[36] He learned this kind of obedience at La Storta. It is obedience because of true communion.[37]

Because of the true communion to which we are called, we care for the Church's teaching and we long for unity between all Christians. To take on the responsibility to reflect the Church's teaching is a burden, but it is necessary in order to work as an ecumenist. The

---

[34] Corella, *Sentir la Iglesia* 115.

[35] Cf. Corella, *Sentir la Iglesia* 121–22: "Es la expresión que brota incontenible, la primera, del corazón enamorado de Ignacio, al referirse a ella."

[36] Cf. Corella, *Sentir la Iglesia* 124: "Es decir, que la obediencia a la Iglesia descrita en esta regla, no podrá ni entenderse, ni ejercitarse sin esa experiencia interior, esponsal y filial a la vez, y caerá ametrallada por mil razonamientos de lógicas humanas, históricas, o de planteamientos personalistas, socioculturales o psicológicos."

[37] Cf. Corella, *Sentir la Iglesia* 119–21, especially at 120: "Aquí 'obedecer en todo' significa obedecer totalmente, hasta el fondo de sí mismo, con una obediencia como la que recomienda siempre Ignacio, que no consiste sólo en la ejecución de lo mandado, sino que le empeña al hombre entero, hasta llegar a ser una verdadera vivencia del misterio de la fe y del amor."

point is that one will really support the ecumenical endeavor if one is faithful to one's own tradition, that is, obeys one's own church out of love, and at the same time is ready to reflect other Christian traditions with a prompt heart to learn from them. Faithfulness and openness do not contradict each other; the opposite is true.

We can conclude that Ignatius's demand for obedience is rooted in the Church as holy mother and in her being the spouse of Christ. Both aspects foster trust in her and thinking and feeling within the Church which leads to true communion.

5.3. To Be Right in Everything (SE 365)

> *Thirteenth Rule.* To be right in everything, we ought always to hold that the white which I see is black, if the hierarchical Church so decides it, believing that between Christ our Lord, the Bridegroom, and the Church, His Bride, there is the same Spirit which governs and directs us for the salvation of our souls. Because by the same Spirit and our Lord Who gave the ten commandments, our holy mother the Church is directed and governed.[38]

The thirteenth rule is certainly the most "difficult" rule of the guidelines. It seems contradictory to what one should believe. If superficially interpreted, this rule appears foolish and irrational and therefore unacceptable to modern believers. But if interpreted in the Ignatian context, that is, within the relationship of love between the believer and the Church as spouse of Christ, a different view opens up and reveals the significance of the rule. Santiago Arzubialde, S.J. shows that the structure of the phrase does not point at the objective problem (whether something is white or black), but at the subjective

---

[38] Fleming, *Into Your Friendship* 286 (SE 365; emphasis in original). Calveras and Dalmases, *Exercitia Spiritualia* 410–412 (emphasis in original): "13ª *regla.* Debemos siempre tener, para en todo açertar, que lo blanco que yo veo, creer que es negro, si la Yglesia hierárchica assí lo determina; creyendo que entre Xpo nuestro Señor, esposo, y la Yglesia, su esposa, es el mismo espíritu que nos gouierna y rige para la salud [. . .] de nuestras ánimas, porque por el mismo Spíritu y Señor nuestro, que dio los diez mandamientos, es regida y gobernada nuestra sancta madre Yglesia."

vision of the individual.[39]

The reference is not the Roman Pontiff as in Erasmus's phrase[40] but the hierarchical Church. It is not a single person but the whole of the Church, that is the catholicity of the Church. The concept of the hierarchical Church alludes to Dionysios Areopagita: the heavenly hierarchy and the ecclesial hierarchy, especially in its three functions: to purify, to enlighten, and to perfect ("purificar, iluminar y perfeccionar").[41]

Jesús Corella, S.J. highlights that Ignatius understood the term hierarchical Church differently than we do today:[42] *First*, for Ignatius the hierarchical Church, based on the medieval tradition, is a much richer concept than the modern understanding of hierarchy. The modern concept refers primarily to giving a person or a group the capacity to command. *Second*, the richness consists of relationship which is at the basis of hierarchy. Hierarchy, therefore, means relationship, receiving of free gifts, participation, union of love, harmony, and divine arrangement. Thus, it fosters communion. *Third*, within the Church there are different institutions of special importance like bishops, ecumenical councils, bishop of Rome, and consecrated life. *Fourth*, the most important reality is, however, that we are all of one and the same dignity.

---

[39] Cf. Arzubialde, *Ejercicios Espirituales* 807 n. to *SE* 365: "La estructura de la frase no apunta al problema objetivo en cuanto tal (si es blanco o negro), sino a la 'visión subjetiva' del individuo." There seems to be an interesting allusion to a phrase of Erasmus of Rotterdam (1469–1536): "Neque enim ideo nigrum esset album, si ita pronuntiaret Romanus Pontifex" (*Supputatio errorum in censuris Beddae*. Erasmi Opera omnia, [Lugduni 1706 in the edition of London 1962]). According to Santiago Arzubialde, S.J. this text points much more to the pure objective issue ("pura objetividad") than Ignatius's text (cf. Arzubialde, S.J., *Ejercicios Espirituales* 807 n. to *SE* 365). In a similar vein: Corella, *Sentir la Iglesia* 139–40. See also Melloni, *Ejercicios* 269 n. 39, who talks about an indirect reference ("referencia implícita") to Erasmus.

[40] See above n. 39.

[41] Cf. Corella, *Sentir la Iglesia* 91–98. See also Melloni, *Ejercicios* 280, who, following Nadal (*Exhortación en España (1554)*, MHSI 90, Nadal V, 93), links the four weeks of the Spiritual Exercises to the three functions.

[42] Cf. Corella, *Sentir la Iglesia* 95–96.

In other words, Ignatius understands by hierarchical Church a life-giving organism which is of existential importance for personal life. It is desirable to be part of it. This union becomes stronger when one trusts the Church and stays in a relationship of love with her. Because the Church is the spouse of Christ, she has the same spirit as Christ. Therefore, the appropriate response to the Church, just as it is to Christ, is trust and obedience, which needs a personal decision and resides on the subjective level.

A biblical example may clarify it further.[43] When Jesus tells his disciples that they will go to Jerusalem, he is moved by the same Spirit as others are who see good reasons to be in favor of the opposite, that is, not to go to Jerusalem. Thomas articulates his feeling and thinking with Jesus declaring: "Let us also go, that we may die with him." (John 11:16[44])[45] Thomas's declaration seems to make no sense, but interpreted as an articulation of his relationship with Jesus, it reveals the deep level of his love and how deeply Thomas is involved with Jesus. It is his personal decision and it resides on the subjective level. Jesús Corella, S.J. suggests that rule 13 can be interpreted similarly. It is about being involved with the Church on a deep level of love with her.[46]

5.4. *Pure Love and Filial Fear (SE 370)*

> "*Eighteenth rule.* Although serving God our Lord much out of pure love is to be esteemed above all; we ought to praise much the fear of His Divine Majesty, because not only filial fear is a thing pious and most holy, but even servile fear—when the man reaches nothing else better or more useful—helps much to get out of mortal sin. And

---

[43] Cf. Corella, *Sentir la Iglesia* 134.

[44] Scripture quotations are, unless indicated otherwise, from the New Revised Standard Version Bible (NRSV), copyright © 1989, 1995 National Council of the Churches of Christ in the United States of America. Used by permission. All rights reserved.

[45] Barbara Aland et al., eds., *Novum Testamentum Graece (Nestle–Aland)* (Stuttgart: Deutsche Bibelgesellschaft, [28]2012) (NA28): *agōmen kai hēmeis hina apothanōmen met' autou.*

[46] Cf. Corella, *Sentir la Iglesia* 134: "Es comprometerse con la Iglesia."

when he is out, he easily comes to filial fear, which is all acceptable and grateful to God our Lord, as being at one with the Divine Love."[47]

Rule 18 is the last rule of the last five rules (*SE* 366–70). These five rules form a distinct part of the guidelines. According to Jesús Corella, S.J., they are intended for people like priests or catechists who want to talk about controversial doctrinal issues and about often misunderstood topics.[48] It seems that the five rules are meant to be anti-Lutheran,[49] especially if considered in the historical context of their creation. Jesús Corella, S.J. discovers rule 14 (*SE* 366) as the basic hermeneutic key to understanding these five rules of the guidelines: "we must be very cautious in the manner of speaking and communicating with others about all these things."[50] In other words, the rule is about applying a particular way of thinking and proceeding (*"modus procedendi"*), a sense of discernment and orientation in dealing with problematic or controversial topics.[51]

The last of the five rules is quite similar to the other four rules, yet, rule 18 becomes especially important because it is not only the last rule of the guidelines for thinking and feeling within the church but the closing of the *Spiritual Exercises*.[52] Not only its place within the *Spiritual Exercises* makes rule 18 so special, but also its content.

---

[47] Fleming, *Into Your Friendship* 290 (*SE* 370; emphasis in original). Calveras and Dalmases, *Exercitia Spiritualia* 414 (emphasis in original): "*18ª regla*. Dado que sobre todo se ha de estimar el mucho seruir a Dios nuestro Señor por puro amor, debemos mucho alabar el temor de la su diuina maiestad; porque no solamente el temor filial es cosa pía y sanctíssima, mas aun el temor seruil, donde otra cosa mejor o más útil el hombre no alcanze, ayuda mucho para salir del peccado mortal; y, salido, fácilmente viene al temor filial, que es todo acepto y grato a Dios nuestro Señor, por estar en vno con el amor diuino."

[48] Cf. Corella, *Sentir la Iglesia* 191.

[49] Cf. Arzubialde, *Ejercicios Espirituales* 810: "Con posterioridad, como respuesta a una problemática diversa, añadió 5 últimas [366–70] de marcado carácter antiluterano." See also Corella, *Sentir la Iglesia* 191.

[50] Cf. Corella, *Sentir la Iglesia* 288 (*SE* 366). Calveras and Dalmases, *Exercitia Spiritualia* 412: "es mucho de aduertir en el modo de hablar y comunicar de todas ellas."

[51] Cf. Corella, *Sentir la Iglesia* 195.

[52] Cf. Corella, *Sentir la Iglesia* 196–97.

Ignatius finishes his *Exercises* with this rule using for the first and only time the term "at one" ("uno").[53] He begins this rule stating that "serving God our Lord much out of pure love is to be esteemed above all." He finishes this rule stating that "filial fear, which is all acceptable and grateful to God our Lord, as being at one with the Divine Love." This is definitive. Ignatius obviously emphasizes love as the aim of the *Spiritual Exercises*, that is, greater love to God and greater love to serve God and human beings. This stance is also strengthened by way of the "Contemplation to Gain Love" (*SE* 230–37).[54] We can follow, thus, Javier Melloni, S.J. in his conclusion that the Ignatian mystagogy culminates in a unifying horizon.[55] This union is not a state but a permanent search for God.[56]

At the same time Ignatius does not ignore "the fear of His Divine Majesty." He differentiates between filial fear and servile fear. Though filial fear is "a thing pious and most holy," servile fear can help "much to get out of mortal sin," if nothing else does better help. The difference is that filial fear means the fear to frustrate the love of God, and servile fear means the fear to lose God from whom one receives life.[57] Thus, true fear of which Ignatius is speaking is always the fear to lose that treasure, that is to say, God.[58]

The search for God is a lifetime task. It is stimulated by love. Sometimes it is also stimulated by filial fear. This kind of fear fears to frustrate the immense love one receives from God, to offend the

---

[53] Cf. Melloni, *Ejercicios* 271 (emphasis in original): "Con esta regla Ignacio concluye el librito de los *Ejercicios*, utilizando por primera y única vez el término *unión*: 'estar uno con el amor divino'."

[54] Fleming, *Into Your Friendship* 174–80. Calveras and Dalmases, *Exercitia Spiritualia* 306–10.

[55] Cf. Melloni, *Ejercicios* 271: "La mistagogía ignaciana, pues, culmina en horizonte unitivo."

[56] Cf. Melloni, *Ejercicios* 271: "Con ello hemos tratado de expresar que tal unión no será un estado adquirido, sino una búsqueda permanente de Dios manifestándose a través de su Voluntad, específica para cada cual en el momento preciso de la historia."

[57] Cf. Corella, *Sentir la Iglesia* 207.

[58] Cf. Corella, *Sentir la Iglesia* 207: "Pero el verdadero temor del que habla Ignacio es siempre el temor de perder ese tesoro."

Father from whom all good things come. In some cases even servile fear might arise, more stimulated by love than by anxiety because one fears to lose God's love more out of one's love for Him than out of being afraid of God. So it is advisable to make use of the various motivations which foster growth in the Lord.[59]

6. The Guidelines and Ecumenism

These findings now need to be applied to Ecumenism. The two key numbers to interpret the guidelines, it seems to me, are *SE* 22 and *SE* 370, that is to say, the "Presupposition" and "Pure love and filial fear." They are a hermeneutical key and are mutually dependent on each other. The "Presupposition" is the fundamental aspect, and "pure love and filial fear" is the goal building on the "Presupposition." The "Presupposition," however, needs "pure love and filial fear" to be lived out authentically.

The "Presupposition" states that "every good Christian is to be more ready to save his neighbor's proposition than to condemn it" (*SE* 22). This is true for any neighbor and therefore especially for Christians of other denominations. It is sometimes tiring to try to understand what another Christian tradition means and how its theological propositions are to be interpreted. In some cases it would be easier to let them go or to agree, respectfully, that they are wrong. Ignatius, however, admonishes us to go deeper and search for what is really meant. In Ignatius's terms, we have to be more ready to save the proposition of other Christian denominations than to condemn it. This will often be the more difficult way to go but also the more fruitful one.

To save the proposition of the ecumenical partner is to relate to one another, which is fundamental to ecumenism. Therefore ecumenism is to a great deal "a model of relationship."[60] A Jesuit who was master of relating to others, friends and enemies alike,

---

[59] Cf. Fleming, *Into Your Friendship* 291.
[60] Corella, *Sentir la Iglesia* 60.

was Peter Faber. In his letter, probably to Bobadilla, from 7 March 1546, he writes that it is better to talk gently and find common grounds with Protestants than to emphasize controversy and that in which they seem to be wrong. He recommends to make friends with Protestants and win their hearts.[61] Peter Faber was strongly influenced by the "Presupposition."[62]

The second key number to interpret the guidelines is rule 18: "Pure love and filial fear" (*SE* 370). This rule builds on the "Presupposition" and at the same time it is the reason for it. Rule 18 finishes the *Spiritual Exercises* and sets down therefore the aim of the *Exercises*, that is to say, love.[63] Love is also the aim of ecumenism. Ecumenism is searching for unity, but we will not reach unity, if we do not love each other. It is not romantic love but the love that Jesus commands: "This is my commandment, that you love one another as I have loved you" (John 15:12).[64] It is challenging and it requires a decision for the other.

Ignatius is very clear: "serving God our Lord much out of pure love is to be esteemed above all" (*SE* 370). Love is the motivation and

---

[61] Cf. Peter Faber, *Memoriale: Das geistliche Tagebuch des ersten Jesuiten in Deutschland*, Christliche Meister 38 (Einsiedeln: Johannes Verlag, ²1989) 374: "Als Erstes muß, wer den Irrgläubigen unserer Zeit helfen will, zusehen, daß er ihnen viel Liebe entgegenbringt und daß er sie in Wahrheit liebt, indem er seinen Geist von allen Überlegungen freimacht, die der Achtung vor ihnen abträglich sein können." Faber continues his reflexion with a second point: "Als Zweites müssen wir ihre Gunst zu gewinnen suchen, daß sie uns lieben und uns einen guten Platz in ihrem Geiste geben. Das geschieht, wenn man sich mit ihnen freundschaftlich über Dinge unterhält, die ihnen und uns gemeinsam sind, und sich vor allen Streitgesprächen hütet, wo einer den anderen herabzusetzen sucht. Zuerst nämlich müssen wir mit ihnen in den Dingen Umgang pflegen, die uns einen, und nicht in den anderen, wo eine Verschiedenheit der Auffassungen zutage tritt."

[62] The serious question that is raised by emphasizing so much love and friendship—as true and important as they are, no doubt—is, whether there is also a duty to articulate issues for truth's sake. When does the moment come to do this? How can this be actualized? It must probably be decided from case to case.

[63] Cf. above, section 5.4.

[64] The Greek text reads: *autē estin hē entolē hē emē, hina agapāte allēlous kathōs egapēsa hymās.*

reason above all to love each other. In our context the others are the faithful of the different Christian traditions. This love, however, has to become a service for God. The purest form of serving God is to serve him out of love. This involves the whole human person. On this ground real encounter can happen. It enables us to encounter each other as brothers and sisters in the Lord. It strongly encourages us to enter into a dialogue of love and truth. I am sure that this will lead us together into filial fear of God, that is to say, into filial love, which is "at one with the Divine Love" (*SE* 370).

To be able to live out love in serving God we need the Holy Spirit. To serve God is fulfilling Christ's command. The Holy Spirit, who also fulfilled Jesus Christ, will lead into the service of God and will lead in the service of God. As the Church is Christ's spouse and as such given the same Spirit as Christ, it is necessary to obey the Church as obeying Christ (cf. *SE* 353). For ecumenism this means that we have first to obey our own church, and second to try to discover Christ's Spirit in the propositions of other Christian denominations, because through baptism all Christians belong to the one and true Church of Christ which is the true spouse of Christ. She has the same Spirit as Christ.

One will obey only in a trustworthy relationship. Trust involves the whole person. To have a loving relationship with one's own church will provide a firm base because it develops a secure identity. This fosters openness in us to other Christian denominations. To listen to the spouse of Christ is to listen to other Christian denominations, too, which will bring us closer to each other and closer to unity.

To love the Church, that is to say, the spouse of Christ, will make one suffer because this same spouse is stained by the divisions within her. These divisions may cause the lover to suffer and to long for wholeness and catholicity which is the traditional third mark of the Church.[65] This suffering is the other side of love, the love which is to be esteemed above all (cf. *SE* 370).

---

[65] The four traditional marks of the church are found in the Nicene-Constantinopolitan Creed: one, holy, catholic, and apostolic.

Love is relationship, and to understand rule 13 ("To be right in everything," *SE* 365) we need to interpret it from the viewpoint of relationship,[66] because it is a question of relationship. It is to trust and acknowledge that the Church as spouse of Christ sees deeper than any single believer does because she is equipped with the same Spirit as Christ, that is to say, with the Holy Spirit. Moreover, she is much, much older than any individual is and, therefore, she is rich in experience. This is a treasure and worth trusting in.

Trust in the Church because of her rich experience, however, is only one part of the story. The more fundamental ground to trust in her is because of the love for the spouse of Christ a believer has. This is the deeper meaning Ignatius tells us with rule 13 of the guidelines. Love will draw the believer closer to the heart of the Church. There we shall encounter others who also love the Church in their tradition. The encounter in the heart of the Church enables dialogue that comes from love and is done in truth.

Rule 13 encourages us to see deeper into reality than reality might appear to us. It is the demand to enter a deep and loving relationship with the Church, that is to say, with the spouse of Christ, and to trust her in everything because she has the same Spirit as Christ has. This testifies to the subjective, not the objective level.[67]

7. Conclusion

The guidelines for feeling with and thinking in the Church support the ecumenical endeavor because they affirm the person involved in ecumenism to be faithful to one's own church. This opens the way to deepen the knowledge of one's own tradition and to draw on the rich experience of the Church universal which is critical for the search for church unity and for engagement in ecumenical dialogue. Ecumenical dialogue, thus, needs to be supported by one's feeling with and thinking in the churches.

[66] Cf. above, section 5.3.
[67] See above, n. 39.

Markus Schmidt, S.J. is Assistant Professor of Ecumenical Theology at the University of Innsbruck, Austria. He was Secretary of the International Society of Jesuit Ecumenists from 2013 to 2015. Since September 2015, he has been Counselor of Fr. General of the Society of Jesus on Ecumenical matters regarding the Protestants.

Thinking with the Church:
From Msgr. Oscar Romero to Pope Francis

Thomas P. Rausch, S.J.*

This article explores how the Ignatian principle of "thinking with the Church" has been understood by Archbishop Oscar Romero and Pope Francis, and asks what it might mean in relation to the 2013 WCC statement: The Church: Toward a Common Vision. *It also raises the question: how can the "new" churches of the Global South affect the future of ecumenism?*

In this presentation I would like to look briefly at how Monsignor Oscar Romero and Pope Francis understand the Ignatian principle, *sentir con la Iglesia*/thinking with the Church. Then, developing an insight of the International Theological Commission's report on *The sensus fidei in the Life of the Church*, turn to the World Council of Churches 2013 statement, *The Church: Toward a Common Vision*, to consider what thinking with the whole Church might suggest in regard to the Church of tomorrow.

Last year I accompanied a group of our students to El Salvador during an "Alternative Spring Break." Our first visit was to the Cathedral of the Holy Savior where Monsignor Oscar Romero is buried. It was a Sunday, and we gathered with a large congregation in the crypt for Mass. Just in front of us was the great bronze sculpture of the four evangelists lifting up the murdered archbishop, marking his tomb. I was moved to read on the red marble slab over the tomb the phrase *sentir con la Iglesia*, "to think with the church." The phrase is Ignatian. Though not in the original text of the Spiritual Exercises,

---

*Rausch, prevented at the last minute from attending, sent his paper for inclusion in these Proceedings.

it was added as a subtitle to introduce Ignatius's "rules for thinking with the church," and it would have been familiar to Romero who had frequently made the Exercises.

While most English-speakers understand the phrase to mean giving assent to official church teaching, for Romero the Spanish *sentir* would have lost none of its rich meaning of "to feel with the church," and "church" meant the suffering people of God for whom he was bishop. According to Ricardo Urioste, Romero's vicar general, for Romero *sentir con la Iglesia* meant to be rooted in God, to defend the poor, and to accept whatever conflicts arose from fidelity to the Lord.[1] Romero represents the kind of church leader Pope Francis describes in his earthy language as "smelling of the sheep." His picture is everywhere in San Salvador, though not upstairs in the nave of the cathedral. Instead, enshrined over a side altar, was a picture of Josemariá Escrivá de Balaguer, the founder of Opus Dei.

Pope Francis's understanding of this hallowed Ignatian phrase is similar. In his famous interview with Pope Francis, Father Antonio Spadaro asked the pope how he understood Saint Ignatius's phrase about "thinking with the church." Francis responded by referring to Vatican II's image of the church as the "holy, faithful people of God," his preferred image, saying that the "people itself constitutes a subject." This means, he said, the *whole* church, the totality of God's people, that "complex web of relationships that take place in the human community" into which God enters. This is the church that enjoys in the Spirit an *infallibilitas in credendo*. "We should not even think, therefore, that 'thinking with the church' means only thinking with the hierarchy of the church."[2] According to Austen Ivereigh, Bergoglio had discovered an early church formula in his reading of Denzinger's *Enchiridion Symbolorum* that said that "the faithful

---

[1] Cited by Douglas Marcouiller, "Archbishop with an Attitude: Oscar Romero's *Sentir con la Iglesia*," *Studies in the Spirituality of Jesuits* 35/3 (2003) 4.

[2] Antonio Spadaro, "A Big Heart Open to God: The Exclusive Interview with Pope Francis," *America* 209/8 (Sept. 30, 2013) 22. http://americamagazine.org/pope-interview

people was infallible *in credendo,* in its believing."[3]

For Pope Francis, all the faithful, considered as a whole, display this infallibility in believing through a supernatural sense of the faith of all the people walking together. He says, "This is what I understand today as the 'thinking with the church' of which St. Ignatius speaks. When the dialogue among the people and the bishops and the pope goes down this road and is genuine, then it is assisted by the Holy Spirit. So this thinking with the church does not concern theologians only."[4] Richard Gaillardetz comments,

> Let us not overlook the audacity of this claim. Francis is saying that we can be confident of an assistance of the Holy Spirit to the bishops on the condition that they are open to listening to others. This perspective stands in startling contrast to the almost mechanistic notions of the assistance of the Holy Spirit often invoked by church leaders.[5]

This is a church in which pastors and faithful listen to each other, not just the faithful listening to the hierarchy.

In his Apostolic Exhortation, *Evangelii gaudium* (November 24, 2013), Francis refers again to the anointing of the people of God by the Holy Spirit, making it infallible *in credendo*:

> This means that it does not err in faith, even though it may not find words to explain that faith. The Spirit guides it in truth and leads it to salvation. As part of his mysterious love for humanity, God furnishes the totality of the faithful with an instinct of faith—*sensus fidei*—which helps them to discern what is truly of God. The presence of the Spirit gives Christians a certain connaturality with divine realities, and a wisdom which enables them to grasp those realities intuitively, even when they lack the wherewithal to give them precise expression. (no. 119)

---

[3] Austen Ivereigh, The Great Reformer: Francis and the Making of a Radical Pope (New York: Henry Holt, 2014) 111.

[4] Spadaro, "A Big Heart. . ." 22.

[5] Richard R. Gaillardetz, "The Francis Moment: A 'Kairos' for Catholic Ecclesiology," *Proceedings of the Catholic Theological Society of America* 69 (2014) 72.

In an address to the International Theological Commission a few weeks later, Francis returned to the image of the church as the entire people of God, speaking of the *"sense of the faith"* as a kind of *"spiritual instinct"* which allows the members to "think with the church" (*sentir cum Ecclesia*) and discern what conforms to the apostolic faith. But the sense of the faith cannot be reduced to majority opinion in the sociological sense. Therefore the magisterium must be "attentive to what the Spirit says to the Churches through the authentic manifestations of the *sensus fidelium*," and it needs theologians to develop criteria for discerning those authentic manifestations.[6]

Pope Francis's Ecclesiology

The ecclesiology that emerges from Pope Francis is one that takes seriously the nature of the church as a true *communio* of the faithful and their pastors in a synergistic relationship, an ecclesiology that calls for a genuine dialogue between pope and bishops, local churches and Rome, pastors and their faithful. And there are a number of indications that he sees his mandate as moving the church in that direction.

First, from the beginning of his papacy Francis has taken much more seriously the voice of national and regional episcopal conferences. In his Apostolic Exhortation *Evangelii gaudium*, he observes that "a juridical status of episcopal conferences which would see them as subjects of specific attributions, including genuine doctrinal authority, has not yet been sufficiently elaborated. Excessive centralization, rather than proving helpful, complicates the Church's life and her missionary outreach" (no. 32). Pope Benedict's approach was different, insisting that episcopal conferences have no magisterial authority, unless unanimous or approved by Rome.

---

[6] "Address of Pope Francis to the Members of the International Theological Commission," (December 6, 2013); http://w2.vatican.va/content/francesco/en/speeches/2013/december/documents/papa-francesco_20131206_commissione-teologica.html.

Second, Francis has not shown himself reluctant to "consult" the church. In preparation for the 2014 Extraordinary Synod on the Family, Cardinal Lorenzo Baldisseri, Secretary General of the Synod, asked bishops around the world to survey their faithful on questions of divorce and remarriage, rules for annulments, children in marriages not recognized by the church, contraception, and how to minister to those in same-sex relations. While not all conferences carried out the survey as requested, including that of the bishops in the United States, a Vatican report on the survey released on June 26, 2014 found that many Christians "have difficulty" accepting church teachings on key issues such as birth control, divorce, homosexuality and cohabitation."[7] One concrete indication of this is Ireland's recent vote on same sex marriage. This effort on the part of Rome to consult the faithful on questions important to their lives was unprecedented. For many it was a sign of hope.

Third, in June 2014 the International Theological Commission published a text entitled "*Sensus Fidei* in the Life of the Church," a doctrine Cardinal Walter Kasper says "is very well established in the biblical and theological tradition, but has often been neglected."[8] After reviewing that tradition, the ITC text argues that the faithful "are not merely passive recipients of what the hierarchy teaches and theologians explain; rather, they are living and active subjects within the Church" (no. 67). They play a role in the development of doctrine, sometimes when bishops and theologians have been divided on an issue (no. 72), and in the development of the church's moral teaching (no. 73). The text notes "that the magisterium needs means by which to consult the faithful" (no. 74). As the *sensus fidelium* is not simply identical with the majority opinion of the baptized, theology needs to provide principles and criteria for discernment (no. 83), echoing what Francis had said in his address to the ITC the previous December.

---

[7] http://www.religionnews.com/2014/06/26/vatican-confronts-shifting-landscape-on-family-issues/.

[8] Walter Kasper, "Open House: How Pope Francis Sees the Church," *Commonweal* 142/7 (April 10, 2015) 13.

There is also an ecumenical dimension to the *sensus fidei*; the text asks if separated Christians can be understood as participating in the *sensus fidelium* in some manner, answering in the affirmative (no 86). This may have some important ecumenical implications.

The ITC document suggests that the old distinction between the church teaching (*ecclesia docens*) and the church taught (*ecclesia discens*), where the church teaching was identified exclusively with the hierarchy, is no longer theologically appropriate. It also suggests that the Catholic Church might have something to learn from other churches.

Towards the end the text notes that problems arise when the majority of the faithful remain indifferent to doctrinal or moral decisions of the magisterium or reject them, perhaps from weak faith or an uncritical embrace of contemporary culture. But it also argues significantly that "it may indicate that certain decisions have been taken by those in authority without due consideration of the experience and the *sensus fidei* of the faithful, or without sufficient consultation of the faithful by the magisterium" (no. 123).

Finally, Pope Francis's understanding of the principle as thinking with the *whole* church was evident at the October 2014 Extraordinary General Assembly of the Synod of Bishops on the Family. Established by Pope Paul VI shortly after the Second Vatican Council, the synod of bishops meets every three or four years to advise the pope on topics of his choosing. Pope John Paul II once referred to the synods, along with ecumenical councils and national or regional episcopal conferences, as "instruments of collegiality."[9] For each assembly of the synod the world's episcopal conferences choose a certain number of their members to represent them, while the pope names other bishops of his own choosing, up to 15 percent of the total. Often he also appoints theological experts or representatives of the laity who take part in the discussions of the smaller language groups but do not have a vote.

---

[9] *L'Osservatore Romano*, September 17–18, 1979; cited by Charles M. Murphy, "Collegiality: An Essay toward Better Understanding," *Theological Studies* 46 (1985) 41.

But previous synods have not realized the hope for a more effective collegiality. As Michael Fahey has written, "Each new synod attracts less and less attention; the structure of their sessions has become unwieldy, they have become rituals with little practical impact on the life of the Church."[10] Many of the bishops see them as a waste of time. Much of the problem results from the fact that control of the synod assemblies has remained in the hands of the Vatican. Conservative curia staffers prepare the *Lineamenta* or text to be discussed and appoint other staffers to collate the synod's work. For example, at the 1987 Synod on the Laity, where several members of the editorial committee belonged to Opus Dei, a number of specific proposals which found considerable support on the floor, such as admitting women to those liturgical ministries not requiring ordination, were deleted, or more accurately, formulated in so general a way in the final list of propositions presented to the bishops for their vote that they were no longer specifically mentioned. This meant that the bishops were not allowed to express their opinion on issues that had been raised.

The 2014 Extraordinary Synod was very different. The meeting in October was itself extraordinary. As it opened, Francis instructed the more than 180 Council Fathers, cardinals and bishops, on the nature of synodality, encouraging them to speak openly and honestly, using the word *parrhesia*, which means "free speech" or "to speak candidly."

> A basic general condition is this: to speak clearly. No one must say: "This can't be said; he will think of me this way or that . . ." It is necessary to say everything that is felt with parrhesia. After the last Consistory (February 2014), in which there was talk of the family, a Cardinal wrote to me saying: too bad that some Cardinals didn't have the courage to say some things out of respect for the Pope, thinking, perhaps, that the Pope thought something different. This is not good; this is not synodality, because it is necessary to say everything that in the Lord one feels should be said, with human respect, without fear.

---

[10] Michael Fahey, S.J., The Synod of America: Reflections of a Nonparticipant," *Theological Studies* 59 (1998) 489.

And, at the same time, one must listen with humility and receive with an open heart what the brothers say. Synodality will be exercised with these two attitudes.

Therefore, I ask you, please, for these attitudes of brothers in the Lord: to speak with parrhesia and to listen with humility.[11]

The Pope's encouragement for more honest conversation was certainly heard by the assembled Synod Fathers. The Synod was unlike any other, with transparency, public disagreement, and cardinals and bishops lining up on different sides of particular issues, with some carrying on the debate in the media. Some took issue with a proposal put forward by Cardinal Walter Kasper to find a way to admit some Catholics in second marriages without an annulment to receive Holy Communion. Others saw this as a violation of church doctrine, or objected to the language in the Synod's initial report, acknowledging the gifts of homosexuals and their desire to find a welcoming home in the Church, asking if Catholic communities could offer one.[12] Others supported this more pastoral approach.

What was perhaps most significant was that the Extraordinary Synod seemed like an effort on the part of Pope Francis and many of the bishops to reclaim the free discussion of difficult issues that had characterized the Second Vatican Council. Not a rubber stamp of earlier conclusions, it was an honest admission of differences in theology and pastoral practice. It represented a transparency not seen since the Council, a true gathering of bishops to work with the pope. In his concluding address Pope Francis spoke of the Synod as a "journey," outlining in blunt language what he saw as the temptations faced by both conservative and progressive members:

> . . . a temptation to hostile inflexibility, that is, wanting to close one-self within the written word, (the letter) and not allowing oneself to be

---

[11] http://zenit.org/articles/synod14-full-text-of-pope-francis-opening-words/

[12] "Relatio post disceptionem" of the General Rapporteur, Cardinal Péter Erdö, no. 50; http://press.vatican.va/content/salastampa/en/bollettino/pubblico/2014/10/13/0751/03037.html.

surprised by God, by the God of surprises, (the Spirit); within the law, within the certitude of what we know and not of what we still need to learn and to achieve. From the time of Christ, it is the temptation of the zealous, of the scrupulous, of the solicitous and of the so-called—today—"traditionalists" and also of the intellectuals.

. . . the temptation to a destructive tendency to goodness [lit. *buonismo*], that in the name of a deceptive mercy binds the wounds without first curing them and treating them; that treats the symptoms and not the causes and the roots. It is the temptation of the "do-gooders," of the fearful, and also of the so-called "progressives and liberals."[13]

Controversial as the Synod was, it showed a church attempting to discuss difficult issues honestly, and while remaining faithful to its doctrine, attempting to find pastoral ways of reaching out to those who so often felt excluded.

As we saw earlier, the ITC document affirms that "separated Christians" can be understood as participating in the *sensus fidelium* in some manner, suggesting that the Catholic Church might have something to learn from other churches on these disputed questions (no. 86). At this point I'd like to ask, what might the Roman Catholic Church learn from other churches ecumenically? To suggest an answer, I'd like to turn to the recent World Council of Churches' statement, *The Church: Towards a Common Vision*.

The WCC on the Church

The Church: Towards a Common Vision was approved by the WCC's Faith and Order Standing Commission unanimously as a convergence (not consensus) statement on June 21, 2012.[14] This and

---

[13] Vatican Radio (October 10, 2014); http://en.radiovaticana.va/news/2014/10/18/pope_francis_speech_at_the_conclusion_of_the_synod/1108944.

[14] *The Church; Towards a Common Vision*, Faith and Order paper No. 214 (Geneva: WCC, 2013). A convergence text would be not so much a statement of agreement among churches, as a consensus of theologians from different traditions.

the 1982 WCC *Baptism, Eucharist and Ministry* text may be the two most significant ecumenical documents since the Second Vatican Council's Decree on Ecumenism. Structured in terms of four ecclesiological issues, the relatively brief text treats successively, in four chapters: (1) the church's essentially missionary origin, (2) its nature as a communion, (3) its growth towards the kingdom, and (4) its relation to the world.

Chapter I locates the church's origin in the saving activity of the Trinity. Visible unity is important for the nature and mission of the church, a point that is emphasized repeatedly. Such unity may require changes in doctrine, practice, and ministry, so that the churches may recognize in each other the "one, holy, catholic, apostolic Church" (no. 9). *Chapter II* stresses the nature of the church as a communion. While diversity is a gift of the Lord (no. 28), the unity and catholicity of the church means that each local church should be in communion with all the other local churches (no. 31).

Chapter III focuses on how the churches can grow towards visible unity in communion: this requires "communion in the fullness of the apostolic faith; in sacramental life; in a truly one and mutually recognized ministry; in structures of conciliar relations and decision-making; and in common witness and service to the world" (no. 37), though many differences remain about the number of the sacraments or ordinances, who presides at the Eucharist, how ordained ministry is structured and whether it is restricted to males, the authority of councils, and the role of the bishop of Rome.

Chapter IV underlines the missional nature of the church. Participating in the Divine Mystery, the church serves God's plan for the transformation of the world. It proclaims the gospel, celebrates the sacraments, and in manifesting the newness of life given by Christ anticipates the kingdom already present in him (no. 58), though it acknowledges a need of the churches to be accountable to each other because of new conflicts over moral principles and ethical questions (no. 63).

This WCC text on a common vision of the church is significant for a number of reasons. First, it presents a trans-denominational ecclesiology that should find resonances in the different churches. Second, sharing a Trinitarian faith means that each church is called to living in visible unity with other Christian communities. Each has a structure, consisting of apostolic faith, sacramental life, and a recognized ministry. The centrality of the Eucharist in the text is remarkable; it clearly sees the Church as a eucharistic community.

At the same time, it has been criticized as being too traditional, and excessively western in its approach. If Christianity is diminishing in the West, it is flourishing in Asia, Africa and Latin America, usually referred to as the Global South where two-thirds of the world's Christians are living today.[15] The WCC text does not deal adequately with the different ecclesial experiences of the new churches of Asia and Africa, many of them Neo-Pentecostal and non-liturgical.[16]

Tomorrow's Church

In the West there are new obstacles to ecumenism. The vision of visible unity seems to be slipping away for many of the Reformation churches. Many are concerned today with a new search for denominational identity, as Cardinal Koch has noted.[17] Some stress justice over unity. There is a lack of agreement on sacramental practice, and the Eucharist is not yet central in many denominations, including many evangelical communities. Mainline churches in the United States and Western Europe continue to lose members. Michael Kinnamon points out that the denominations that were once pillars of the ecumenical movement are in many places experiencing

---

[15] Philip Jenkins, *The Next Christendom: The Coming of Global Christianity* (Oxford: Oxford University Press, 2002) 6–7.

[16] See Thomas P. Rausch, "Towards a Common Vision of the Church: Will It Fly?" *Journal of Ecumenical Studies* 50/2 (Spring 2015) 265–85. Veli-Matti Kärkkäinen's *An Introduction to Ecclesiology: Ecumenical, Historical & Global Perspectives* (Downers Grove: InterVarsity, 2002) is one study that takes the churches of Asia, Africa, and Latin America seriously.

[17] Kurt Koch, "Developments and Challenges in Ecumenism Today," July 29, 2011; http://www.katolsk.no/tro/tema/ekumenikk/artikler/developments-and-challenges-in-ecumenism-today.

diminishing numbers and resources, with a resulting toll on ecumenical organizations. Those that are member churches of the WCC constitute little more than 20 percent of world Christianity, and their number is diminishing.[18]

But if Christianity is diminishing in the West, it is flourishing in Asia, Africa and Latin America, as Christianity's center of gravity shifts from Europe and North America to the southern hemisphere.[19] A recent Pew Forum study finds that more than 1.3 billion Christians live in the Global South (61%), compared with about 860 million in the Global North (39%).[20] Much of this growth has been the Church's evangelical, Pentecostal, and Neo-Pentecostal expressions. According to David Barrett, there are over 126 million charismatics and Pentecostals in Africa, over 140 million in Latin America, and over 134 million in Asia,[21] and these numbers are more than ten years old. Allan Anderson cites studies that claims that "there are 628 million 'Pentecostals, Charismatics and Independent Charismatics,' collectively termed 'Renewalists,' in the world in 2013, 26.7 percent of the world's Christians."[22] Also rapidly growing are the independent indigenous churches, whose members comprise about one-fifth of all Christians today and are thus not members of traditional denominations or churches. Mark Noll notes that "This past Sunday it is possible that more Christian believers attended church in China than in all of so-called 'Christian Europe'."[23] Thus the profile of global Christianity has changed dramatically, and the Western Church cannot afford to ignore it.

---

[18] Michael Kinnamon, "New Contours of Ecumenism in the 21st Century," *Ecumenical Trends* 42/11 (December 2013) 11–12.

[19] Philip Jenkins, *The Next Christendom: The Coming of Global Christianity* (Oxford: Oxford University Press, 2002) 6–7.

[20] http://www.pewforum.org/2011/12/19/global-christianity-exec/.

[21] David Barrett and T. M. Johnson, "Global Statistics," in *New International Dictionary of Pentecostal and Charismatic Movements*, ed. Stanley Burgess and Eduard M. Van der Mass (Grand Rapids, MI: Zondervan, 2002) 287.

[22] Allan Heaton Anderson, *An Introduction to Pentecostalism*, 2nd ed. (New York: Cambridge University Press, 2014) 307.

[23] Mark A. Noll, *The New Shape of World Christianity* (Downers Grove: InterVarsity, 2009) 20.

This recentering of the majority Christian population to the Global South poses significant challenges for ecumenism. Much less concerned with doctrine, confessional difference, or ecclesiology, these new communities have a different agenda. They sense the nearness of the supernatural, unlike the Enlightenment-influenced West; they place great emphasis on healing—of body, mind, soul, spirit, and society—and stress life issues such as AIDS, violence, and poverty. Their denominational boundaries are often porous and multiple Christian identities are not unusual. As Noll notes, whether Anglican, Baptist, Presbyterian, Roman Catholic, or independent, "almost all are Pentecostal in the broad sense of the term."[24] And not a few Christians in these churches are decidedly anti-ecumenical, as was evident at the Busan WCC 10th Assembly (2013), where hundreds were protesting not just the assembly but the ecumenical movement in general. We might let our attention briefly circle the globe.

Asian Churches

Noting the enormous diversity of forms of Christianity in Asia, with evangelical, Pentecostal, Neo-Pentecostal, and independent house churches, Peter Phan speaks of Asian Christianities in the plural.[25] In China, Christianity is growing rapidly, though exact numbers are difficult to come by. It is estimated that there are some 16 million Catholics, while estimates for Protestants vary from 20 to 120 million, though a more realistic estimate, based on cross-checked data, suggests 39 million as of 2007.[26] The overwhelming majority of Protestants in China are Pentecostal or Neo-Pentecostal in their theological orientation; this includes 90 percent of house church Christians and perhaps 80 percent of the total Christian population. Classical Pentecostals represent a minority, but they still represent 25 percent of house-church Christians.[27]

---

[24] Ibid. 34.

[25] Peter C. Phan, ed., *Christianities in Asia* (Malden, MA: Wiley-Blackwell, 2011).

[26] Benoit Vermander, "Religious Revival and Exit from Religion in Contemporary China," *China Perspectives* 4 (2009) 10.

[27] Luke Wesley, "Is the Chinese Church Predominantly Pentecostal," *Asian*

These house churches emphasize the miraculous, with prayers for healing playing an important role in the life of their communities.[28] According to Phan, these house and indigenous churches, present also in Japan, South Korea, the Philippines, Malaysia, and Indonesia, "do not have any central authority and have minimal, if any sacramental practice and ordained ministry," so that church union as envisioned by the WCC text, "founded on a common set of theological and ecclesiological principles, is totally out of question for the foreseeable future."[29] Nor am I aware of any efforts to build bridges between these house church Christians and China's Roman Catholics, a situation made worse by the fact that in some parts of Asia Catholicism and Protestantism are considered separate religions.

African Churches

In Africa the Roman Catholic and Anglican churches have experienced enormous growth, but the continent has also seen an explosion of new churches, usually identified as African Independent, African Indigenous, or African Instituted Churches (AICs). Roughly two thirds of the AICs are in South Africa, Democratic Republic of the Congo, and Nigeria. While AIC typology is complex, with some tracing their roots to the Ethiopian movement in the late nineteenth and early twentieth centuries, some from the prophet-founded movements after the First World War, the most significant expression emerged after the 1970s and is Neo-Pentecostal.

Many see these churches as an authentic expression of African religious impulses and cultures. They are communitarian in style,

---

Journal of Pentecostal Studies 7/2 (2004) 251; Allan Anderson says that "The rapidly growing house church movement in China is mostly of an autochthonous Pentecostal type, even though it may not recognize itself as 'Pentecostal'," *An Introduction to Pentecostalism* 303.

[28] Ibid. 226.

[29] Peter C. Phan, "The Church toward a Common Vision: A View from the Asian Churches," unpublished article from a not-yet-published lecture given at St. John's College, Oxford, U.K. April 11, 2014.

pneumatological in ecclesiology, and more comprehensive in their doctrine of salvation. Many are Neo-Pentecostal. Their liturgy is known for "its exuberance, spontaneity, free expression, and corporate reverence."[30] But most are not eucharistic communities; while some might celebrate the Eucharist at Easter, others believe that it is not necessary. More emphasis is placed on the work of the Spirit in dreams, prophecy, visions, and other spiritual gifts. Many preach the "Prosperity Gospel," an emphasis developed from bases in the United States that is growing rapidly in Africa, China, Korea, and Latin America. Its theological profile stresses healing, prosperity, and "positive confession," meaning the believers' laying claim to God's provisions and promises in the present, combined frequently with support for current regimes and national pride.[31] Mainstream evangelicalism has long opposed prosperity theology as unbiblical, if not heretical.

Latin America

The Catholic Church has learned much from the Pentecostals in Latin America. Some speak today of its "Pentecostalization," particularly through the widespread Catholic Charismatic Renewal (CCR). Far more Latin American Catholics have been involved with the Renewal than with Christian Base Communities: 73.6 million have participated to some degree in the Charismatic Renewal, 16 percent of all Catholics in Latin America; Christian Base Communities have engaged only 20 to 30 million, 2 to 5 percent of the Catholic population.[32] While these charismatic Catholics "report holding beliefs and having religious experiences that are typical of Pentecostal

---

[30] See Cephas N. Omenyo, "Essential Aspects of African Ecclesiology: The Case of the African Independent Churches," *PNEUMA: The Journal of the Society for Pentecostal Studies*, 22/2 (Fall 2000) 241.

[31] Simon Coleman, The Globalization of Charismatic Christianity: Spreading the Gospel of Prosperity (New York: Cambridge University Press, 2000) 28–40.

[32] Jacob Egeris Thorsen, "Charismatic Catholicism in Latin America," Aarhus University, Denmark, 7–8; see also Edward L. Cleary, *How Latin America Saved the Soul of the Catholic Church* (NY: Paulist Press, 2009) 53.

or spirit-filled movements," they appear able to incorporate renewalist or charismatic practices without displacing their Catholic identity and core beliefs, and most do so without formal participation in Catholic charismatic organizations.[33] Something similar is occurring in the Philippines where the Catholic Bishops' Conference is working actively with the popular charismatic movement, El Shaddai.

While not all pluralism is a blessing, it can make it possible for churches to share their gifts with each other and learn from each other. The liturgical movement has helped many churches to recover a greater appreciation of the Eucharist in their ecclesial lives. Some evangelical theologians today lament the "real absence" of the Eucharist in many American evangelical communities and call for a return to the sacramental ontology and eucharistic practice of the great tradition.[34]

It is also true that some of the churches of the Global South may have something to learn from older, more established churches. Pentecostal churches are more known for divisions than for unity. They may need to rethink their emphasis on the Prosperity Gospel, which too easily substitutes the false hope of material prosperity for the inevitability of suffering and the cross in the following of the poor Jesus. The 23rd Pentecostal World Conference at Kuala Lumpur, Malaysia, called attention to the errors of this prosperity teaching.[35] Others may need to pay greater attention to the place of the Eucharist in the WCC's statement on the Church.

[33] Pew Forum Survey, "Changing Faiths: Latinos and the Transformation of American Religion" pewforum.org/newassets/surveys/hispanic/hispanics-religion-07-final-mar08.pdf, 32.

[34] John Jefferson Davis, *Worship and the Reality of God: An Evangelical Theology of Real Presence* (Downers Grove, IL: InterVarsity Press, 2010) 113–14; Hans Boersma, *Heavenly Participation: The Weaving of a Sacramental Tapestry* (Grand Rapids, MI: Eerdmans, 2011).

[35] *Global Christian Forum News*, 1 (2014) 3.

How Can We Move Forward?

So what will tomorrow's church be like? Will it be a truly catholic church, a communion of local churches living in visible unity? Or will it be a multiplicity of churches and communities, even more divided in faith and life? Will these churches be able to receive the WCC statement on the church as a challenge to renewal of ecclesial life, commitment to justice and peace, mission, and unity?

How might we move forward towards the WCC's vision of a Church that is a eucharistic community, sharing a Trinitarian faith, nourished by the word of God and the sacraments, guided by a ministry with oversight and a teaching authority, and living in visible community with other Christian communities? Let me make some suggestions.

One approach would be to dismiss the WCC's ecclesial vision[36] as too traditional, too western, not sufficiently attentive to the experience of the largely Pentecostal-Charismatic churches in the Southern Hemisphere, as does Veli-Matti Käakkäinen in his comments on an earlier version of the WCC statement:[37] a failed effort, not helpful with today's religious pluralism. But this would mean reducing the theological meaning of church to any group that claims the name. Even those who advocate a broadly inclusive "inductive ecclesiology" or "ecclesiology from below," stress the centrality of the Eucharist. Paul Lakeland says unequivocally, "without the Eucharist we have no Church,"[38] while Roger Haight points to BEM's common apostolic understanding of the Eucharist "as the central act of the church's worship."[39]

---

[36] See above n. 14.

[37] Veli-Matti Käakkäinen, "'The Nature and Purpose of the Church': Theological and Ecumenical Reflections from the Pentecostal/Free Church Perspectives," *Ecumenical Trends* 33/7 (2004) 5–7.

[38] Paul Lakeland, *Church: Engaging Theology: Catholic Perspectives* (Collegeville, MN: Liturgical Press, 2009) 179.

[39] Roger Haight, *Ecclesial Existence: Christian Community in History*, vol. 3 (New York: Continuum, 2008) 210.

A second approach would be to argue that these new churches or ecclesial communities are not churches in the proper sense, as does the Vatican declaration *Dominus Iesus*. A strict interpretation of the WCC statement *The Church* would do the same thing, checking off the missing elements. But that would be to ignore the obvious vitality of these new churches.

The WCC text *The Church* presents an ecclesiology strongly rooted in the tradition. It can continue to serve as a goal, a *terminus ad quem* for the ecumenical movement. But we are not there yet. Perhaps there was considerable wisdom in Vatican II's language of "churches and ecclesial communities." It may be that not every Christian community realizes what it means to be church "in the proper sense." Are there not "churches" today that are more accurately Christian communities, with rich apostolic lives, their own traditions, a unique mission, and their own structures of governance, but which are not eucharistic communities, may not have sacraments, lack a teaching authority or a ministry of unity or even a concern for visible bonds with other churches? Thus, they do not fulfill the vision that the WCC statement presents describing church. But they bring unique gifts that could enrich the life of the entire church. Perhaps we could describe them as movements in search of a church, which might appropriately find a home within the larger communion of the church. Among such Christian communities we might include the Moravians, the Hutterites, the Mennonites, and the Quakers; perhaps also some indigenous, Pentecostal, or emergent church communities.

We might take as an analogy Catholic religious orders. Catholics have a saying, a cliché really, like most clichés, simplistic but still with a certain truth, that when a Protestant has a new vision of the Christian life and mission he or she establishes another church, while a Catholic in the same position establishes a religious order or community. A religious order is a community within the Church, with its own charism, mission, ministry, and structures of governance. Part of the genius of Francis of Assisi was his ability to find a home for his movement, part of a larger apostolic movement that revitalized European Christianity in the twelfth century, within the church.[40] It became the Franciscan order. The Reformation gave us denominations. How many denominations do we have today? Presently, roughly 43,000 according to the Center for the Study of Global Christianity at Gordon-Conwell Theological Seminary. In 1900 the number was 1600. If Christianity is now truly a world religion, as Noll argues, it is not yet a global church. He quotes Lamin Sanneh's remark about the new dynamics of world Christianity, which "compels a fundamental stocktaking of Christianity's frontier awakening, and an imperative of partnership with it. When opportunity knocks the wise will build bridges, while the timorous will build dams."[41]

Thus the WCC statement presents a challenging vision for all the churches. Its great strength is its trans-denominational ecclesiology. But it also calls for the recovery of a vision of the Church rooted in the fullness of apostolic faith (no. 37). It is testimony both of how far the ecumenical movement has come and of how far it needs to go. All the churches are being challenged to renewal and perhaps change, while the statement suggests that it may not be possible to recognize just any Christian community as church. The church has certain endowments or gifts which need to be incorporated into its life.

The Roman Catholic Church will need to continue to renew its structures of governance, making them more truly "personal, collegial and communal in their exercise" (no. 52), a renewal which hopefully has already begun under Pope Francis but still has a long way to go. It will need to find ways to give expression to the principle of subsidiarity in the church's life, allowing local and regional churches more latitude for making pastoral decisions in light of their own social contexts as well as more input from local churches in the selection of their bishops. While the Synod of Bishops could provide a consultative structure for more than the Catholic Church, it would first need to be reformed in its exercise.

---

[40] See M.-D. Chenu, *Nature, Man, and Society in the Twelfth Century* (Chicago & London: University of Chicago Press, 1969) 239–69.

[41] Noll, *The New Shape of World Christianity*, 196–97; Lamin Sanneh, *Disciples of All Nations* (New York: Oxford University Press, 2008) 287.

The Orthodox lack a clear consensus about the ecclesial and salvific character of the non-Orthodox churches, sometimes even about the validity of their baptism, and they lack the distinction between full and partial communion, so important to Roman Catholic ecumenical theology, as Walter Kasper has argued.[42] They will also have to find ways to accommodate a diversity of theological expression with an underlying consensus in the church's faith and consider how to develop structures of visible communion with other Christian communities. As Herman Pottmeyer notes, without a center of unity and ministry of communion, the Eastern Churches "saw its unity disintegrate into a multiplicity of autocephalous or autonomous churches, which have not found their way to a workable communion among themselves."[43]

Protestant churches are in different places ecumenically. Some have yet to engage in the search for unity, or to see visible unity as a goal. Some may need to examine their worship life, recovering the centrality of the Eucharist in the Church's life. Others may need to establish or formalize a teaching office, or to renew their teaching or practice in light of the great apostolic tradition, providing a creedal or liturgical context for the interpretation of Scripture, preventing the Reformation Scripture principle from becoming a warrant for private or non-traditional interpretations such as the Prosperity Gospel so popular with some Neo-Pentecostal communities.

Some need to develop structures for conciliar relations and decision-making. Some non-eucharistic churches might better be seen as apostolic communities within the communion of the Church, sharing in its sacramental life, rather than being churches themselves "in the proper sense." Ultimately communion with the Catholic Church means that the churches must face the question of an office of unity exercised by the bishop of Rome, though reformed in light of the Gospel.

---

[42] Walter Kasper, *That They All Be One: The Call to Unity Today* (London: Burns and Oates, 2004) 59.

[43] Hermann J. Pottmeyer, *Towards a Papacy in Communion: Perspectives from Vatican Councils I & II* (New York: Crossroad, 1998) 134.

Conclusion

In concluding, I might suggest that the principle of "thinking with the Church" means taking the ecclesial reality of other churches more seriously. What the churches most need to do is to begin taking the steps towards reestablishing bonds of communion in life, witness, and worship that would symbolize a common ecclesial life. What if the Catholic Church and the Orthodox churches could find ways to occasionally bring other Christians to share in their sacramental life? If both could find ways to relax somewhat their sacramental discipline, extending occasional eucharistic hospitality to those other Christians who share a eucharistic faith and desire to live in communion with them, rather than proselytizing their members, these established churches might help those Christians and their communities to recover a deeper understanding of the Church as a eucharistic community. This would represent significant progress on the road to visible unity.[44]

Thomas P. Rausch, S.J. is the T. Marie Chilton Professor of Catholic Theology at Loyola Marymount University in Los Angeles. A member of the Anglican/Roman Catholic Consultation USA (2009–), he co-chairs the Catholic/Evangelical Committee and the Theological Commission for the Archdiocese of Los Angeles. He was a consultor to Father General Adolfo Nicolás, for ecumenical affairs (2010–14).

[44] On precisely this point, see the recent article by Robert J. Daly, S.J., Gary Macy, and Jill Raitt, "The Ecumenical Significance of Eucharistic Conversion," *Theological Studies* 77 (2016) 7–31.

A Theology of Brokenness as a Source for Ecumenical Unity: Collaborative Efforts to Support People with Mental Illness and Their Families

PATRICK HOWELL, S.J.

Mental illness knows no denominational barriers. Addressing the needs of people thus afflicted can advance ecumenical understanding and friendships in a practical vibrantly religious way. Many of the mentally ill have deeply embedded religious questions that need addressing. Most importantly, the Bible provides occasions for preaching and for opening up ways in which religious communities can offer welcome and restoration to wholeness.

Mental illness is a human condition that knows no boundaries. It strikes a wide variety of people, across cultures, across religions, across diverse families, and across genetic and social conditions.

Someone said once that you can gauge the health of a community or society by how well it cares for children and for those with mental illness. The assumption is fairly obvious. Care for the most vulnerable in our society is a strong indicator of a community's compassion and efforts to work together. Just as it takes a village to raise a child, it takes a strong network of caring, committed, and skilled individuals to address the multiple needs of those with profound mental illness, as well as to support their families.

I would like to suggest that addressing the needs of people with mental illness—of those who are broken or homeless or at risk for multiple reasons—can be a source of strong ecumenical ties and can advance ecumenical understanding and friendships in a practical, as well as a vibrantly religious, way.[1]

---

[1] Almost every mainline denomination, with the exception of Roman Catholics, has a substantial set of guidelines and information for supporting people with

Some years ago I spent part of a sabbatical at the Tantur Ecumenical Institute in Jerusalem. While there someone mentioned, the "Jerusalem syndrome." Apparently, Jerusalem can be a favorite spot for "messiahs"—those beset by schizophrenia—from the three major religions. They not only have a messianic calling, but they come to the launching pad for messiahs—Jerusalem itself:

- if they are Christian, they are Jesus reincarnate;
- if they are Jewish, they are Moses or sometimes David;
- or, if they are Muslim, they are Mohammed.

It's rather common, according to one of my Jewish friends, and it's another indicator of how mental illness cuts across all religions.

My own personal entry into the "ecumenism of mental illness," if I can coin that term, came 40 years ago this month when I suffered an acute psychosis. I was principal of one of our Jesuit high schools and during my eight-day retreat that July, 1975, I had an onset of an acute psychosis which, a few days after the retreat concluded, became a full blown breakdown with a maze of delusional thinking. I won't go into all that except to say that one of the delusions was that "I was being sent to the Vatican to discern and straighten it out!!" An obvious delusion.[2] Get help quickly, if this ever occurs to you!! This little humorous distinction between a neurotic and a psychotic might be helpful if you're unfamiliar with the nature of a psychosis:

- A neurotic builds castles in the sky;
- A psychotic moves into them;
- And a psychiatrist collects the rent.

mental illness and their families. Here's a sample of a few: "Comfort My People: a Policy Statement on Serious Mental Illness with a Study Guide" (Louisville, KY: Presbyterian Church [USA], 2008); "A Leader's Guide for Congregational Study ELCA Message on Mental Illness," *God's Work. Our Hands* (Chicago: Evangelical Lutheran Church of America). See also Pathways to Promise at www.Pathways2Promise.org, an interfaith network with multiple resources.

[2] E. Fuller Torrey, M.D. *Surviving Schizophrenia: a Family Manual*, 6th ed. (New York: Harper Publishers, 2013) describes the nature, causes, symptoms, treatment, and course of schizophrenia and also explores living with it from both the patient's and the family's point of view.

In other words, the nature of a psychosis is the loss of boundaries and filters so that reality floods in upon the brain. To grasp it better, consider what it would be like if you moved into one of your dreams and lived it out in real life.

I was fortunate in having good friends who got me to the psychiatric ward, followed by first-rate psychiatric care. This began a whole new journey. Emerging from what I call now my "psyche ward spirituality," I learned and relearned Ignatian discernment and the power of the examen from the inside out. But I won't go into all this. I have written about it all at some length in an autobiography published 30 years ago.[3] Rather I'd like to simply focus on the unexpected ecumenical gift that arose out of this experience of brokenness.

First off, the psychiatric ward itself is a safe place of great ac-ceptance—radical acceptance. One of the psychiatric nurses, Lillian, was a wonderful gift. She could walk onto the floor at the beginning of her shift, and immediately sense the climate and level of sanity or insanity. Surprisingly, she shared with me her deep, abiding devotion to St. Thérèse, the Little Flower. Lillian explained that Thérèse suf-fered a great deal but her "little way" of trusting in Jesus to make her holy and her reliance on small daily sacrifices, instead of great deeds, appealed to thousands of Catholics.[4] "Pat, we live day by day, step by step," she quietly said.

A Lutheran pastor led a weekly discussion around faith or religion. He provided grounding. The Catholic chaplain, on the other hand, was quite dreadful. He was high strung, nervous, eager to bless and move on. And among the patients our bond was our brokenness.

---

[3] Patrick Howell, S.J., *Reducing the Storm to a Whisper: the Story of a Breakdown* (Kansas City: Sheed & Ward, 1985) new ed. (Spokane: Ulyssian Publications, 2000).

[4] John Clark, O.C.D., trans. and ed., *The Story of a Soul: The Autobiography of St. Therese of Lisieux*, 3rd ed. (Washington, D.C.: Institute of Carmelite Studies, 1997).

Breaking out of the Stigma

A great amount of stigma is still attached to mental illness, and religion can play a key role in either exacerbating it or in providing acceptance and support and hospitality. Early on, I received a grace—I can only call it that—one of many. The attending psychiatrist asked me after I was in the hospital about 10 days, if I would be willing to share my experience with a group of police officers that he was training so that they could respond appropriately with people on the streets who were experiencing a breakdown or severe mental illness. At many levels I wanted to say, "no," but instead, I said, "yes," and from that moment on decided that I would not hide my illness or be driven by the stigma, but would share what I went through—whenever it seemed helpful.

Months went by, healing came slowly. Eventually, three years later, I served again, successfully, as a high school principal. Still later I wrote the book that I referred to earlier and did a doctorate in pastoral theology.

A Bond of Brokenness

People started coming to me for spiritual direction—somehow sensing that their own brokenness or lack of perfection would be accepted and understood. I started receiving invitations to speak at various churches about mental illness, faith and spirituality, all of them Protestant: Presbyterian, Episcopalian, United Church of Christ and so forth. My friendships developed naturally, warmly, and deeply. They were obviously ecumenical, but a whole lot more.

In addition to conferences, I was at times invited to preach at Protestant churches during "Mental Awareness Week" in October each year or other times. We shared stories of brokenness, healing, pervasive challenges of obtaining psychiatric help, and, of course, trying to build networks of advocacy for people with mental illness.

Together with a United Church of Christ minister—Craig Rennebohm,[5] and a Presbyterian layman, we sponsored an annual symposium on mental illness—called "Soul, Psyche, and Spirituality"—at Seattle University for ten years. It was like the annual family gathering: friendships, stories, insights abounded. We had expert witnesses—psychiatrists, police officers, nurses, and "consumers" speak about their experience—but it was always from a perspective of faith.

When I became dean of our School of Theology and Ministry at Seattle University in 2000, I was drawn away for some years from this community of brokenness and family. But because of the ecumenical nature of the School, I was promoting ecumenism, theologically and institutionally, a very different world. Still later Father General Adolfo Nicolás, to my surprise, appointed me rector of the Jesuit Community, and so I drifted further away from my grassroots ecumenical family—until this last year.

Then, last fall (2014), for the first time in the history of the Catholic Archdiocese, the Archbishop sponsored a symposium for pastors and lay leaders on Spirituality and Mental Illness (hosted by a former student of mine) and I was the keynoter on the topic "Transforming Stigma to Stigmata—The Cross at the Heart of our Human Experience."[6] Though it now seems obvious, I began to see how the Cross was the point of convergence for all our ecumenical, compassionate responses.

Then a year ago I was invited by the American Psychiatric Association to be part of a team of psychiatrists and faith leaders that

---

[5] Craig Rennebohm, *Souls in the Hands of a Tender God: Stories of the Search for Home and Healing on the Streets* (Boston: Beacon Press, 2008). For two decades Craig met and supported people with mental illness on the streets, and he founded the Mental Health Chaplaincy in order to accompany people in their illness and trials.

[6] Stigma in Christianity has a transformative effect. The Cross itself of the Crucified Lord is the ultimate sign of infamy, but it also became a sign of new life. Christians later also incorporated the *sphragis* or seal with which Romans would "brand" their slaves in the baptismal ceremony. In the *sphragis* ritual the priest seals the person or child baptized with the sign of the Cross.

met in Washington D.C. to develop guidelines for all faith leaders—clergy, ministers and so forth—for responding to people with mental illness, not just as a person but as communities. We were Jewish, Hindu, Black Christian Church, Lutheran, United Church of Christ, Muslim, and yes, a few Catholics. The two-page overview and 28-page guide were just approved in May 2015 and are now available on line.[7]

OK. All this is far too much about my own experience, but I had to lay the groundwork. My thesis is that a Theology of the Cross, a sharing of our life in Christ through our brokenness, sinfulness, healing, and redemption, can be the source of profound ecumenical unity.

Restoration to Community

Earlier in our conference here in Vienna we had some discussion about our connectedness through suffering. Jan described his surprising welcome at the Orthodox Monastery on the Sea of Galilee, and then Peter suggested that perhaps it was occasioned by the monks' sympathetic cords with the nearby Benedictine monastery Tabgha which had been torched and burned earlier this spring.

It was a clear example of how redeemed suffering builds and binds communities, even those which have been alienated from each other.

In fact, Christian healing is always about restoration to community. Most often when Jesus heals, he tells the person, "Go show yourself to the priests." Now, finally, they'll welcome you back to worship and community. Biblical healing is always about restoration to community and often enough about discipleship. The healed person not only wants to follow Christ, but spontaneously shouts it out with loud enthusiasm about how the hand of God is here.

---

[7] To my surprise, I was part of this dynamic group, and this last year, we constructed an online guide for faith leaders (priests, ministers, rabbi's, imam's, and so forth) to respond to their parishioners. *Mental Health: A Guide for Faith Leaders* and the *Quick Reference on Mental Health for Faith Leaders*. Available at www.psychiatry.org/faith

A colleague of mine, Gunnar Christiansen, who has been a leader in the movement in California for support of people with mental illness, has said: "Whereas being cured is a complete restoration to the normal state, I interpret healing as the presence of solace and a sense of wholeness, which are gifts from God."

Isn't this precisely what Pope Francis has affirmed through his episcopal motto *Miserando atque eligendo*," a phrase taken from the Venerable Bede's homily on the Calling of St. Matthew, which means "because he saw him through the eyes of mercy and chose him."[8]

Challenges in Faith Communities Response

Let me highlight some of the challenges and differences in how various faith communities respond to mental illness. Here are some of the problematic attitudes:

1. The biggest single response is silence. A pall of silence hangs over the subject and, though it has changed significantly over the years, it is still a hidden illness with significant stigma attached to it.

2. Biblical-based healing is especially strong in fundamentalist and some evangelical communities. It has been expressed as, "just believe strongly enough and you will be healed." This stance lays a further burden on the person with the illness. It implies that it's the person's fault that they continue to be ill—because their faith is inadequate. Another way it is expressed is, "Those of us in the biblical counseling movement are the only ones who know that the construct of mental illness actually has to do with problems of the heart and require the gospel of God's grace for

---

[8] The Latin phrase is stronger than our English translation. It might best be read as "the Lord *mercy-d* him." For an exploration and application of this experience of human brokenness, see Walter Kasper, *Mercy: the Essence of the Gospel and Key to the Christian Life*, trans. William Madges (New York: Paulist Press, 2014).

healing."[9] The claim has a strong element of truth. Often enough a person's faith can carry them through tremendous pain and suffering, and even result in a further conversion experience that brings about a deeper healing. But too often biblical healing eschews effective psychiatric resources of both medications and psychoanalytic, therapeutic counseling. Medication and/or psychological analysis are of utmost importance in treating abnormalities of the body and mind, but, of course, they cannot be expected to fulfill the needs of the spiritual aspect of our being.

3. Some denominations may attribute mental illness to a person's sinfulness or lack of faith.[10]

4. A biblical literalism can lead to a practice of exorcism, which can have a highly negative effect and exacerbate the illness. The revival of a strong interest in exorcism among younger Catholic clergy can at times seem more like a narcissistic, power trip than a genuine encounter with the person seeking God.

These religious attitudes are pervasive and significant, but they are not the whole story. Many, I would say most, mainline Protestant and Catholic communities are open to and welcome solid scientific, psychiatric approaches—a combination of medication and counseling. Some faith communities are particularly good at outreach—Presbyterian USA, Lutheran Social Services, United Church of Christ, and a few Catholic dioceses. Most often in the Catholic Church, mental illness is lumped with an Office of Disabilities and gets short shrift. An exceptional, contrasting example is St. James

---

[9] Kevin DeYoung, "Guest Post: the Gospel and Mental Illness," http://thegospelcoalition.org (April 3, 2014).

[10] See Sarah Griffith Lund, "Lies Christians Tell about Mental Illness" (October 11, 2014). https://sarahgriffithlund.com/2014/10/24/5-lies-christians-tell-about-mental-illness. Griffith Lund is the author of *Blessed are the Crazy: Breaking the Silence about Mental Illness, Family & Church* (St. Louis, MO: Chalice Press, 2014).

Cathedral parish in Seattle, which has a full-time psychiatric nurse on staff—for emergency response, educational training, and building support systems for families. It's funded by the cathedral parish, the Knights of Malta who have a commitment to parish nursing, and by the father of an adult daughter with chronic mental illness.

Some Consequences

This ministry to people with mental illness is a frontier for any Jesuit or, for that matter, any Christian. But one needs to know one's gifts and limitations. For instance, I'm not good at street ministry with the homeless or with people with profound mental illness. But I can give voice to their experience. All of us can be advocates. All of us can avoid the stereotype of lumping people together as "the mentally ill." We don't speak of people with heart problems as "the cardiacs." We can make an effort to speak of a *person* who suffers from mental illness. Then we encounter each other person-to-person.

We need to use the obvious texts in the Gospels to preach a message of hope. About one-third of the Gospel of Mark is miracle stories, and about half of these are dealing with some form of mental illness. So one-sixth of all of Mark deals with mental illness. The only category that Jesus and his contemporaries had for dealing with mental illness was demonic possession. The personalities of people with mental illness were so dramatically changed that only possession by an evil spirit could begin to explain it.

Mark 5:1-21 is a great example. The Gerasene demoniac is chained in a cemetery. Living in the cemetery, he's already considered dead, exiled from the community. And by attending to him, Jesus breaks one taboo after another. Jesus is in the land of foreigners: Gentiles. He deals directly with an unclean spirit, he drives them into the swine. And, perhaps most importantly, he wrecks the local economy and overturns the dominant social categories.

The community says—as it says to so many people with mental illness—"Please go away, please don't bother us anymore." Yet the person with mental illness who is healed has a radiance that can only remind us of the angelic man at the tomb of Christ—announcing the Resurrection.

These texts, these experiences, these stories of brokenness go beyond all our ecumenical differences. They provide us entrée into the most intimate heart of other Christian traditions and worship services. They allow us to plunge into the mystery of our baptism into the one Lord the Christ—who died and is risen—who went down into the waters of Chaos, and upon emerging from the baptismal waters, he sensed and felt and was enveloped by the Spirit. In that profound chthonic moment arising out of the waters, he heard the words of the Father, "You are my Beloved Son in whom I am well pleased."

Or, in my own translation of the Greek: "You are my agaped one *(ho agapētos)*—you are my beloved in whom I am absolutely delighted." God takes delight in us. He invites us into the intimacy of the banquet *(agape)*. He loves us into being and never quits. If God can accept us as we are—in all our brokenness and imperfection—who are we to do less![11]

All are welcomed. Let us join the AGAPE together! And let us celebrate our unity in Christ across the divide.

Patrick J. Howell, S.J., specializing in spiritual discernment, sacramental theology, the theology of Vatican II, and contemporary Catholicism, has, since 1985, served as both professor and sometime dean at Seattle University's innovative School of Theology and Ministry, a major ecumenical center both for training Catholics for ministry and for providing an ordination track for 12 Protestant denominations.

---

[11] See Chapter One of Peter G. van Breemen, S.J., *As Bread That is Broken* (Denville, NJ: Dimension Books, 1974).

Selected Resources

The Body of Christ and Mental Illness. Chicago: ELCA, November 2011.

"For I am Lonely and Afflicted." New York Catholic Conference of Bishops, February 2014.

Mental Health: A Guide for Faith Leaders and the *Quick Reference on Mental Health for Faith Leaders.* Available at www.psychiatry.org/faith

The National Catholic Partnership on Disability (NCPD) Council on Mental Illness, "Welcomed and Valued." Mental Illness Resource and DVD, July 2009 (First Edition).

Pathways to Promise: Putting Faith in Mental Health Recovery at www.Pathways2Promise.org, an interfaith network with multiple resources.

Presbyterian Church (USA), *Serious Mental Illness: Resources.* Louisville, KY: 2006.

Ecumenism and Inculturation or, Thinking and Feeling with the Churches in an African Context

What model or image can serve as an ecumenical bridge for the Churches in Africa? This paper wants to show that, thinking and feeling with the Churches, *from an African perspective, must take into account the social-cultural riches of the latter. Such riches will serve as common ground for reflecting on the nature and the mission of the Churches as well as their relationship towards unity.*

Introduction

This paper intends to reflect on the theme of this Congress from an African perspective. The theme *Thinking and Feeling with the Churches* invites the following questions: what has been done or achieved in the continent in terms of ecumenical dialogue? What can be done to improve it? The Christianity that came to Africa was and continues to be a divided Christianity. Christian division still affects the life of African people in the core of their life which is the family, especially at this time when many religious movements exponentially emerge. Our reflection will be conducted in three steps. *First,* it tries to read the ecumenical achievement of the African churches. This will be done by the evaluation of and reflection on the work of the *All Africa Conference of Churches* (AACC). *Second,* it will look at the role and importance of inculturation in the ecumenical dialogue in Africa. *Third,* it will propose some ways of approaching ecumenism in an African context as a way of responding to the theme *"Thinking and Feeling with the Churches."*

African Churches and Christian Unity

This section will not have enough space to write about the history of ecumenism in Africa. In fact, however, "African Christian participation in ecumenism lapsed between the fifth and twentieth centuries," and to write such a history would impel us to go back to the life of the early Christian community. It might be enough to borrow J. N. K. Mugambi's praise of such a contribution which says:

> It is worthwhile emphasizing that African Christians in the early Church contributed immensely to the preservation of unity of Christian faith, and this contribution is memorably embedded in the ecumenical creeds promulgated at the early Ecumenical Councils of Nicea (CE 325), Constantinople (CE 381) and Chalcedon (CE 451) [. . .] this early contribution should serve to rejuvenate the participation of African Christians and churches in the Ecumenical Movement.[1]

Indeed, the aim of this section is to look at and evaluate the place and role of the African Christian churches in the Ecumenical Movement during the past century up to today. For this we can rely on two important works of Efiong Utuk to uncover the role and importance of the African churches since the beginning of the ecumenical movement. Utuk's first book, which is his dissertation, explores "the relation of Africa to the making of ecumenical mission and mandates during the formative years, 1900-1958."[2] In other words, his research deals with Black Africa's role, involvement in, or contribution to the early formative process of the Protestant ecumenical development, which would later become the World Council of Churches (WCC). His method consists of analyzing "the proceedings of some of the movement's early conferences and meetings." In doing so, he asks the following questions:

---

[1] Jesse Ndwigda Kanyua Mugambi, "The Ecumenical Movement and the Future of the Church in Africa," in J. N. K. Mugambi and Laurenti Magesa, *The Church in African Christianity: Innovative Essays in Ecclesiology* (Nairobi, Kenya: Initiatives Ltd., 1990) 5.

[2] Efiong Utuk, *From New York to Ibadan: the Impact of African Questions on the Making of Ecumenical Mission Mandates, 1900-1958* (New York: Peter Lang, 1991) 1.

1. What was the impact of the African social conditions on mission thinking and doing?
2. How did the persistence of indigenous cultural and primal religious values affect Christian evaluation of non-Christian religions?
3. How did the rise of indigenous African churches affect church-mission relations?
4. How did the race problem and calls for equality and justice affect ecumenical consciousness?
5. What in Africa necessitated unity in church and civil life on the one hand, between mission and church, and on the other hand, mission and government?
6. Who were some of the principal figures, "adopted" as well as "African Africans," and how did they reflect on, and respond to, these questions?[3]

Without entering into the details of his analysis, we can say that his concluding observations stress the role and importance of Africa in the "construction of ecumenical mission mandates." For examples, while in Europe the Industrial Revolution had badly affected the social role of the Churches, "encounter with African conditions helped to reorient the Protestant social conscience and, with this reorientation, came the need for liberalism and united action in the social sphere."[4] The same progress of understanding can be perceived regarding the Churches' attitude towards the so-called "primal religions." Utuk says:

> While, throughout our survey, we have seen arguments for and against an all-out effort to baptize values into Christianity, it is indisputable that, progressively through these conferences, the *tabula rasa* image of Africa was modified, if not completely abandoned. . . , churchmen and churchwomen came to consciousness of what had remained unconscious for too long, namely, that in modern Africa, just as in ancient Britain, Germany, and other European nations including

[3] Ibid. 4–5.
[4] Ibid, pp. 253–54.

Russia, Christianity and primal religion borrowed heavily from each other especially in the early years.[5]

Regarding Indigenous Churches, Utuk's analysis is even more interesting. According to that analysis, the Conferences held between 1920 and 1925 happened "against the backdrop of increased pressure from the Pan-African movement and the rise and spread of Independent Churches such as the Kimbanguist Church in Zaire, and the Prophet Harris Movement as well the Garrick Movement in West Africa."[6] He further says:

> The rise of these indigenous churches fostered ecumenism and brought African writers and interpreters of the continent to the fore. These Africans, gradually, became vocal and strident. They made clear their desire to be part of a *new order*, not just to make small gains in the *old order*. Their quest for *self-identity*, not merely for recognition, helped to arouse the movement to look more favourably at pluralism within the ecumenical body. Their steady growth in spirituality and the important doctrines associated with Christianity helped the ecumenical movement to find a hospitable home in Black Africa.[7]

Utuk's second book focuses on the proclamations of the All African Conference of Churches (hereafter AACC) from independence to the early 1990s. Since its foundation in 1963, the AACC, through its assemblies' reports, has wanted to assert and develop the authenticity of African Christianity. Prof. J. N. K. Mugambi, in his introductory comment of the book, points out Utuk's main ideas among which the following are important for our reflection: the need to include Catholic and evangelical expressions of Christianity; openness to Orthodoxy which has been excluded from the mainstream of ecumenical social thought and action in Africa; the importance of African cultural heritage as the foundation of ecclesial life, and so forth.[8] Indeed, despite the efforts shown

[5] Ibid. 255.
[6] Ibid. 259.
[7] Ibid. loc cit.
[8] See Efiong Utuk, *Visions of Authenticity: the Assemblies of the All Africa*

during the past decades, the reality on the ground seems to reveal the opposite; there is more competition than cooperation between the Roman Catholic Church and other denominations. Such practice definitely slows down the movement towards visible unity among Christians. Mugambi says,

> In the twenty-first century, African Christianity has to assert its identity in such a way that it becomes a catalyst for constructive transformation of African culture, without becoming a cultural replica of other forms of Christian expression from other parts of the world.[9]

Again, Utuk explores this vision of authenticity by analysing the outcome of the first six assemblies of AACC using five important lenses: (1) African self-identity, (2) acculturation of Christianity, (3) African socioeconomic order, (4) cementing ecumenical relations, and (5) the business aspect of authenticity. His summary reflection on the first two aspects of authenticity are important for our own reflection. Utuk is convinced that "the Assemblies would not have been able to carve a place for a genuine African understanding of Christianity without some emphasis on self-identity."[10] Indeed, self-identity was a process in the sense that it came along with the "political and economic aspirations" of the "emerging states" in which the different Assemblies saw Christ at work.[11] Regarding the acculturation[12] of Christianity, Utuk's analysis is very important. He observes:

> ... As the analysis shows, each Assembly felt at once embarrassed and challenged when it realized that African Christianity existed largely in name only, because its language, liturgy, rituals and ceremonies were mostly foreign and undeciphered. After criticisms revealed the need

Conference of Churches 1963-1992 (Nairobi, Kenya: All Africa Conference of Churches, 1997) 13.

[9] Ibid. 24–25.

[10] Ibid. 231.

[11] See Ibid. 232.

[12] Utuk uses the term *acculturation* in his book whereas in this reflection paper I prefer using the term *inculturation* that is now widely accepted and used by many if not all African theologians and others.

to naturalize the essential Christian message, frantic effort produced several definitions of African theology.[13]

In addition to the importance of inculturation, Utuk's analysis unearths the necessity of "building coalitions across confessions," which should first begin with the "disparate Protestant groups" before any inclusion of other "Christian Confessions;" he also regrets the lack of attention by the Assemblies to the "splendid work of the Orthodox Churches over the centuries in Egypt and Ethiopia."

At the beginning of the 21st century and the third millennium, Utuk's observations, analysis and criticism remain current and relevant. African Christians are still divided, not only along ethnic, socio-economic and political lines, but also and especially along their faith lines. It would be wrong to say that nothing has been done. Yet both the churches' *ad extra* and *ad intra* challenges continue to question the relevance of Christian faith in the continent. The ongoing intra and international conflicts and the socio-economic as well as political predicaments of the African people defies the Church's self-understanding as communion, yet in search of unity. *Thinking and Feeling with the Churches* must first be grounded in the reality, whether cultural, social, economic, or political of the people. As Hamilton Dandala says, "to emphasize denominational divisions in such circumstances is to undermine the mission of the Church to bring healing and transformation to the situations that the people face."[14] Thus, inculturation remains imperative as far as the search for Christian unity in Africa is concerned.

Ecumenism and Inculturation

The Second Vatican Council's assertion on the role and importance of local culture in evangelization still remains valuable today. It says:

[13] Utuk, *Visions of Authenticity* 232–33.
[14] Hamilton M. Dandala, "The Challenges of Ecumenism in African Christianity Today," in Diane B. Stinton, ed., *African Theology on the Way: Current Conversations* (London: SPCK, 2010) 104.

The seed which is the word of God grows out of good soil watered by the divine dew, it absorbs moisture, transforms it, and makes it part of itself, so that eventually it bears much fruit. So too indeed, just as happened in the economy of incarnation, the young churches, which are rooted in Christ and built on the foundations of the apostles, take over all the riches of all nations which have been given to Christ as an inheritance. . .[15]

Different documents that came after the council explain this in a broader context of evangelization. *Evangelii Nuntiandi*, for example, asserts that "evangelisation means bringing the Good News into all the strata of humanity, and through its influence transforming humanity from within and making it anew."[16] For the Church in and of Africa, the 1994 Synod of bishops gave an important place to the theme of inculturation. Indeed, through the Synod, not only does the Church in and of Africa re-emphasize the importance of inculturation as "a priority and urgent matter," but also affirms that "inculturation is a demand of evangelization."[17] As it says:

Inculturation is a movement toward full evangelization. It seeks to dispose people to receive Jesus Christ in an integral manner. It touches them on the personal, cultural, economic, and political levels so that they can live a holy life in total union with God the Father, under the action of the Holy Spirit.[18]

According to the Nigerian theologian, Oliver Alozie Onwubiko,

The task of inculturation since the Second Vatican Council has been to convince some theologians and particularly those Christians with more of colonial than Christian missionary zeal that Christianity could enter into marriage with other cultures.[19]

---

[15] *Ad gentes divinitus* no. 22.

[16] Paul VI, *Apostolic Exhortation Evangelii Nuntiandi* (Rome: Vatican Polyglot Press, 1975) no. 18.

[17] *Propositio*, nos. 29 and 30 = among the Propositions given to the Pope by the synod fathers after the synod. See: Maura Browne (dir.), *The African Synod: Documents, Reflections, Perspectives* (Maryknoll, NY: Orbis Books, 1966) 97.

[18] Ibid. 32.

[19] Olivier Alozie Onwubiko, *The Church in Mission in the Light of Ecclesia in Africa* (Nairobi, Kenya: Paulines Publications Africa, 2001) 385.

Inculturation, however, from the African perspective goes back to the year 1956 when African theologians published their "first distinctive statement" in *Des Prêtres Noirs s'interrogent*.[20] Since then, African theologians have been searching and writing on African Traditional Religion (hereafter ATR), especially its role for a meaningful encounter with Christianity. Inculturation has become the "mot d'ordre" of doing theology in Africa. It has been used as methodology to decipher both the contents and meaning of Christian faith so that it may be understood and properly lived by African people. A recent book by Laurenti Magesa stresses the place of African Religion in the dialogue debate, a subject that has been neglected in "formal religious discourse in Africa today."[21] It is important to notice that Magesa talks about African Religion not African Traditional Religion. He takes the understanding of inculturation to another level by taking African Religion as a "distinct and distinctive entity" so that in the process of dialogue "there can be no question of arbitrarily collapsing identities together even where, from the point of view of African theology, the process of inculturation is concerned."[22] The main goal of the different above-mentioned definitions is to show the central role of cultures in the practice of evangelization in general but especially in Africa.

Why then is inculturation important in the search for Christian unity in Africa? Such a question invites us to evaluate the way ecumenical dialogue has been done in Africa for the past fifty years. It would be wrong to say that the Churches of Africa have done little or nothing. The section above already shows the contribution of the Protestant denominations to the early formation of the ecumenical movement. Generally, ecumenical dialogue in Africa takes place in three ways: (1) bible translation, (2) common worship, and (3) cooperation. In his book entitled *African Christianity: Its Public Role*,

---

[20] Albert Abble, et al., *Des Prêtres Noirs S'interrogent* (Paris: Les Éditions du Cerf, 1956).

[21] Laurenti Magesa, *African Religion in the Dialogue Debate* (Zweigniederlassung Zurich: LIT Verlag GmbH & Co. KG, Wien, 2010).

[22] Ibid. 69.

Paul Gifford devotes the first two chapters to Africa in general and the global context of the African Churches.[23] Gifford's description of the socio-political life of post-independence Africa remains relevant today. Despite the achievement of independence fifty years ago, Africa is still underdeveloped and still lives in uncertainty. The different crises such as HIV/AIDS, refugees, corruption, conflict, and terrorism are but examples of this uncertainty. According to Gifford, "the explicit involvement of Africa's churches was drawn to the world's attention in the late 1980s, when francophone countries began national conferences and Catholic bishops were appointed to chair them."[24] In many other countries, such an involvement has been conducted by a particular Church or, by some National Council of Churches.

An evaluative example of the ecumenical movement drawn from my own country, Madagascar, may elucidate further the above statement and what Gifford described regarding the churches' involvement in the public sphere.[25] The Fiombonan'ny Fiangonana Kristianina eto Madagasikara (hereafter FFKM) or the Ecumenical Council of Christian Churches of Madagascar is already thirty-five years old. At the end of the week of prayer for Christian unity, January 20, 1980, Christians from the four main Churches that compose the FFKM[26] came together responding to the invitation of their respective leaders to pray and welcome the official constitution of the FFKM. On July 13 of the same year, the Ecumenical Council was equipped with its first central committee followed by the creation of the different commissions such as that of Theology, Youth, Women,

[23] Paul Gifford, *African Christianity: Its Public Role* (London: Hurst & Company, 1998) 1–56.

[24] See Ibid. 21. Gifford mentions, for examples, Mgr. Isidore de Sousa (Benin), Mgr. Basile Mve Engone (Gabon), Mgr. Sanouko Kpodzro (Togo), Mgr. Ernest Kombo (Congo), Mgr. Laurent Monsengwo Pasinya (Zaire).

[25] Part of this evaluation is taken from the author's doctoral thesis entitled "Ecumenism in the light of the Church as God's Family: A Malagasy Perspective." (Ph.D. diss., The Catholic University of Eastern Africa, 2015).

[26] FFKM is composed of four mainline Churches: Roman Catholic, Anglican, Lutheran, and Protestant (Church of Jesus Christ in Madagascar).

National Affairs, and Education, among others. Indeed, the current ecumenical activities in Madagascar can be grouped in three areas: common translation of the bible, common worship, and political mediation. But the Ecumenical Council of the Christian Churches is well known by the majority because of its intervention in politics since independence.

First, the common translation of the bible is an area where ecumenism is fruitfully taking place in Madagascar. This project started immediately after independence, but could not continue due to the reluctance of some denominations. It could, however, resume after the installation of FFKM or the Ecumenical Council of Christian Churches of Madagascar, and received a lot of help from the Biblical Society. All the Bible, all the Old and New Testament books, have now been translated ecumenically into the Malagasy language. The translation is currently being used by many local parishes of different denominations in many parts of the country.[27]

Second, the Malagasy ecumenical movement stresses common worship as the centre of ecumenical activities. Church members of the Ecumenical Council only meet a few times a year to celebrate particular events: New Year, Independence Day, and one day of the week of Christian unity in January. Yet, little has been done in terms of research and practice in areas such as the liturgy. In an interview with the Anglican Bishop, Ranarivelo S. Jaona, he regrets the lack of research in the area of liturgical celebration, for instance in the celebration of the Eucharist as well as in the reception of Communion. His opinion stems from his understanding of the Malagasy culture of meal and sacrifice, especially their role in affirming and building up the community.[28] It is indeed interesting to observe the contradictions that occur when celebrating a sacrament. On the one hand, the

---

[27] It is to be noted that although the publication of the ecumenically translated Bible has been a decisive step in the ecumenical life of the Malagasy Church, some denominations, for instance the Lutheran Church, decided to oppose the use of the translation.

[28] Jaona Ranarivelo, *Interview* on June 15th, 2011. The interview took place during the research conducted for the dissertation mentioned above in n. 25.

Church does not allow intercommunion during the celebration of a sacrament, so much so that some members of a family prefer staying outside the Church's main door during such a celebration; on the other hand, the same family members would later celebrate as one family the so-called event of grace by sharing food as well as dancing. This fact requires a deeper theological reflection on who we are as we search for the unity of the Church.

Third, the FFKM has been instrumental in its efforts at solving the different political crises in the country during the past four decades. Both the crisis of 2001 and that of 2009 are still fresh in memory to illustrate such an ecumenical engagement in reconciliation and justice. The crisis of 2001 came from a protest against the result of an election on December 16 of the same year, whereas the one of 2009 came as a result of a long frustration among the majority of people being subjected to an ongoing tendency of near dictatorship by one man. The involvement of the Ecumenical Synod/Council in such a situation always brings to surface the challenging question regarding the Church-state relationship. Gilbert Raharijatovo, a journalist and politician, sees this ambiguous role of the FFKM as so powerful that it is a threat to politicians in power or in search of power in the country. He says :

> La puissante congrégation œcuménique des églises chrétiennes de Madagascar, connue sous le nom de Fiombonann'ny Fiangonana Kristiana eto Madagasikara, FFKM, fait peur à tous les politiciens au pouvoir ou en quête de pouvoir. Ce n'est pas parce qu'elle est politique, mais justement parce qu'elle dit apolitique, qu'elle dispose d'une marge de manœuvre suffisante, pour arbitrer quand les besoins se font sentir ou pour prendre de position, quand elle juge que c'est nécessaire, comme c'est le cas dans les divers événements politiques qui ont secoué, d'une manière périodique, le pays.[29]

[29] Gilbert H. Raharizatovo, *Madagascar 2002: Genèse et Silences d'une Crise* (Antananarivo: Editions Antanimena, 2008) 278: "The powerful FFKM frightens all politicians in power and in quest for power. This is not because the FFKM is political; but precisely because it is non-political it is free to arbitrate when necessary, as in the case of the different political events that have shaken the country."

Despite the achievement of the FFKM in terms of political mediation or reconciliation, a lack of serious theological reflection that should accompany the work of the FFKM is noticeable. It seems that ecumenism does not really constitute a pastoral priority for any of the Church members of FFKM, or for the FFKM itself. The enthusiasm at the beginning of the ecumenical movement in the 80s seems to be fading away despite the many efforts of popularizing the movement among the Christians through publications, conferences, and diverse sessions. The involvement of the FFKM in politics, which has been seen by the Church leaders as a symbol of its prophetic role, has not really impacted the faithful. On the contrary, such an involvement has been interpreted as political. In the eyes of the majority, whether politicians or not, the FFKM plays as a counter-power to the different regimes in the country. An interesting question to ask is whether Christians at the grassroots really understand what ecumenism is all about, even after thirty years of existence of FFKM. In fact, interviews conducted with Catholic lay leaders of Small Christian Communities reveal that none of them perceived or understood the challenges of Christian unity in their communities. This unawareness obviously stems from the lack of theological reflection, especially in ecclesiology, and as a result of it, the neglect of its pastoral dimension. Despite the riches of Vatican Council II in terms of ecumenism and the subsequent post-conciliar documents, the Roman Catholic Church has never entered into serious reflection on the movement it has engaged in for the benefit of its faithful. The same observation can be said about other church members of FFKM.

The evaluation of the Malagasy ecumenical movement can illustrate and reflect the experience of the Christian churches in the continent of their search for Christian unity. Although the commitment to reconciliation and justice might indeed be necessary, it must be rooted in a solid theological grounding. Such a theological reflection also requires a methodology that takes into account the sociocultural context of the people. In other words, for the Christian churches in and of Africa to be a symbol of communion and unity, they must embrace what they hold in common not only as Christians but also as Africans.

Thinking and Feeling with the Churches

Despite the diversity of cultures in Africa, African people, especially those of sub-Sahara, to some extent share the same "value systems, beliefs and practices." African culture is believed to be a communitarian one in which the understanding of a person cannot be separated from the community to which he or she belongs. I find the concept *Ubuntu* which is the "most abiding principle of African worldview"[30] relevant in reflecting on the relationship among Churches.

What is *Ubuntu?* Archbishop Desmond Tutu speaks of it against the backdrop of apartheid and the "Truth, Justice, and Reconciliation Commission" in his book *No Future without Forgiveness.* A sample of his descriptive definition of the term would be useful for our purpose.

> It [*Ubuntu*] speaks of the very essence of human being . . . We say, "A person is a person through other persons." It is not, "I think therefore I am." It says rather: "I am human because I belong. I participate, I share." A person with *Ubuntu* is open and available to others, affirming of others, does not feel threatened that others are able or good, for he or she has a proper self-assurance that comes from knowing that he or she belongs in a greater whole and is diminished when others are humiliated or diminished, when others are tortured or oppressed, or treated as if they were less than who they are.[31]

Drawing from different scholars, Munyaka and Molthabi came up with the following definition:

> Although there is no single definition, all those cited imply that *Ubuntu* is more than just a manifestation of individual acts. It is a spiritual foundation, an inner state, an orientation, and a disposition towards good which motivates, challenges and makes one perceive, feel and act in a humane way towards others. It is a way of life that

---

[30] Muleki Munyaka and Mokgethi Motlhabi, "Ubuntu and Socio-Moral Significance," in Munyaradzi Felix Murove, ed., *African Ethics: An Anthology of Comparative and Applied Ethics* (South Africa: University of KwaZulu-Natal Press, 2009) 63.

[31] Desmond Mpilo Tutu, *No Future without Forgiveness* (New York: Doubleday, 1999) 31.

seeks to promote and manifests itself and is best realised or made evident in harmonious relations with society.[32]

Laurenti Magesa succinctly defines it as the "value of ultimate or accomplished humanness."[33] The nature and characteristic of *Ubuntu* is generally summed up in the saying "I am because we are" whose "components can be identified such as respect for persons and the importance of community, personhood and morality."[34] At the centre of *Ubuntu* resides the sharing of human nature and life. The person, not considered as pure individual like an atom, finds fulfilment in belonging to a community of people who share the same life, values, beliefs and customs. The community is the place for formation of personhood.

Using the culture of *Ubuntu* may enhance the effort towards Christian unity in Africa. Indeed *Thinking and Feeling with the Churches* in an African context demands a solid theological framework rooted in the socio-cultural reality of the African people. The weakness of the ecumenical movement in Africa, as mentioned earlier, resides in the lack of theological reflection that sustains it. If Church is truly understood as "people of God" or "Family of God," then *Thinking and Feeling with the Churches* means thinking and feeling with the people in their own context and reality. It requires an ecumenism from below that speaks to and serves the people of God with compassion and love. This leads to an important question whether the culture of *Ubuntu* could provide such a theological framework. In other words what can Christian faith learn from this cultural value that is cherished by the majority of African people?

---

[32] Munyaka and Motlhabi, "Ubuntu and Socio-moral Significance," 65.

[33] Laurenti Magesa, *What is not sacred? African spirituality* (New York: Orbis Books 2013) 13. In fact, according to Magesa, it is expressed in various names among different groups of Sub-Saharan Africa: *Ubuntu* (among the Zulu, Xhosa, Ndebele—South Africa), *Botho* (Sotho, Tswana—Botswana), *Umunthu* (Chewa—Malawi), *Obuntu* (Ganda—Uganda), *Utu* (Swahili—East and Central Africa), *Unhu* (Shona—Zimbabwe), *Obunu* (Kwaya/Jita—Tanzania) etc.

[34] Ibid.

Michael Battle, in his book on reconciliation, explores the riches of *Ubuntu* and builds what he calls the *Ubuntu* theology of Desmond Tutu. He develops this theology by pointing out "four vectors":

> First, this theology builds up true, interdependent community. Second, it recognizes persons as distinctive in their identities. Third, it combines the best of European and African cultures to produce a new and distinctive theology. And fourth, it is strong enough to address—even overthrow—apartheid.[35]

My reflection will be on the community dimension of *Ubuntu* from an African perspective and how such an understanding will help shun Christian division and help truly think and feel with the churches. Christian division is not an African-made division. The Christianity that came to Africa was and is still a divided Christianity. As such it came as an addition to the already existing divisions such as ethnic, social or cultural. African Christians are being entangled in this challenge every day. More particularly the reality of division in its multiple aspects occurs at the heart of African society, which is the family.[36]

However, we have no hesitation in saying that any division, whatever its origin or nature, is against the spirit of *Ubuntu*. *Ubuntu* finds its foundation in God who created human beings in God's own image (Gen 1:27). Indeed, the story of creation reveals the connectedness that exists between creatures. The root of such a connectedness is *life*.[37] God, human beings and other creatures share the same *life* from the beginning, through the act of creation, as Cecil McGarry submits:

> In this way the Bible reveals God's plan for the human race and for the world. Love and communion are at the heart of human life

[35] Michael Battle, *Reconciliation: The Ubuntu Theology of Desmond Tutu* (Cleveland, Ohio: The Pilgrim Press, 1997) 40.

[36] This reality is recognized by the Synod of the Bishops for Africa in 1994 as we will see later.

[37] It is important to know that life in the African understanding is more than biological life; it takes its root from God the creator through the ancestor. That is why ancestral veneration has an important place in African culture.

and express its deepest meaning. A human person finds happiness and fulfilment in communion and friendship with God, with other persons and with nature. The condition for this communion is the inner peace and harmony that comes from accepting ourselves and God's plan for our life and in living it fully.[38]

Seen from this perspective, division, especially Christian division is against God's will from the beginning. It is within that context of bringing humanity back to life in its fullness that we can understand the history of salvation culminating in the death and resurrection of Jesus, in which the churches participate in their being and mission. The practice of *Ubuntu* therefore stems from the awareness of sharing life with God, the community, and God's creatures (the cosmos). *Thinking and Feeling with the Churches* would remain just an ideal, or indeed a veritable impossibility unless it is founded on this awareness of belonging through the sharing of divine life.

The foregoing reflection clearly shows that the principle of *Ubuntu* can enhance the search for unity among Christians. As we set aside our division, we become more aware of our vulnerability[39] and embrace what we share together. When describing the mystery of the Church, the Second Vatican Council began by saying that the purpose of the creation of the universe was "to raise up men to share in his [God's] own divine life."[40] The culture of *Ubuntu* can explain and expand our understanding of unity or communion in an African context. The Church as communion or communion ecclesiology has a long history in the tradition of the Church. The term communion itself comes from the Greek *koinōnia* whose "root *koin* suggests what is common; hence words such as fellowship, participation, communion and solidarity, always with a personal element,

---

[38] Cecil McGarry, "We are God's People: the Church as Communion." in Terry Charlton, ed., *Exploring our Christian Life: in the Light of the African Synod* (Nairobi: Paulines Publications Africa, 1994) 79.

[39] See Battle, *Reconciliation* 40.

[40] *Lumen gentium* no. 2.

contribute to the sense of *koinōnia*."[41] In fact, the Church as people of God or Body of Christ is the image which explains the mystery of communion. Communion ecclesiology involves relationship, divine and human as well. According to Dennis M. Doyle:

> It [communion ecclesiology] represents an attempt to move beyond the merely juridical and institutional understandings by emphasizing the mystical, sacramental, and historical dimensions of the Church. It focuses on relationships, whether among the persons of the Trinity, among human beings and God, among the members of the Communion of Saints, among members of a parish, or among the bishops dispersed throughout the world. It emphasizes the dynamic interplay between the Church universal and the local churches.[42]

This quotation from Dennis M. Doyle reveals that communion ecclesiology includes all the dimensions of the Church: divine, mystical, sacramental, historical, and social. Those dimensions obviously "overlap and interpenetrate" and cannot be viewed separately. It is not surprising to see that the Church in/of Africa, through the Synod of Bishops in 1994, adopted "Family" as the image of the Church appropriate for Africa. The image of Family, whose centre is *Ubuntu* or the sharing of life, reveals and fosters the communion with God and the unity of humanity. Indeed, in his exhortation, taking from the propositions of the Synod fathers, John Paul II says:

> The Synod Fathers acknowledged it [the Church as God's Family] as an expression of the Church's nature particularly appropriate for Africa. For this image emphasizes care for others, solidarity, warmth in human relationships, acceptance, dialogue and trust. The new evangelization will thus aim at building up the Church as Family. . . .[43]

---

[41] Christopher O'Donnell, *Ecclesia: a Theological Encyclopedia of the Church* (Collegeville, Minnesota: The Liturgical Press, 1996) 94.

[42] Dennis M. Doyle, *Communion Ecclesiology: Vision and Versions* (Maryknoll, New York: Orbis Books, 2000) 12.

[43] John Paul II, *The Church in Africa: Post-Synodal Apostolic Exhortation Ecclesia in Africa* (Nairobi: Paulines Publication Africa, 1995) nos. 63, 48.

Such an understanding of the Church definitely has an ecumenical dimension and implication. The Synod for Africa whether in the preparatory documents or in the Post-Synodal Exhortation, speaks of ecumenism within the context of dialogue. The *Instrumentum Laboris* (hereafter IL), for example, sees the dialogue (ecumenical and/or interreligious) as an important part of the Church's mission. It states:

> Hence, the Church is not free with respect to dialogue nor does she enter into it with ulterior motives. Striving to live in a state of continual conversion and of docility to the Holy Spirit, she cooperates with his activity wherever it is found. To a certain extent, the Holy Spirit is also active in the other Churches and Christian Communities as well as in the other religions of the world. The Church has a duty to discern this activity and to promote it to the best of her energy, and this calls for dialogue and mutual challenge. In this way, she grows into the fullness of Christ, the foundation of God's self-manifestation and self-communication to man.[44]

Drawing from the riches of the Church's documents, the IL insists that dialogue is constitutive of the evangelizing mission of the Church in that "dialogue is not an alternative for proclamation or a substitute for it; one implies the other, and both are different aspects of the same mission of the Church."[45] In Africa particularly, the document continues, "religious pluralism cuts across national, tribal and at times even family lines" so that the risk of conflict and discord is unavoidable. With regard to ecumenism, Africa is host to "older Churches truly indigenous" such as the Coptic Orthodox Christians in Egypt and Sudan and Ethiopian Orthodox Christians. Other Christian Communities emanating from the Christian divisions of the 16th century have been present in Africa for centuries. Yet, challenges remain due to "differences on the level of doctrine and of the interpretation of the bible, on the nature and mission of

[44] *Instrumentum Laboris* no. 76.
[45] Ibid. n. 77.

the Church, on moral questions and Church discipline."[46] John Paul II, in his Post-Synodal Exhortation, obviously acknowledges all this and reiterates the importance of ecumenical dialogue with other Churches and Ecclesial communities, and of dialogue with African traditional religion and Islam.[47]

Thus, the Church understood as Family, and whose centre is *Ubuntu*, is not confined to any particular Church such as the Roman Catholic. It not only concerns the Church of Africa, but even possesses a universal character that reaches out to the unity of the human family. The culture of *Ubuntu*, through which we become more aware of our humanness in relation to others, brings our understanding of baptism to a new and deeper level. Baptism does not make one join a particular community or a particular family; instead, through baptism one joins a wider family or extended family. Baptism possesses an ecumenical characteristic in that the baptized Christians can truly call one another "brothers and sisters," as announced by the Council.

Thinking and Feeling with the Churches impels Christians to become symbols of *Ubuntu* in their daily life. The Second Vatican Council's invitation to Church renewal implies the fostering of *Ubuntu* among Christians in view of unity. The Council says:

> There can be no ecumenism worthy of the name without interior conversion. For it is from newness of attitudes of mind, from self-denial and unstinted love, that desires of unity take their rise and develop in a mature way. We should therefore pray to the Holy Spirit for the grace to be genuinely self-denying, humble, gentle in the service of others and to have an attitude of brotherly generosity toward them. . .[48]

Furthermore, the Churches commitment to peace, justice and reconciliation must begin at home by fostering *Ubuntu* among Christians first and, second, in the wider community. Pope Francis,

---

[46] Ibid. no. 83.
[47] See John Paul II, *Ecclesia in Africa* no. 49.
[48] *Unitatis redintegratio* no. 7.

in his recent Apostolic Exhortation, speaks of the search for unity as a journey which Christians are invited to fulfill and finish together. He says:

> We must never forget that we are pilgrims journeying alongside one another. This means that we must have sincere trust in our fellow pilgrims, putting aside all suspicion or mistrust, and turn our gaze to what we are all seeking: the radiant peace of God's face. Trusting others is an art and peace is an art. Jesus told us: "Blessed are the peacemakers" (Matt 5:9). In taking up this task, also among ourselves, we fulfil the ancient prophecy: "They shall beat their swords into ploughshares" (Isa 2:4).[49]

Conclusion

The first rule in the *Spiritual Exercises* for thinking with the Church deals with personal judgment and obedience to the Church (*Ex.* 353). For instance it invites us to "put aside all judgment of our own" and "obey in all things, the hierarchical Church." This should be understood within the context of the time, namely the Reformation. Yet, the intention of Ignatius could be understood as an effort to bring change or reform from within the Church. Such an intention has, to this day never been fully achieved. The search for Christian unity has come a long way. It is a challenging process. The role of a theologian and ecumenist is always that of a bridge that connects the tradition of the Church with the present reality. That is what I have been trying to do in this paper. *Thinking and Feeling with the Churches* in an African context basically requires a dialogue between the theme itself and the African socio-cultural riches. I have chosen the culture of *Ubuntu* to do that. African worldview is rich, and *Ubuntu* constitutes one of its pillars. *Thinking and Feeling with the Churches*, when seen through the practice of *Ubuntu*, implies awareness of what we share together as Christian brothers and sisters as well as a true growth of communion towards unity.

---

[49] Pope Francis, *The Joy of the Gospel: Apostolic Exhortation Evangelii Gaudium* (Nairobi: Paulines Publications Africa, 2013) no. 244.

Jocelyn Rabeson, S.J. belongs to the Jesuit province of Madagascar. He is currently the head librarian and a lecturer in systematic theology at Hekima College, Nairobi, Kenya.

Sentir con la iglesia and Ecumenical Rapprochements of the Sixteenth Century: An Indian Reality

Antony Mecherry, S.J.

Clear-cut differences of opinion prevailed among the early Jesuits in Rome and elsewhere—such as in sixteenth-century Malabar in southwest India—regarding the application of the Ignatian principle of "thinking with the Church." The Jesuits in Rome, in contrast to those in Malabar, actually did a better job of adjusting to the ecumenical climate of the sixteenth century, despite the limited understanding of ecumenism in that century.

Historically speaking, the Ignatian dictum *sentir con la iglesia*, inadvertently led to an understanding of the ecclesial exclusivity of the hierarchical Roman Church. At the level of interpretation, Ignatius of Loyola had, in his "rules for thinking with(in) the Church," prompted the Jesuits to recognize the working of the Spirit even in a different way of thinking and in a plurality of opinions, whether those opinions pertained to the theological, liturgical, or canonical life of the church.[1] Supposing that this interpretation is significant also with regard to plurality and diversity in ecclesial expressions, a question arises here: did the Jesuit missionaries who set out for India, from the mid-sixteenth century onward, follow this Ignatian attitude of openness that operated within the "rules for thinking with the Church"?

As far as the ancient church in Malabar was concerned, this Ignatian message went through evolutionary phases even during the time of Ignatius of Loyola (d. 1556), the founder of the Jesuit order. Note that in 1557, the Jesuits in Malabar played a crucial role

---

[1] Antonio Guillén, "Praise: the Fundamental Attitude in the Church," *The Way* 52, no. 2 (2013) 101–112 at 105.

in ousting from India Mar Abraham, the bishop of the Christians of St. Thomas. Mar Abraham then belonged to the Assyrian Church of the East, in other words, to the Nestorian Church, as understood in the sixteenth century. Quite unexpectedly, by 1565 the Jesuit curia in Rome had sent clear-cut instructions to the Jesuit superiors and missionaries in India, asking them to welcome Mar Abraham on his way back to India. By that time, the pope and the Chaldean patriarch had named Mar Abraham the metropolitan of the see of Angamaly in the Malabar Church, respecting his communion with Rome.[2]

Despite the order from Rome, no religious, including the Jesuits in India at that time, were prepared to welcome Mar Abraham in Malabar. Accordingly, one can observe a considerable opposition between the official position of the Jesuits in Rome regarding the acceptance of the new ecumenical context and the outlook of the Jesuit missionaries in India. For, having become aware of the rite difference of the Malabar Church, which always had followed the East Syrian rite, the Jesuits in India began to act on the assumption that they were supposed to adhere rigorously to the Ignatian point of departure by thinking, judging, and feeling with the Roman Church. Furthermore, the presupposition of the missionaries in general regarding the superiority of the Latin rite played a crucial role in prompting the Jesuits to take a precautionary approach towards the Chaldean bishops and their rites. In addition to the preoccupation of the orthodoxy of the Catholic Church, a thrust for uniformity played a key role in the outlook of the missionaries, especially in a Counter-Reformation epoch. Consequently, the Ignatian message regarding the praise of a plurality of opinions did not bear much fruit in the Malabar Church.

---

[2] Joseph Wicki, ed., *Documenta Indica* (hereafter *DI*), vol. 6, (Rome: Institutum Historicum Societatis Iesu) 451, letter from Francis Borgia, the vicar general of the Society of Jesus, to the rectors and the superiors in India on 23 March 1565.

A Question of Incompatibility

The first generation of Jesuit missionaries in India, confounded as they were by the presence of an already existing church in Malabar, a church different from their Latin Church, considered the Malabar Church as incompatible with the Ignatian vision of *sentir con la iglesia*. Consequently, the Jesuits in Malabar behaved in such as way as if the Ignatian vision presupposed the existence of only the Roman Church, its Latin rite, and papal primacy.[3] Furthermore, the spirit of Counter-Reformation, Reconquista, and Inquisition played a crucial role in the encounter between the *Padroado* missionaries, including the Jesuits and the Christians of St. Thomas in ancient Malabar.[4] At the same time, unaware of and unaffected by the confessionally divided church in the West, the Christians in Malabar held in high esteem their jurisdictional affiliation with the East Syrian Church of Mesopotamia. That respect for the East Syrian Church brought forth in the Malabar Church an independent ecclesiastical hierarchy

---

[3] Ignatius of Loyola gave eighteen rules in his *Spiritual Exercises* (nos. 352–370) regarding thinking with the church, otherwise known as the rules for thinking, judging, and feeling with the church. On the surface, these rules presupposed the authority of the hierarchical Roman Church. Furthermore, according to the *Constitutions of the Society of Jesus*, "the unity of the Church is cherished and any schismatic tendencies are regarded a threat to that unity. 'To have separated oneself for a time from the bosom of the Holy Church (*gremio de la santa Iglesia*) is considered as an impediment for acceptance to the Society of Jesus'." See Fredrik Heiding, "Ignatian Spirituality at Ecclesial Frontiers," (D.Phil., diss. University of Oxford, 2012) 35. *Sancti Ignatii de Loyola Constitutiones Societatis Iesu, MHSI, Monumenta Ignatiana*, vol. 2 (Roma: 1936) 285.

[4] The *Padroado* refers to the Portuguese patronage of the Catholic missions. During the reign of Afonso V (1438–1481), the popes handed over plenipotentiary power to Portugal by means of a number of papal documents. Subsequently, the exploration of the new world resumed during the reign of King João II (1481–1495). Pope Sixtus IV confirmed to João II the privileges previously granted to the king of Portugal by his predecessors, Nicolas V and Callixtus III. The crucial papal bulls regarding the *Padroado* rights were *Romanus Pontifex* by Nicholas V (January 8, 1455), *Inter Caetera* by Calixtus III (March 13, 1456), and *Aeterni Regis* by Sixtus IV (June 21, 1481). See Frances Gardiner Davenport, ed., *European Treaties Bearing on the History of the United States and Its Dependencies to 1648* (Washington, DC: Carnegie Institution of Washington, 1917) 9–55.

that had functioned for centuries, even before the arrival of the Portuguese in Malabar, without being under the direct control of the pope in Rome.[5]

Perceiving that the jurisdiction of the Chaldean patriarch over the local church in Malabar would be an impediment both to the *Padroado* and papal jurisdiction over the Christians of St. Thomas, Jesuit visitor Alessandro Valignano laid out, in 1584, a clear-cut mission policy regarding the gradual reduction of the Christians of St. Thomas.[6] Subsequently, Valignano decided to establish a Latin seminary in Malabar with a view to uprooting the vestiges of the Chaldean period, including the Syriac language of the Malabar Christians. Besides the strategies mentioned, Valignano further maintained that ancient Christianity in Malabar, with its social privileges in a caste-based society, had a key role to act as a catalyst in the conversion of the high castes.[7] In other words, Valignano decided, at least for the time being, to view the caste distinctions in Malabar as conversion potential. However, note that by the term *caste*, the Jesuits in Malabar did not mean the postcolonial construct of caste as a system, but the "castas"—that is, the occupational groups and

---

[5] Andrews Thazhath, *The Juridical Sources of the Syro-Malabar Church: A Historico-Juridical Study* (Kottayam: Paurastya Vidyapitham, 1987) 68–72. Pope Julius III (1550–55) extended the jurisdiction of the Chaldean patriarch to India and China. See Giamil Samuel, *Genuinae relationes inter Sedem Apostolicam et Assyriorum Orientalium seu Chaldaeorum Ecclesiam: nunc maiori ex parte primum editae, historicisque adnotationibus illustratae* (Rome: Ermanno Loescher, 1902) 15–23.

[6] The verb *reduzir* in Portuguese implies "to reduce," "to reclaim," "to reform," and "to mend." Etymologically speaking, it could mean "bring back," "lead back," and "restore." Nevertheless, in Malabar, the Jesuits understood the term *reduzir* as a process of separating the Christians of St. Thomas from the influence of the Nestorian Church and its rites by leading them to the rites and usages of the Latin Church. According to the interpretation of Vincenzo Poggi, the Jesuits used the term *reduzir* with regard to the Malabar Christians meaning "reduction into the fold of Peter," without any reference to the Jesuit reductions of Paraguay and the other Latin American territories. See Vincenzo Poggi, "Gesuiti e Diamper," in *The Synod of Diamper Revisited,* ed. George Nedungatt, 105–133 (Rome: Pontificio Istituto Orientale, 2001) 117.

[7] *DI*, X, 267, 753.

divisions of Malabar society with strict codes of societal frontiers and pollution rules.

For their part, the Malabar Christians always had held in high esteem the church of East Syria and its patriarch. From 1553 onward, the patriarch of the Uniate Church in Chaldea enjoyed jurisdiction over the Christians of St. Thomas. In addition to the hierarchical dependence on the Chaldean Church, the Law of Thomas, Syriac language, Chaldean rite, social privileges, and participation in cultural and social life ensured the unique identity and place of the St. Thomas Christians in Malabar society.[8] Even upon the arrival of the Jesuits in Malabar, the local Christians faced coercive methods employed by the *Padroado* missionaries who tried to reduce the local Christians forcefully to the Latin Church and its rite. Accordingly, until 1577—that is, until the official entry of the Jesuits in the Malabar Church—the local Christians effectively prevented the *Padroado* missionaries from entering into their ecclesial and social life.[9]

The Jesuits in the Face of Ecumenical Rapprochements

Among the ecumenical endeavors of the patriarchs of the church of East Syria, the most celebrated result, the union of Patriarch Yukhannan Sulaqa with the Roman Church, occurred in 1553, during the reign of Pope Julius III.[10] But in 1552, before the birth of the Catholic patriarchate of the East Syrian Church, Antonio de Heredia, S.J., encountered the Malabar Christians. And even prior to the arrival of Heredia in Malabar, Jesuit Francis Xavier had made every attempt to introduce the Jesuit mission into the Malabar

[8] The Malabar Christians defined their particular law as the Law of Thomas, distinguishing their law from the Law of Peter. See *DI*, XIV, 804.

[9] Joseph Wicki, "How the Jesuits Began to Work among the Christians of St. Thomas, 1575–1577," in Jacob Vellian, ed., *Malabar Church*, Orientalia Christiana Analecta 186 (Roma: Pontificium Institutum Orientalium Studiorum, 1970) 193–202.

[10] Giuseppe Beltrami, *La Chiesa Chaldea nel secolo dell'Unione* (Rome: Pont. Institutum Orientalium Studiorum, 1933) 86–100.

Church.[11] Accordingly, Ignatius of Loyola assured Xavier that he would send Jesuits to the Malabar Church. However, Ignatius could not send Jesuits to Malabar because of the lack of clarity that prevailed between the Jesuits and the Portuguese king regarding the provision of the mission. By the time of the death of Ignatius in 1556, Mar Abraham, who later would become the metropolitan of the see of Angamaly, reached Malabar, even though at that time Mar Abraham did not yet belong to the Uniate Church in Chaldea.

As part of the ecumenical endeavors of the sixteenth century, Bishop Ambrosio Buttigeg, OP, and Antonio Zahara, O.P., entered the Malabar Church by the end of 1557, accompanied by two Catholic bishops from Chaldea, Mar Joseph and Mar Elias. I view the arrival of the Catholic bishops in Malabar as part of the ecumenical initiatives of the Uniate Church in Chaldea with the Roman Church.[12] Although these bishops represented the Catholic patriarch, the Portuguese detained them in Goa, north of Malabar on the west coast of India. Afterwards, the *Padroado* missionaries in Malabar, including the Jesuits, efficiently employed these Chaldean bishops in ousting Mar Abraham from Malabar. At the same time, the Jesuit missionary Melchior Carneiro, who came to Malabar in 1557, found that the reputed Nestorianism of the Malabar Church did not exist in actual practice in the Malabar Church. Consequently, alluding to a rudimentary form of the methods of adaptation in mission, Carneiro thought of encouraging the positive customs of the Christians of St. Thomas. Realizing that the liturgical language of the local Christians was Syriac, Carneiro informed the Jesuit general in Rome that the Malabar mission was in an urgent need of a talented Jesuit, well versed in both Syriac and Latin, to help the

---

[11] Xavier, Francis, *The Letters and Instructions of Francis Xavier*, ed., M. Joseph Costelloe (Anand: Gujarat Sahitya Prakash, 1992) 222.

[12] *DI*, IV, 10. In 1558, Bishop Ambrosio Buttigeg passed away while he was in Cochin (Beltrami, *La Chiesa Chaldea* 46). On the other hand, Mar Elias and Mar Joseph tried to convert Mar Abraham into the Catholic Church (Beltrami, *La Chiesa Chaldea* 50).

Jesuits to enter into the linguistic and cultural world of the local church and to help the local Christians.[13]

On the other hand, the Jesuit missionary Melchior Nunes Barreto came to Malabar with an inquisitorial mindset, and he was successful in ousting Mar Abraham from India. Nevertheless, when Archbishop Mar Abraham joined the Uniate Church in 1565, Pope Pius IV permitted the archbishop to keep some of the customs and usages of his see of Angamaly. The pope found that the customs and usages of the local church in Malabar were not in opposition to the dogmas of the Catholic faith.[14] In other words, this provision further indicated that Mar Abraham had requested, on his visit to Rome, that the pope protect the identity of the local church in Malabar. Notwithstanding the intelligent moves on the part of Mar Abraham, the Portuguese viceroy detained the archbishop a second time when Mar Abraham reached Goa in 1568. Note that Mar Abraham had secured legitimate credentials from both the pope and the Chaldean patriarch in order to govern the see of Angamaly respecting the jurisdiction of the Chaldean patriarch.[15]

From 1575 onward, recognizing that only amiable approaches would help the Jesuits to enter the Christian community in Malabar, Valignano thought of a new mission method, *entrare con amore* ("entering with love"), which historiographers have come to call the method of accommodation.[16] However, Valignano did not reveal to the local Christians his strategies regarding the gradual Latinization of the Malabar Christians and the elimination of the Syriac language.

---

[13] *DI*, III, 810–11.

[14] *DI*, XI, 64–65. Biblioteca Nacional, Lisbon, *Fondo Geral.*, *Codice*. 464, f. 8ʳ.

[15] *DI*, XI, 64–65.

[16] *DI*, X, 168. *A Glossary of Jesuit Terms and Phrases* defines accommodation as "originally a device of humanistic rhetoric, the ability to adapt oneself and one's speech in order to be in touch with the feelings and needs of the audience, this became a device of all Jesuit ministries which spanned many cultures and contexts." As cited in Ines G. Zupanov, "One Civility, But Multiple Religions: Jesuit Mission among St. Thomas Christians in India (16th–17th Centuries)," *Journal of Early Modern History* 9, no. 3 (2005) 284–325 at 286.

While Mar Abraham was struggling to ensure his jurisdiction over the church in Malabar in 1563, Juan Alfonso de Polanco, the secretary of the Society of Jesus, asked Jesuit provincial Gonçalo Vaz de Melo of Portugal to obtain a directive from the Portuguese king Sebastião I that would prevent the white Jews and the Syrian bishops from entering India.[17] Furthermore, Polanco stated that the reduction of the heretics would be more difficult a task than the conversion of the infidels.[18] Accordingly, Polanco's opinion clearly shows that he had upheld an exclusive rather than inclusive understanding of the Ignatian *sentir con la iglesia*. At the same time, the church in general lacked an awareness of the right spirit of ecumenical endeavors especially in the context of the confrontational spirit of the Counter-Reformation. Meanwhile, in 1565, Mar Abraham reached Rome and obtained papal credentials, thereby asserting his legitimate authority over the Christians of St. Thomas. Furthermore, he received the supporting letters of the superior generals from all the major religious orders in Rome, including the Jesuits. It is likely that the appearance of Mar Abraham in Rome had given Polanco an opportunity to think differently regarding the union of the churches.

Regarding the Catholic missions in general, suspicion of heresy played a crucial role even in the outlook of the missionaries toward the ecumenical rapprochements of the sixteenth century. However, Jesuit General Diego Laynez (1558–1565) took concrete steps to prepare the Jesuit missionaries to face the new ecclesial climate of ecumenism, despite the lack of a clear definition of *ecumenism* at the time. Even though Polanco was not hopeful about the reduction of heretics to the Catholic fold, Laynez informed João Nunes Barreto, S.J., in 1563 that Audishu IV Yukhannan, the patriarch of the Chaldean Church had united with the Roman Church. Furthermore, Laynez expressed hope that the churches in India subjected to Patriarch Audishu, the successor Yukhannan Sulaqa, would persevere in the union.[19]

---

[17] *DI*, V, 651.

[18] *DI*, V, 703, Polanco to Melchior Carneiro on 6 January 1563.

[19] "Que en ello persevere con las muchas yglesias a él subjetas, que parece se

Again, note that the Jesuits in the later decades of the sixteenth century generally viewed the union of the Eastern churches with the Catholic Church only as acts of reduction and victory over what the Western Church considered heresy. However, the question of the differences of the Eastern rites remained untreated in subsequent decades. Still, after knowing from Melchior Barreto, S.J., about the importance of the Syriac language in the Malabar Church, Laynez ordered Antonio de Quadros, the provincial of India, to organize Syriac lessons in the Jesuit college in Goa. Moreover, Laynez asserted that the knowledge of the Chaldean language among the missionaries was very important to ensure their authority among the Christians of St. Thomas, since the local Christians did not admire the Latin language.[20] Meanwhile, after seriously considering the request from Polanco regarding the Syrian bishops, King Sebastião of Portugal ordered Francisco Coutinho, the Portuguese viceroy, to prevent the schismatic Syrian bishops from entering Malabar.[21]

Ecumenical Rapprochements under Suspicion

Despite the enthusiasm of Laynez regarding the ecumenical rapprochement of the Chaldean Church, the Jesuits in India found it difficult to welcome in Malabar Mar Joseph, another Uniate bishop from the Chaldean Church. In 1565, in an unexpected turn of events, Francisco Borgia, the vicar general of the Society of Jesus, ordered the Jesuit rectors and superiors of India to receive and to give due honor to Uniate Archbishop Mar Abraham at his arrival in India.[22] Before the arrival of Borgia's letter in India, however Jesuit Vice-Provincial

estiende hasta esa India." *DI*, V, 693, Diego Laynez to João Nunes Barreto on 1 January 1563. The seventh session of the Council of Trent formally recognized Patriarch Audishu IV Yukhannan (1555–1570) in 1562. See Van Den Berg Heleen Murre, "The Patriarchs of the Church of the East from the Fifteenth to Eighteenth Centuries," *Journal of Syriac Studies* 2.2 (1999) 250–51.

[20] *DI*, V, 699.

[21] *DI*, VI, 12, Sebastião I to Francisco Coutinho on 6 March 1563.

[22] *DI*, VI, 451, Francis Borgia to the rectors and the superiors in India on 23 March 1565.

Barreto informed Diego Mirón, S.J., the provincial of Portugal, that the Bishop George Temudo, O.P. of Cochin had already reduced the Malabar Church to the "perfect obedience" and customs of the Roman Church. According to the vice-provincial, it was not wise, then, to allow even Mar Joseph to stay in Malabar. Barreto feared that Mar Joseph would resist the further reduction of the Christians of St. Thomas into the Latin Church.[23]

The comment of Barreto on the "perfect obedience" of the local Christians bears ample testimony to the attitude of the missionaries in Malabar regarding the superiority of the Latin rite. By *perfect obedience*, Barreto probably meant the Latinizing attempts of the bishop of Cochin and the formal obedience that the leaders of the Malabar Christians accorded to the bishop in 1563, when both of their Chaldean bishops were in exile.[24] However, that formal obedience did not effectively result in the Latinization of the local Christians. For as soon as Mar Joseph reached Malabar, the local Christians renewed their allegiance to him. On the other hand, the historiography that the agents of the *Padroado* propagated began to portray Mar Joseph and Mar Abraham as "professed Nestorians."[25]

Conclusion

The discrepancies in the Jesuit outlook regarding the reception of the Uniate Churches reflect a general perplexity prevailing in the sixteenth century at the differences in ecclesial expressions. Many factors contributed to the rise of such confusion. Primarily, the sixteenth century ecclesial climate, affected by the confessional divisions within the Catholic Church, did not favor deeper ecumenical endeavors. Secondly, the Ignatian dictum *sentir con la iglesia*

---

[23] *DI*, VI, 699, Melchior Nunes Barreto to Diego Mirón on 20 January 1566.

[24] Archivum Romanum Societatis Iesu, *Goa-Malabar*, LXV, f. 6.

[25] Antonio de Gouvea, *Jornada of Dom Alexis de Menezes: A Portuguese Account of the Sixteenth Century Malabar; Jornada do Arcebispo originally written in Portuguese in 1603 by António de Gouvea*, ed. Pius Malekandathil (Kochi: LRC Publications, 2003) 33.

presupposed, at least at the level of its literal understanding and in specific missions, an uncompromising loyalty to the Roman Church and Latin rite. Thirdly, the *Padroado* missionaries functioned as the agents of a complex system in which both crown and altar worked together to make decisions regarding missions in distant lands like Malabar in India. In addition to the three factors mentioned above, the inherent conflicts about the presentation of the Catholic faith in cultures with an unyielding disposition overwhelmed the ecclesial climate of the sixteenth century.[26]

In other words, conflicts between faith and culture prompted the Jesuits in Malabar in the later decades of the sixteenth century to formulate the rudimentary methods of adaptation or accommodation (*accommodatio*) in the Malabar mission before they set out for the other centres like Japan, China, and Madurai. Yet even at this stage of vague openness to the cultural realities of individual missions, a few Jesuits attempted a different approach—one emphasizing the need to accommodate creatively the Catholic faith in the context of emerging ecclesial and ecumenical realities. Nevertheless, in those attempts, the Ignatian point of departure *sentir con la iglesia* embraced a wider perspective at the practical level. Furthermore, that perspective required of the missionaries an openness to appreciate the Spirit at work in ecclesial expressions different from those operative in the Roman Church.

Antony Mecherry, S.J. is a member of the teaching staff at the Pontifical Oriental Institute in Rome. He is specialized in the early modern history of the church, in particular, in the history of the Christians of St. Thomas in ancient Malabar seen from the perspective of mission methods and of the relationship between faith and culture.

---

[26] Antony Mecherry, S.J., "Francis Ros, SJ, and the Method of Accommodation among the Christians of St. Thomas in Malabar (1584–1624)" (Ph.D. diss., Rome: Pontificia Università Gregoriana, 2016) 95–108.

Responding Together to an Anti-Christian Climate: The Gujarat United Christian Forum for Human Rights (GUCFHR)

CEDRIC PRAKASH, S.J.

This Case Study attempts to highlight not only the "thinking" and "feeling" with the Churches but also the "acting together." Dialogue, however necessary, often devolves, entering into hair-splitting theological discourse. But what ultimately wins the day is an ecumenism that is practical at the grassroots and that finds ways to help create that "union of hearts and minds"' that is so dear to us in the Society of Jesus.

Introduction

India has been regarded as the "cradle of great religions" giving to the world some of its major religions like Buddhism, Jainism, and Sikhism, as well as Hinduism. The Muslim population is the second largest in the world; and Christians are roughly about 2.5 percent, making us more than 50 million in a billion-plus population. Religious pluralism, cultural diversity, harmony, and tolerance have been India's forte. This acceptance, however, in recent years, is under great stress with the upsurge of right-wing Hindu groups who have been systematically targeting the minorities, particularly the Christians. (India may also have today the largest number of Christian denominations in the world!)

1998–99 was a defining year for the Christians of Gujarat.[1] A series of attacks all over the country on Christians (personnel and on their institutions) resulted in massive demonstrations in several

---

[1] Gujarat is the westernmost state of India, on the coast, south of Pakistan and north of Mumbai.

parts of the country. Gujarat was not to be left behind and more than 30,000 Christians were on the streets in Ahmedabad (Gujarat's former capital and largest city) on December 4th 1998 saying "**stop these attacks.**"

The Christians of Gujarat then came together under a loose banner hastily assembled called "**The United Christian Forum for Human Rights**" (GUCFHR). It brought together all the mainline Churches and also several of the evangelical Churches that were working in Gujarat.

The then right-wing Government of Gujarat and their cronies were definitely not amused that such a large number of Christians would come onto the streets in protest—in a city that was dominated by Hindus.

Beginning on Christmas day, 1998, Christians in several parts of Gujarat were attacked as never before. The Dangs district in the South of Gujarat bore the brunt of these attacks. While no deaths were reported, there were several Christians who were beaten up by right-wing Hindus, and several Churches/prayer halls, and vehicles belonging to Jesuits were destroyed. All this in the land of Mahatma Gandhi, the apostle of peace and non-violence, who was born and brought up in Gujarat!

The Christians of Gujarat raised a hue and cry that prompted the then Prime Minister of India Atal Bihari Vajpayee to rush down from New Delhi in order to calm the Christians. Several other political leaders also came out in support of the Christians. The National Minorities Commission had a hearing and its report against the Government was severe.

As the violence lessened, the Christian leaders from the various denominations felt the need to come together in a more cohesive way, and in March 1999 they formed the **Gujarat United Christian Forum for Human Rights (GUCFHR).**

The Gujarat United Christian Forum for Human Rights

The main objectives of the GUCFHR are:

1. To provide fellowship and a common forum for dialogue and for fostering common concerns among the Churches in Gujarat.
2. To promote Christian Unity as a basic requirement for the life and work of the Church and as an essential step for restoring the wholeness of the human community.
3. To communicate the mission of the Church, relating it to every aspect of life.
4. To preserve, promote, and defend all **Fundamental and Minority Rights** as enshrined and guaranteed in the Indian Constitution.
5. To promote inter-religious dialogue with a view to maintaining a spirit of brotherhood, religious harmony, and communal peace.
6. To engage in and enhance the quality of the educational, social welfare, relief, development, and health services by the churches.
7. To represent the Churches/Christian Congregations before the public, the Government, and other appropriate agencies.
8. To initiate and to promote action in the area of the socio-political needs of the poor and the marginalized, including those of the Christian community in Gujarat.

The first signatories of this unique collaborative venture are the Bishops/Elders of the following twelve mainline Churches that work in Gujarat:

1. The Church of North India (Gujarat Diocese)
2. The Catholic Archdiocese of Gandhinagar (the Capital of Gujarat)
3. The Catholic Diocese of Ahmedabad
4. The Catholic Diocese of Baroda
5. The Catholic Diocese of Rajkot

6. The Gujarat Regional Conference of the Methodist Church in India
7. The Salvation Army Indian (Western)
8. The Malankara Orthodox Syrian Church
9. The Mar Thoma Syrian Church
10. The Seventh Day Adventist Church (Gujarat Conference)
11. The Syrian Orthodox Church
12. The Christian Missionary Alliance of India (Gujarat Synod)

Ever since its inception, the GUCFHR has been meeting regularly (once every three months) under the able leadership of the Catholic Archbishop of Gandhinagar, Stanislaus Fernandes, a Jesuit (he resigned as Archbishop upon reaching the age of 75 years. The Bishop of Ahmedabad took over as Archbishop of Gandhinagar, Gujarat on September 12th 2015). Fr. Cedric Prakash, S.J. has been the Convenor/Secretary of the GUCFHR since its inception.

The quarterly meetings are attended by most of the Bishops/Elders/Heads of Churches and or their representatives. The meetings normally begin and end with a prayer and fellowship: common issues are discussed, concerns/problems are shared; plans of action/joint programmes are chalked out. The forum tries in several ways to address the growing human rights violations that are perpetrated not only on the Christians of Gujarat but also on the poor and other vulnerable sectors of society.

The joint annual programmes include: the Christmas Prayer and Fellowship of priests/pastors and religious; ecumenical prayer services in different Churches during the Christian Unity Octave in January; and training/workshops on particular issues for priests/pastors/religious/lay leaders.

The Freedom of Religion Law of Gujarat 2003

One important issue which the GUCFHR has taken up is to challenge the "Gujarat Freedom of Religion" law which was promulgated by the Gujarat Government in 2003 and made implementable five years later in 2008. This law is one of the most draconian laws in the history of any democracy in the world and was piloted by the then Chief Minister of Gujarat, Narendra Modi, who is currently the Prime Minister of India.

One needs to look into some basic aspects of this law to understand why the Christians of Gujarat from across their respective divides have come together to challenge such a law that clearly targets the Christians and other minorities of the State.

The provisions of this law include the following:

- It prohibits forcible conversion by allurement or fraudulent means. "Allurement" is defined as "any gift or grant of any material benefit, either monetary or **otherwise.**" "Force" is defined as "show of force or a threat of injury of any kind, including threat of divine displeasure or social ex-communication." "Fraudulent means" is defined as "misrepresentation or any other fraudulent contrivance."

- It provides for punishment of those who seek to forcibly convert for a period up to three years imprisonment and a fine up to Rs.50,000. But if the person being forcibly converted is a "minor, a woman, or a person belonging to a scheduled caste or scheduled tribe," the punishment is for a term of up to four years imprisonment and a fine of Rs. 1 lakh.

- Anyone seeking to convert someone from one religion to another, either by performing a ceremony as a religious priest, or who takes part directly or indirectly in the ceremony, shall have to obtain **prior permission** from the district magistrate (a civil authority) using a prescribed format.

- The person who is sought to be converted **shall have to inform** the district magistrate about the ceremony within a prescribed period, to be laid down in the rules. In case of default, the converted shall face up to one year imprisonment or a fine of Rs.1,000 or both.

That Narendra Modi is the Prime Minister of India today assumes great significance in the "freedom of religion" debate. In his election campaign of 2002 in Gujarat he promised to introduce an anti-conversion law if elected. True to his word, on March 26th 2003, the Gujarat Assembly passed the above **"Gujarat Freedom of Religion Act 2003."**

In keeping with this law, in February 2006, at a Shabri Kumbh (a mass gathering of Hindus) program in the Dangs (supported by the Gujarat Government), Modi warned the Christians *"It is my constitutional duty to prevent conversions. Our Constitution disapproves of them, and yet some people turn a blind eye."* Morari Bapu accused the Christians of bringing in planeloads of missionaries from the Vatican *"who come here to carry out conversion activities but when we organise a 'ghar wapsi' why should it be termed as bad?"* Both Modi and Morari Bapu clearly endorsed the "ghar wapsi" programs which were part of that program (and today this is a burning issue in many parts of India).

The moot point is certainly not whether one has the right "to convert another," but whether citizens of India have the right to adopt a religion of their own choice. This is not only guaranteed in the Constitution of India, it is also enshrined in the Universal Declaration of Human Rights: *"everyone has the right to freedom of thought, conscience and religion; this right includes freedom to change his religion or belief, and freedom, either alone or in community with others and in public or private, to manifest his religion or belief in teaching, practice, worship and observance"* (Art. 18).

Eminent Jurist and former Solicitor General of India, Mr. Soli Sorabjee addressing a public gathering on the subject at the Nehru Centre in London on June 11th 2003, stated:

> The Gujarat legislation goes one step further and provides that the person who is converted has also to seek permission from the District Magistrate about the fact of such conversion. Failure to comply with these statutory provisions invites severe punishment of imprisonment and fine. These provisions are objectionable. They intrude on a person's right to privacy. One's religious belief is essentially a private

matter as is conversion from one's religion to another. It is a result of deep-seated inner convictions. The State laws have the effect of deterring genuine conversions and impairing the substance of religious freedom guaranteed by the Constitution. These laws have further shaken the confidence of the minority communities and accentuated their sense of insecurity.

This law is very obviously directed at the Christian minority of Gujarat. Already in 1998–99, as we have said earlier, Christians were roughed up in the Dangs district and in several parts of South Gujarat. Now, with Modi as the PM, the community continues to be intimidated and harassed though not as blatantly as what the Muslims are subjected to.

Rallies against Attacks on the Christians

Besides the rally that was organized on December 4th 1998, the GUCFHR has successfully organized two other major rallies in the city of Ahmedabad bringing together Christians of all denominations and also other men and women of goodwill on a common platform.

In September 2008, in the wake of the attacks of the Christians in Orissa (a state on the east coast), Karnataka (a state in the southwest) and in other parts of India, more than 25,000 people were once again on the streets of Ahmedabad demanding justice for the Christians and that the perpetrators of these dastardly acts be brought to book.

Again on March 20, 2015, in response to concerted attacks on the Christians since May 2014 (listed as at least 200) all over the country, the GUCFHR organized a major rally in the city of Ahmedabad saying, *"enough is enough."*

Challenges in Working Together

It is good to think together, to feel together and to "act together," but the last mentioned is certainly not easy to do. We have had several challenges ever since we began "working together." These include:

- One upmanship games; "it is your need to come together not ours."
- "You Catholics have the money so as long as you foot the bill, then we 'may' come for the joint programmes."
- We come together on human rights; but we would rather play footsie with the Government even if they are the biggest perpetrators in the attacks against the Christians.
- As Christians, we should be engaged only in the proclamation of our faith—nothing else!
- It is good to talk and share but, after that, the Churches do what they want.
- Problems of communication: decisions made by the Bishops/Elders do not reach the grassroots.
- Concern about the way some evangelical groups operate/proselytise— often in very insensitive ways.

Conclusion

Yes, there are drawbacks/obstacles, and certainly some serious ones, but we do see them as challenges in our quest to come closer together. Our former Superior General Fr. Peter Hans Kolvenbach in an opening address to the Rome Consultation in 2004 entitled "Sentire cum Ecclesia" said:

> In our day, this can mean that it is appropriate to make a scandalous situation public if there is no other way to correct it. Ignatius believed that if our love for Christ, inseparable from love and solidarity for the Church, his Spouse, prompts us, after a prayerful discernment, to speak out, the result will always be constructive.

While it is clear what he was speaking about, and also its context, we can certainly apply these words to our efforts in the Gujarat United Christian Forum for Human Rights. We have come a long way these past years, and we certainly look forward to a more effective and meaningful coming together in the years ahead.

Cedric Prakash, S.J. from Gujarat, widely honored for his work in human rights, inter-religious dialogue, and ecumenism, was founding director (2001—15) of PRASHANT, the Ahmedabad-based Jesuit Centre for Human Rights, Justice, and Peace. Since 2016 he has been based in Beirut with the Jesuit Refugee Service (MENA Region) responsible for Advocacy and Communications.

Both Thinking and Feeling with the Churches: Catholic-Orthodox Ecumenism and Christian Spirituality

Dorian Llywelyn, S.J.

Efforts to rebuild unity between the Orthodox and Catholic Churches by theological dialogue have moved slowly. Underlying these discussions are cultural factors and different conceptions of the nature of theology. "Spiritual ecumenism" offers the possibility of helping overcome theological impasses, and the academic discipline of spirituality, with its emphasis on experience, provides a conceptual framework to address the often under-explored impact of cultural factors on ecumenical progress.

I frequently tell my students that all intellectual interests contain some element of autobiography. Experiences that do not appear in our official areas of research or our current CVs are likely to be reflected in what academics study and teach. This paper has as its formal topic the long, slow, tortuous path toward unity between the Catholic and Orthodox Church, in both United States and international arenas. But equally important in any study is emotional motivation and practical method. One's particular intellectual foci are likely to be closely related to context, and often reflect passionately held convictions and concerns. By way of explanation, therefore, it is important to note that the emotional motors of this paper—the things that concern me—include the current state of American Catholic theology, especially the distance between academic theology and the realities of the faithful; the connections between religious and cultural experience; and the academic study of spirituality.

Background

Some nine years ago, the university at which I then worked invited me to set up and run a new ecumenical institute, the aim of which is fostering relations between the Catholic and Orthodox Churches at local, regional, national, and international levels. The institute's founding donor is a wealthy Orthodox businessman. On a visit to Germany with his family, he could find no Orthodox church one Sunday and so attended Mass at a Catholic parish. Given the restrictions on eucharistic reception, he found the experience of being Orthodox among Catholics in equal parts congenial, puzzling, and disturbing. That seminal experience in turn led to his dream of the possibility of being able, in his lifetime, to be able to receive Holy Communion in a Catholic Church. His hope—one which is shared by many—is courageous, yet its realization seems to remain locked up in a distant, permanently receding, and eschatological future. Full, visible, doctrinal, and jurisdictional unity, in whatever form that might take, seems to be an unattainable desideratum. Indeed the disunity concerning the nature of what unity consists of is itself the symptom, the symbol, and the cause of profound disagreements.

There is a sense in which Catholic-Orthodox theological dialogue has reached a certain plateau. That is, we have moved along far since the heady days of the lifting of the mutual excommunications between the Holy See and the Ecumenical Patriarchate in 1965, but the pace of movement seems to have slowed. That having been said, it is also important to note that, particularly during the pontificate of Pope Francis, there are areas of new growth. Yet some of these developments seem to precede theological exploration or even to override it. In 2014, the Prior and founder of the Comunità Monastica di Bose, and consultor of the Pontifical Council for Promoting Christian Unity, Enzo Bianchi, speculated that the Pope might call upon Orthodox bishops to assist him in governing the Church.[1]

---

[1] http://www.thetablet.co.uk/news/1024/0/pope-francis-could-invite-orthodox-to-help-run-the-church-

Ecumenical Patriarch Bartholomew I, in an interview given in April 2015 to *La Civiltà Cattolica* said that "thankfully today the spirit of fraternal love and mutual respect has replaced the old polemic and suspicion . . . [W]e have learned to forgive one another for the mistakes and mistrust of the past; and we have taken significant steps toward rapprochement and reconciliation."[2] He added that "the central, critical points are 'difficult to unpack' giving as the reasons for that difficulty, the presence of 'prejudice and polemic on both sides'." Importantly, moreover, precisely how church leaders conduct themselves while these issues are being discerned "will have a significant impact on how authority is perceived in the church." In other words, Bartholomew was teaching that content and meaning are intimately connected with style, the medium being at least part of the message. In the meantime, at the level of practical ecumenism the Ecumenical Patriarch affirmed that there is much the Orthodox churches "can do together with Pope Francis in order to respond to the vital needs of our world," suggesting as examples of such solidarity between Catholics and Orthodox, (1) service to the poor, (2) addressing climate change, and (3) concern for the situation of Christians in the Middle East.

"Unity" Pope Francis recently said, "cannot be created in a congress on theology."[3] He also confirmed the story that Patriarch Athenagoras had said to Paul VI: "Let us quietly go forward; we can put all the theologians on an island to carry on their discussions, while we keep walking on in life!" Given this recent stress on practical unity, it might well seem that theology is either a hindrance or irrelevant. At one level, then, current Catholic-Orthodox relations are warmer, more practically urgent, and less concerned about theological differences. Or rather, as this article will suggest, they might be based on a different conception of the sources, role, and nature of theology

---

[2] English translation from https://www.patriarchate.org/-/interview-of-the-ecumenical-patriarch-bartholomew-inherit Redirect=true

[3] https://w2.vatican.va/content/francesco/en/speeches/2014/may/documents/papa-francesco_20140526_terra-santa-conferenza-stampa.html

than the one which has been operative in ecumenical discussion up to this point.

Keeping in mind Patriarch Bartholomew's strictures concerning polemic, prejudice, and the behavior of church leaders, it is useful to look back to the 2007 Ravenna meeting of the Joint International Commission for Theological Dialogue between the Roman Catholic Church and the Orthodox Church. One participant told me that even getting participants in the same room had been a minor miracle, given the height of emotions. Contrary to Russian objections, the Ecumenical Patriarchate had invited members of the Estonian Apostolic Church to attend. Russian Orthodox representatives, led by Bishop Hilarion Alfayev, then of Vienna, walked out in protest.

The theological fruit of that meeting was a document called "Ecclesiological and Canonical Consequences of the Sacramental Nature of the Church: Ecclesial Communion, Conciliarity and Authority." Understandably, in the light of the tensions, the Ravenna document is theologically cautious, minimalistic even. On the matter of primacy and synodality, it states: "It remains for the question of the role of the bishop of Rome in the communion of all the Churches to be studied in greater depth."[4] In other words, the level of authority of the meeting and the conditions and climate were not right. The document limits itself to posing the question "How should the teaching of the First and Second Vatican councils on the universal primacy be understood and lived in the light of the ecclesial practice of the first millennium?"[5] The question is consonant with the suggestion made by Pope John Paul in *Ut unum sint* 96: "Could not the real but imperfect communion existing between us persuade Church leaders and their theologians to engage with me in a patient and fraternal dialogue on [papal primacy], a dialogue in which, leaving useless controversies behind, we could listen to one

---

[4] http://www.vatican.va/roman_curia/pontifical_councils/chrstuni/ch_orthodox_docs/rc_pc_chrstuni_doc_20071013_documento-ravenna_en.html, 45.

[5] Ibid.

another?" The same issue of the Petrine office has been discussed further in the meetings of Paphos in 2009 and Vienna in 2010. Yet reconciliation, if indeed there is any reconciliation in this matter at all, seems to creep forward in geological time, almost imperceptible to human perception.

The difficulties of that "patient, fraternal" listening are expressed in a single, telling footnote to the Ravenna document:

> Orthodox participants felt it important to emphasize that the use of the term "the Church" . . . in this document and in similar documents produced by the Joint Commission in no way undermines the self-understanding of the Orthodox Church as the one, holy, catholic and apostolic Church, of which the Nicene Creed speaks. From the Catholic point of view, the same self-awareness applies: the one, holy, catholic and apostolic Church "subsists in the Catholic Church". . . . This does not exclude acknowledgement that elements of the true Church are present outside the Catholic communion. [6]

So one of the key theological ideas, that is, who the Church is, remains non-negotiated and non-negotiable. As a result, with no mutual recognition of each other's identity, it is difficult to see how the parties could value what each other said.

Cultural Analysis

In teaching ecumenism, I frequently invite students to compare Catholic-Orthodox relations to marital therapy. Let us imagine a couple who cannot live together peaceably. Separated now for as many years as they lived together, they cannot nevertheless bring themselves to divorce. For many years the spouses have been meeting regularly in difficult sessions in which the Holy Spirit is a well intentioned but frustrated therapist whose skills they/the couple cannot (or will not) avail themselves of. Where partners in relationships have experienced

---

[6] http://www.vatican.va/roman_curia/pontifical_councils/chrstuni/ch_orthodox_docs/rc_pc_chrstuni_doc_20071013_documento-ravenna_en.html. n.1.

a long history of hurt and miscommunication, apparently innocent words and small gestures can unexpectedly explode an arsenal of half-buried ancient resentments. Anecdotally, I have found that my own relations with the Orthodox in Los Angeles and other places vary from the genially cordial to the politely distant. But when apparently minor practical questions have arisen—who sits where in a liturgy, who gets to talk first, and last, and for how long, at a symposium— prejudice and polemic can re-emerge as it were from nowhere. I have discovered to my surprise that as a member of the Catholic hierarchy I bear a share of responsibility for all the offenses committed by my Church to the Orthodox, including the conquest of Constantinople by Frankish troops in 1204! All of this is to confirm Bartholomew's conviction that in ecumenical encounter, the emotional tone can be effectively as important as its ostensible content, if not more so.

In therapeutic encounters, the initial presenting symptoms are rarely the real issues at stake. It is true that the theological sticking points of Orthodox-Catholic relations are truly sticky. According to the Romanian Catholic monk Maximos Davies, "old disputes over the Filioque . . . and the modern Roman dogmas of the Immaculate Conception and Assumption . . . are usually agreed to be subspecies of the problem of papal assertions, the Catholic understanding of papal primacy being the greatest difficulty."[7] Yet my conviction is that relations between the Churches of East and West are not only— and perhaps not even primarily—a matter of theology, much less of dogmatic theology. I wonder rather whether the question of papal primacy—that is to say the Orthodox understanding of the Catholic understanding of papal primacy and vice versa—is as much about inter-cultural epistemology. By way of illustration, in discussing the quest to restore unity between the Chalcedonian and non-Chalcedonian Orthodox Churches, John Erickson argues:

> the chief reason for Christian division today is division itself. What-
> ever may have been the issues initially leading to division, a division

---

[7] http://americamagazine.org/issue/636/article/what-divides-orthodox-and-catholics

once established very quickly takes on a life of its own, as each side tries to justify its own role in the division. Differences that would not in themselves have been church-dividing are invested with new meaning, to the point of becoming symbols of division rather than examples of legitimate diversity.[8]

That extra level of new meaning is most distinctive at the level of ecclesial cultures. Collective, cultural psychologies were clearly operative in Archbishop Hilarion's decision to walk out of the aula at Ravenna. Even without the presence of Catholics (and thus no significant theological bone of contention) inter-Orthodox relations are inevitably fiery, involving, as they do, competition between parallel hierarchies and a tangle of ethnic, national and political considerations. In this milieu, intellectual considerations are frequently hypercharged by emotions which do not necessarily correlate directly to the matter at hand. Differences between collective psychologies, especially when they are at most only half-consciously acknowledged, are the deep source of those disproportionate reactions that too easily demolish the work of years of building up cordiality.

What affects theological discussions to a degree not often recognized are what the historian Ramon d'Abadal i de Vinyals called *mythomoteurs*—the constitutive myth of a society. These deep stories about itself provide a group with a sense of roots in the past, an identity in the present, and a purpose for the future. A *mythomoteur* does not define the content of discussion, yet inevitably sets its tone and, therefore, affects the possibilities of reconciliation where there is rupture. Orthodoxy is unlikely to impinge much on the *mythomoteurs* of many individual Catholics or most Catholic communities, for historical and geographical reasons: the papacy is located in Western Europe, the imagined center of Catholicism for much of its history; the dominant strains of Catholic culture and imagination have been predominantly European; and few of the historical centers of Catholic population in Western Europe and North and South America, or the

---

[8] https://www.svots.edu/content/beyond-dialogue-quest-eastern-and-oriental-orthodoxy-unity-today

more recent centers in Asia and Africa have Orthodox populations. The traditional Orthodox homelands, in contrast, frequently present elements of what anthropologists call negative identity formation, where a communal sense of self is constructed in contradistinction to a neighboring but alien polity. Catholics, Maximos Davies says, are perceived in the Orthodox mind as being radically "other."[9] Orthodox identity is construed partially as being intrinsically suspicious of Catholicism on the one hand and adversarial to Islam on the other.

Collective identities easily fuse religious allegiance with ethno-national belonging. The solidarity between altar and throne, dating back to Constantine, continues for example in the instinct that, "to be Croatian is to be Catholic"[10] (with the implied corollary that "to be Serbian is to be Orthodox" and that Croatian-Serbian relations are therefore necessarily Catholic-Orthodox relations). Religio-political *mythomoteurs* are particularly likely to exhibit striking continuity and longevity. With the waning of Christian commitment in the West, Russian anti-Western attitudes continue to be cast in a religious mold, proposing Russia as the messianic champion of traditional values. This modern ideological posture is the current manifestation of an *antemurale*, bulwark identity based on territory and religious frontiers. The Russians, says one commentator,

> deeply believe that Europe would have succumbed to the Mongols and could not have either retained its Christianity or developed culturally and scientifically if Russia had not absorbed the shock of Mongol invasion. Therefore, they believe that the West owes a debt of gratitude to Russia, [which] still sees itself as a bulwark against the Islamic South, which continues to threaten Europe . . . Russia developed a sense of duty to perform a civilizing role, both in parts of Europe and in Asia, especially among its Muslim subjects.[11]

[9] Davies, "What Divides Orthodox and Catholics" (see above, n. 7).

[10] Zlatko Skrbiš, "The Apparitions of the Virgin Mary of Medjugorje: The Convergence of Croatian nationalism and her Apparitions," *Nations and Nationalism* 11, no. 3 (July 2005) 2.

[11] Shireen Hunter, Jeffrey L. Thomas, and Alexander Melikishvili, eds., *Islam in Russia: The Politics of Identity and Security* (London: Routledge, 2005) 5.

The 2016 pan-Orthodox Synod has the potential to lead to major ecumenical transformations, negative as well as positive. One of the particular *mythomoteurs* underlying the Synod is that there exists a unique Orthodox civilization, construed as a religio-cultural force in opposition to the liberal secular West. In Catholicism, the pastoral ecclesiology of *Gaudium et spes* has long supplanted the dogmatic image of the Church as *coetus perfectus*—itself an *antemurale* conceit. In contrast, among the Orthodox, the image of the Church and particular people as eschatological bastion of civilization perdures, and seems to be strengthening under fire.

In addition to these cultural factors, Orthodox relations with Catholicism, are also affected by differences in the nature, locus and culture of doing theology. It is commonplace to note the slow separation in the West between, on the one hand, theology and, on the other, religious experience, that is, between the *fides quae* and the *fides qua*. The separation of these tectonic plates is often dated to the development of medieval scholasticism with its need to define, delineate and distinguish in the face of error, along with the growth of the university and the resultant professionalization of theology. Today, in the official bodies of ecumenism, it is rare to find a Catholic representative who does not have a doctorate in theology, and many either work in academia or have a strong background in it. As academics, we necessarily partake in the particular culture of academia, which includes the dominance of lexical intelligibility, the passion for *disputatio*, and the deployment of various forms of logic. More subtly, we are also affected by the micro-culture of contemporary secular academia, with its own internal debates, tensions, ideologies, and preferential options.

Participants in ecumenical dialog at the top level include such eminent figures as Bishop John Zizioulas and Cardinal Walter Kasper, professional academic theologians both before they were elevated to the episcopacy. On the Orthodox side, however, Bishop Zizioulas is something of an exception. The development of theology as an academic enterprise is a comparatively recent development for Orthodoxy, which did not experience the growth of the influence of the university that Western Catholicism did. In Orthodoxy, *theologia* cannot be considered as an enterprise separate from the whole life of the Church. If theologians could be put on an island, as Athenagoras suggested to Paul VI, doing theology could not be so easily isolated. Evagrius's oft-quoted dictum "the theologian is the one who prays truly, and the one who prays truly is a theologian" reflects the fact that the monastery rather than the university, is the cradle of Orthodox theology, and theology is composed in the tones of doxology. Nor has Orthodoxy for the most part developed a philosophically assisted systematic theology on the Western model. Our Orthodox brothers (and a few sisters) thus speak out of a *theologia* conceived of as a body of wisdom rather than from the fissiparous nano-specializations of Western thought.

The Eastern Churches did not pass through the Renaissance, Reformation or the Enlightenment, all of which have molded Western theology, Catholic and Protestant alike. Within Orthodoxy, therefore, such contemporary Catholic concerns as feminism or social justice are innovative, and not always assimilated or welcomed. What Catholic theology can receive from Orthodox thought is at least its finely tuned sensitivity to the spiritual implications of theology and canon law. The fact that the Church is conceived of as an "icon of the Trinity" means for example that the Orthodox have historically perceived the addition of the *Filioque* not only as an imperialistic innovation by/of the Western Church. The *Filioque*, they argue, also homogenizes Father and Son, and subjugates the Spirit to them, a deviation of belief which results and supports a monarchic model of the Church. Theologically, including the Estonian Church at Ravenna was for the Russians a denial of the synodal ideal of the *koinonia* which should participate in and reflect the inner life of the Trinity. Culturally and politically, that inclusion was seen as an exercise in Constantinopolitan quasi-papalism.

I share a Romantic nostalgia for the pre-scholastic intimacy between the *fides qua* and the *fides quae*. Two different kinds of theology emerge from each of these aspects of faith. Robert Taft has frequently highlighted the difference between the two by contrasting *theologia prima* with *theologia secunda.* In the memorable description of Bob Taft, *theologia prima* is

> the faith expressed in the liturgical life of the Church antecedent to speculative questioning of its theoretical implications, prior to its systematization in the dogmatic propositions of theologia secunda or systematic reflection on the lived mystery of the Church. Liturgical language, the language of theologia prima, is typological, metaphorical, more redolent of Bible and prayer than of school and thesis, more patristic than scholastic, more impressionistic than systematic, more suggestive than probative . . . it is symbolic and evocative, not philosophical and ontological."[12]

Theologia secunda—what Western theology for much of the last thousand has thought "theology" consists of—came early to involve systematization into discreet dogmatic tracts – *De Ecclesia, De Deo Uno, De Deo Trino,* and so forth. Such differentiations are pedagogically useful and intellectually coherent. But they have also engendered as a by-product a tendency toward fragmentation and disunity. In the Catholic universities of North America, many theologians reject the word "systematic" in favor of "constructive," arguing that this latter adjective implies that the theological enterprise is an ever-expanding universe. The advantage of this construal is that theology can indeed add an infinite number of specialist extensions to its house, when new considerations arise. It does so, however, at the risk of losing the design and sense of there being a rational and intelligible whole. Rejecting hierarchies of importance leads to fragmentation. Adjectival theologies of gender, race, class, or geography concentrate on particular methodologies or contextual viewpoints. When such perspectives are deployed primarily or preferentially as projects of social vindication, theological discourse becomes the handmaid of power relations rather than the glorification of God. As a result, there is no longer a unified Catholic theology, but multiple, and sometimes competing Catholic theologies. Moreover, in the face

---

[12] Robert F. Taft, S.J., "The Liturgy in the Life of the Church," *Logos* 40 (1999) 187.

of widespread diffidence in the secular academy about the very existence of objective truth, theologians struggle to sustain the belief that dogmatic theology is intellectually respectable. Metaphysical considerations yield to the more socially conventional field of ethics. None of these tendencies in Catholic academic theology makes much sense in Orthodox minds and hearts, with the danger that they may actually lessen rather than enrich the possibilities of ecumenical dialogue. Other approaches are needed.

Spirituality in Ecumenical Dialogue

The term ecumenical *dialogue* is significant, for it suggests the importance of words. Human intimacy certainly involves talking. But talking only makes sense from within an economy of shared life. In addition, intimacy is also physical and symbolic. For this reason, the term "ecumenical encounter" might be more accurate and comprehensive, for it allows for the task of cultural comprehension complementary to other ways of searching for unity. Byzantinists, such as Stephen Runciman and Frantisec Dvornik, have pointed out that the so-called Great Schism was a "bottom-up" split caused by mutual cultural dissonance.[13] The fundamental cause of this estrangement was the drifting apart over centuries of cultural tectonic plates, representing different languages, mentalities, theological styles and particular historical circumstances. For schism to become entrenched, it had to be experienced as a fundamental and mutual estrangement between laity as well as clergy and political authorities. The lifting of the anathemas of 1054 by Paul VI and Athenagoras happened just over fifty years ago. But that was *only* fifty years ago. An estrangement of a thousand years might take a thousand years to heal. To a great extent *where* it heals might also well shape *how* it heals. If the split was from the grassroots up, then it seems logical

---

[13] On this, see the essay of Margaret Trenchard-Smith, "East and West: Cultural Dissonance and the 'Great Schism' of 1054," http://www.stsophia.org/orthodoxy/great_schism_of_1054.pdf

that reconciliation must also happen in that direction. Without "a long, slow process of re-acquaintance,"[14] theological dialogue will be ultimately rootless, and symbolic gestures merely symbolic. In his *Handbook of Spiritual Ecumenism*, Cardinal Kasper asserts that "only in the context of conversion can the wounded bonds of communion be healed,"[15] and suggests that conversion can best happen within communities of faith.

Communities, however, are cultural beings, and cultural encounter is thereby inseparable from the mutual comprehension that theological dialogue aims at.[16] As is well known, the Thirty-Fourth General Congregation of the Society of Jesus talked in the context of interreligious relations of (1) the dialogue of life, (2) the dialogue of action, (3) the dialogue of studying and (4) the dialogue of religious experience.[17] These four planes of dialogue are easily translated into ecumenical terms, and have much to commend themselves, especially when they are seen as a sort of Trinitarian perichoresis in which each dialogue occupies its own autonomous realm and has its proper mode of being but at the same implicates all the other kinds, in a constant hermeneutical cycle.

The (1) *dialogue of life* is inevitably local and particular, and particularly important today in places such as Ukraine or the Middle East, where the dialogue between Christian communities and individuals is simply about how to remain alive. The (2) *dialogue of action* includes the propagation of truly human moral values. Kasper's *Handbook* for example devotes much space to looking at what can already be done together. More shared endeavors in peacemaking, in the protection of human dignity, and in social and ecological justice

---

[14] Davies, "What Divides Orthodox and Catholics" (see above, n. 7).

[15] Walter Kasper, *A Handbook of Spiritual Ecumenism* (New York: New City Press, 2007) 11.

[16] Kasper, *Handbook of Spiritual Ecumenism* 12.

[17] GC 34, n. 131, quoting *Dialogue and Proclamation: Reflections and Orientations on Interreligious Dialogue and the Proclamation of the Gospel of Jesus Christ* (Pontifical Council for Interreligious Dialogue and Congregation for the Evangelization of Peoples, 1991) no. 42.

for example, would inevitably ease and enrich the other kinds of dialogue. The (4) *dialogue of religious experience*, concerns the process of coming to know the religiously other by attempting to understand her spiritual universe and is likewise well developed, at least among ecumenical cognoscenti.

Complementary to these aspects, we might add what Bishop John Zizioulas, speaking at the presentation of *Laudato Si*, called "an existential ecumenism—the effort to face together the most profound existential problems that preoccupy humanity in its entirety—not simply in particular places or classes of people,"[18] ecology being the most obvious form of this. We also have what Pope Francis calls the "ecumenism of blood, which further encourages us on the path toward peace and reconciliation."[19] In varying ways, most of these forms of ecumenism represent a *fides* requiring an *intellectum*, what Bishop Zizioulas, called "ecumenism in time . . . theological discussion, the predominant form of ecumenism"[20]—effectively the same as the (3) *dialogue of study*. The fact that a Joint International Commission for Theological Dialogue Between the Catholic Church and the Orthodox Church even exists is a beacon of hope. Its statements are the first documents written by representatives of both the Catholic and Orthodox Churches since the Council of Florence in 1443–45. In ten plenary sessions over the last thirty-six years, the Commission has produced agreements on the Church and Eucharist; on faith, sacraments and Church unity; on the sacrament of orders and apostolic succession; with special attention to Uniatism and papal authority. In the United States, the North American Orthodox-Catholic Theological Consultation has met over eighty times since it was established in 1969, and it has produced valuable joint statements on inter alia, mixed marriages, respect for life, on

---

[18] http://press.vatican.va/content/salastampa/en/bollettino/pubbli-co/2015/06/18/0480/01050.html#ziziou

[19] https://w2.vatican.va/content/francesco/en/messages/pont-messag-es/2015/documents/papa-francesco_20150510_messaggio-tawadros-ii.html

[20] http://press.vatican.va/content/salastampa/en/bollettino/pubbli-co/2015/06/18/0480/01050.html#ziziou

pastoral office, on the principle of oikonomia, on marriage, and on the spiritual formation of children of mixed marriages. The pastoral bent of these documents is noteworthy.

The successes and impact of these dialogues of study have, however, been limited. The intended audience of such documents is unclear and the accords are not widely known. Michael Fahey noted that such statements have sought consciously to speak in a neutral language that avoids the in-house dialects of Catholic scholasticism and Orthodox Palamitism, and which is sometimes abstracted from lived realities.[21] Official statements speak in the terms of wish and possibility. There remains, Fahey said, much ignorance and prejudice that needs to be overcome by proper education and changes of heart. But I wonder if theologians are also among those who need education and change of heart. Effectively, the university is the home of Catholic theology. We cannot assume that the perspectives of academic theologians are identical to the convictions and experiences of the rank and file in their churches.

The category of experience—particularly in its cultural and communal aspects—leads me to consider the potential imports for ecumenism of Christian spirituality. Since "spiritual" and "spirituality" are notoriously slippery terms, it would be useful to delineate and differentiate at this point. Spiritual ecumenism is, of course, a familiar, and venerable approach, originally articulated and championed by the pioneer ecumenist Abbé Paul Couturier (1881–1953). *Unitatis redintegratio* 5 defines this approach as being a matter of conversion and worship: "This change of heart and holiness of life, along with public and private prayer for the unity of Christians, should be regarded as the soul of the whole ecumenical movement, and merits the name of 'spiritual ecumenism'." Elaborating on this sentence, Cardinal Walter Kasper explains that spiritual ecumenism is

[21] Michael A. Fahey, S.J., *Orthodox and Catholic Sister Churches: East is West and West is East. The Père Marquette 1996 Lecture in Theology* (Milwaukee, Wis: Marquette Univ. Press, 1996) passim.

rooted in the foundations of Christian spirituality, requiring more than ecclesial diplomacy, academic dialogue, social involvement and pastoral cooperation. It presupposes a real appreciation of the many elements of sanctification and truth wrought by the Holy Spirit both within and beyond the visible boundaries of the Catholic Church.[22]

"Spiritual" in this context refers primarily to the Holy Spirit, understood as the dynamism of the ecumenical endeavor, and also as the ultimate agent of a unity which awaits the Churches in a future and in a way yet to be revealed. "Spiritual" is also, secondarily by way of derivation, something that involves the participants in ecumenical relations in the work of repentance, reconciliation and prayer.

In contrast, in common parlance in the United States, "spiritual" refers not primarily (if at all) to the third person of the Trinity, but rather something more generic by far, and often to the human spirit rather than to any transcendental reality. "Spirituality" thus understood is a loose and polymorphous *fides qua*, one that does not necessarily involve any theistic belief, has a flexible moral code and no requirement for collective belonging. And it is often placed in contradistinction to "religious," characterized as institutional, moralistic, constraining, and propositional.

Having summarily dismissed (and admittedly, simplified) some aspects of contemporary American Catholic academic theology, I also believe that some of its insights might also have something to offer the field of Orthodox-Catholic relations. Taft's words for *theologia prima*: "faith expressed . . . life . . .metaphorical . . . impressionistic . . . symbolic . . . evocative, " sound to me like the leitmotifs of spirituality, at least in the way I have understood the field. It is Patriarch Bartholomew's category of "the manner in which we exist" that makes me hopeful about deploying some of the methodologies of the American academic discipline of spirituality.

Long before I ever became a student of theology, the first theological book I ever read was Tanquerey's 1924 classic, *The*

---

[22] Kasper, *Handbook of Spiritual Ecumenism* 12.

Spiritual Life: A Treatise on Mystical and Ascetical Theology. "Mystical and Ascetical Theology" represents one conception of a sub-field of theology. This academic endeavor has no mutually agreed name, definition, object of study, or method. Different currents have traditionally placed it in close relationship to dogmatic or moral theology, with differing emphases. Many see the field as a guide towards Christian perfection, rising towards the heights of mystical experience. The current guidelines for the training of priests in Italy states that spiritual theology—the preferred term in European Catholic circles—

> reflects theologically on the "spiritual life" of the Christian, and therefore the action of the Spirit of Jesus in him. It listens to the living faith of individuals and communities, to make it as consistent as possible with doctrine. In the Christian tradition, and especially in the New Testament, spiritual theology seeks the essential elements of the "spiritual man," in order to offer guidance to help direct the spiritual experience of the believer.[23]

In contrast, in North America, Sandra Schneiders delineates spirituality in far broader terms, as a common anthropological experience that may or may not include conventional categories of religion. Schneiders's version can embrace those secular and popular *zeitgeistlich* understandings of the category of the spiritual that set it up against the religious. Consequently the academic study of spirituality, in this version, is not even *necessarily* Christian or theological:

> Spirituality—as the subject matter of the (academic) discipline (of that name)—is the experience of conscious involvement in the project of life-integration, through self-transcendence toward the ultimate value one perceives. In Christian spirituality, the horizon of ultimate value is the triune God revealed in Jesus Christ; and the project involves the living of his paschal mystery in the context of the Church community through the gift of the Holy Spirit. (The) relationship to the whole of

[23] http://www.santamariadelmare.it/msm/Portals/0/documenti/spiritualita/ Per uno studio della spiritualitá.pdf. Translation my own.

reality . . . in a specifically Christian way . . . constitutes (the experience of) Christian spirituality.[24]

Less abstractly, Philip Sheldrake understands the practice of Christian spirituality to be more or less synonymous with discipleship, being engaged in the mission of God.[25] Discipleship and mission invite Christians to share publicly what they believe. Sharing publicly involves "learning how to be truly hospitable to what is different and unfamiliar, and establishing and experiencing a common life."[26]

Common to all definitions of spirituality is a focus on some variety of lived experience. Philip Sheldrake notes that the study of Christian life has refocused itself to include all aspects of human experience, re-engaged with mainstream theology, and has often been a medium for ecumenical growth.[27] An older stance, rooted in the conviction that "theology was a stable body of knowledge, rich in the tradition of the past and secure enough to answer the questions of the present and future" has yielded to a paradigm in which, he says "the frontiers of theology increasingly seek articulation in a process and method that is experiential." A given spirituality says Matthew Ashley, "can define . . . the atmosphere in which theology is undertaken and which permeates its methods and results."[28] Theology, when infused with spirituality, provides a "fruitful locus for posing questions correctly and interrelating them productively." Effectively, in the terms sketched out above, a "theology interlaced with spirituality" represents a reintegration of *theologia prima* and *theologia secunda*.

---

[24] Sandra Schneiders, "The Study of Christian Spirituality: Contours and Dynamics of a Discipline," *Christian Spirituality Bulletin* 6 (Spring 1998) 1, 3.

[25] Philip Sheldrake, "Christian Spirituality as a Way of Living Publicly: A Dialectic of the Mystical and Prophetic," *Spiritus* 3 (Spring 2003) 19.

[26] Sheldrake, "Christian Spirituality . . . " 27.

[27] Sheldrake, *A Brief History of Christian Spirituality* (Hoboken, NJ: Wiley-Blackwell, 2004) 4.

[28] J. Matthew Ashley, "The Turn To Spirituality? The Relationship between Theology and Spirituality," chap. in Elizabeth Dreyer and Mark S. Burrows, eds., *Minding the Spirit: The Study of Christian Spirituality* (Baltimore, MD: Johns Hopkins Univ. Press, 2004) 162.

The very broad domain "experience" leads us inevitably to wonder "whose experience and which kind of experience?" and "how are such experiences evaluated?" These questions render Sheldrake's experience-based "frontier" spirituality problematic as an ecumenical approach. Three reasons for this difficulty suggest themselves immediately. *First,* although an experiential element is certainly part of the approach of spiritual ecumenism as outlined above, spirituality considered primarily as an experiential process and an academic methodology seems to include experiences which might be secular, psychological rather than spiritual, and include the heterodox. *Secondly,* some Orthodox instincts have a strong a-historical bent. In their most fundamentalist form, they tend to hold that all doctrinal, liturgical, canonical and other features of Christianity were preordained at Pentecost and have been unaffected by change and development. Within that tendency, Christian experience is unlikely to be seen as a solid base for doing theology. *Thirdly,* the theological preference of Orthodoxy is broadly speaking for descending, Alexandrian, perspectives that show the influence of Neoplatonism: incorporating anthropologically based perspectives could easily smell of Western secularist anthropocentrism.

Yet for all that, and for all the confusing polyvalence of the term spiritual and its related domains, taking religious experience as a *locus theologicus* in ecumenism should not be lightly dismissed. A deeper consideration reveals that it offers an enrichment of theological perspectives. The membership of Catholic-Orthodox theological bodies reflects assumptions about what are regarded as the constitutive disciplines of ecumenism. My impression is that Catholic theologians who are members of such panels tend to be experts in the field of biblical studies, patristics, dogmatic theology, and church history.[29] This selection reflects a preferential option

---

[29] The preponderance of academic backgrounds among Catholic members of ecumenical bodies also helps explain why one participant in high-level discussion told me that he found his Orthodox counterparts to be "weak on theology."

for eternal verities of revelation, for the common patrimony of the Church Fathers, and for a *ressourcement* from tradition as the preferred medications for the current ailments. Michael J. Fahey advocated for the need in ecumenical discussions for "solid historical and theological scholarship . . . the power of ideas, the probative impact of critical and serious historical research" along with the "complementary magisterium of theologians and other scholars such as church historians."[30] I agree. But I would like to add pastors, ethicists, spiritual directors, liturgists, and many more to Fahey's "complementary magisterium."

According to David Tracy, "the peculiarly modern genre for theological reflection has been the rational argument."[31] That genre assumes a preferential option for the textual not only as medium of communication, but also as object of study. Yet *fides* is not limited to concepts and words, and its *intellectum* may be expressed in a variety of idioms. In many cultures, spiritual literacy and religious experience cannot be adequately understood in terms of texts, writers, and readers alone.

If we are to understand the religiously other, we must thus look beyond doctrinal formulations. Or rather, we must consider the relationship of religious dogma and doctrine to spiritual experience. It is precisely here in that nexus that the modern study of Christian spirituality, with its starting point in anthropology and its investigation of experience in the light of revelation, might serve Catholic-Orthodox relations well. Sandra Schneiders points out that we cannot return to the medieval synthesis of theology and spirituality—"we" being, I think, in her mind, North American academics.[32] Yet Orthodox theology has retained the memory that dogma has an "a posteriori existential character."[33] In a 1997 address, at Georgetown Patriarch

---

[30] Fahey, *Orthodox and Catholic Sister Churches* 45.

[31] See Mark McIntosh, "Lover Without a Name—Spirituality and Constructive Christology Today," in Dreyer and Burrows, *Minding the Spirit* 215ff.

[32] Schneiders, "The Study of Christian Spirituality" 5.

[33] Andrew Sopko, *For a Culture of Co-Suffering Love: The Theo-Anthropology of Archbishop Lazar Puhalo* (Los Osos, CA: Archive Publications, 2004) 138.

Bartholomew made a claim for the experiential nature of dogma and doctrine.[34] His semi-veiled criticism of Catholic theology proposed a Christian hope that starts from a lived, spiritual experience rather than from intellectual conceptions.

In that same address, the Patriarch set the bar for the possibilities of unity very high. He famously said that the problem of Orthodox-Catholic division is

> assuredly . . . neither geographical nor one of personal alienation. Neither is it a problem of organizational structures, nor jurisdictional arrangements. Neither is it a problem of external submission, nor absorption of individuals and groups. It is something deeper and more substantive. The manner in which we exist has become ontologically different.[35]

In Orthodox-Catholic relations then the spiritual question that needs to be brought out into the open in the therapist's office, as it were, is precisely the one that caused it: differences in identity and culture.

To help heal that deep wound, Catholic-Orthodox ecumenism might be enriched by a cultural theological approach. It would not be a "theology of culture," derivative of systematics and which makes general or normative statements about the role of culture in the human condition,[36] or which looks at culture from a purely missiological perspective. Rather, what I am struggling to chisel out is an approach that breaks down a wall between cultural anthropology and theology.[37] In the context of ecumenical encounter, this approach would take cultural experience as an important source of theological reflection, using the insights of cultural studies, but moving beyond

---

[34] https://www.patriarchate.org/-/address-of-his-all-holiness-ecumenical-patriarch-b-a-r-t-h-o-l-o-m-e-w-phos-hilaron-joyful-light-georgetown-university-washington-dc-october-21-1997

[35] Ibid.

[36] E.g., the work of Reinhold Niebuhr.

[37] In this direction, see Gailyn Van Rheenen, "A Theology of Culture: Desecularizing Anthropology," *International Journal of Frontier Missions* 14/1 (Jan–March 1997) 33–38.

them too by putting them into dialogue with revelation. Analogous to historical theological method, its hallmark would be the theologizing of particular experience, deploying what anthropologists call "thick description," that is, explaining behavior in its context, so that it becomes comprehensible to the other.

Awareness of the deep patterns of the thought and feeling of the Churches—particularly those that are only semi-conscious and those buried deeper in the soul of a community—can only help mutual understanding. What would Catholic-Orthodox theological discussion look like if, for example, it began not with delineating points of dogmatic, ecclesial, sacramental, and canonical convergence and divergence, and carefully explaining what particular propositions mean or do not mean, but rather, say, with an approach rooted in *theologia prima*? This would mean understanding others not primarily by what they say or think, but rather how they act and feel. That, I think is what *sentire cum ecclesiis* might involve, and the reflection on this *sentire* would find a natural home in the methods and concerns of the academic discipline of spirituality.

Schneiders insists that the first step in the study of spirituality is embracing a wider range of ancillary disciplines. The very interdisciplinarity of the contemporary study of spirituality could be both gift and challenge to Catholic-Orthodox ecumenism. It would be gift because the Orthodox mind is already predisposed towards an organic, holistic theology. At the same time, incorporating insights from psychology, sociology, natural sciences, anthropology, social geography, comparative religion, aesthetics, ritual studies, and gender studies into theological discourse would indeed represent an innovation in the patterns and loci of most Orthodox theological discourse.[38] We will also need experts able to theologize nationalism and ethnic identity (rather than merely describe them), given that these are deeply implicated in intra-Christian divisions. Far more

---

[38] This is not to claim, of course, that Orthodox thinkers do not consider these perspectives. Since the cradle of these disciplines is largely Western professional academia, however, they occupy a space far smaller than they do in Catholic theological discourse.

attention must be given too to popular religiosity—particularly in its connections with and distinctions from the liturgy of the Church—as an expression of the *sensus fidelium*.[39] In short, the more perspectives employed to examine the division between East and West, the more profound will be our mutual recognition—the question of that Ravenna footnote.

When our marital spats are examined in full, from many perspectives, our blind spots brought to our own attention, and when we have tried to enter into the experience of the other, we might get a better sense of who each other is. Only at that point can we truly proceed to the final stage of Schneiders's methodology namely, critical analysis, which involves considering how we ought to be or wish to be. This ontological perspective—itself a form of existential askesis—is needed lest we reduce description to normativity and thereby fall ineluctably into a void of uncritical subjectivism. The light of scripture and tradition illuminates and purifies the experiences of what exists currently. This revelation is propaedeutic to that work of conversion called for in Kasper's notion of spiritual ecumenism. At this point, the ecumenical encounter becomes properly moral and properly theological. The insights of the human sciences are the *natura* on which the *gratia* of ecumenical encounter can build a solid foundation and point to the ultimate goal of all learning and all reconciliation, the glorification of God.

Dorian Llywelyn, S.J. is Executive Director of the Ignatian Center for Jesuit Education at Santa Clara University, and former director of the Huffington Ecumenical Institute at Loyola Marymount University. He writes on theology and culture, with a specific emphasis on ethnic and national identity. His current research focuses on popular Marian devotion and its relation to both theology and politics.

[39] Spirituality, says Schneiders, is "the aspect of organized religion . . . least under the control of the religious institution . . . more impervious to institutional scrutiny and much more powerful at times in its appeal to the ordinary membership in the church." Sandra Schneiders, "The Study of Christian Spirituality" 7.

Thinking and Feeling with the Churches about Islam: Changes from the Early 20th Century to the Early 21st Century

PATRICK J. RYAN, S.J.

Asking what Jesuits can do to help the Catholic Church to think and feel the way it should about Islam, this article begins to lay the foundation for a proper answer by outlining a history of attitudes towards Islam in the years 1915–2015, first among Roman Catholics, then among the Byzantine Orthodox, and finally among Protestants. The article suggests how helpful it is—especially in this time of increased tension—to be aware not only of what is distinctive in these histories, but also to be aware of the more eirenic aspects and more eirenic potential contained in them.

Saint Ignatius appended to the text of the *Spiritual Exercises* a set of "rules to follow in view of the true attitude of mind that we ought to maintain [as members] within the Church militant" (*Sp. Ex.* 352).[1] They arise, quite obviously, from the context of the Catholic Church at the time of the Protestant Reformation and the Council of Trent, a time when the Catholic Church was much troubled by internal corruption, rabid dissension, multiple schisms and rampant criticism of authority inside and outside the Church. The first rule Ignatius formulated was the most basic: "Laying aside all our own judgments, we ought to keep our minds open and ready to obey in everything the true bride of Christ Our Lord, our holy mother, the

---

[1] *Saint Ignatius of Loyola: Personal Writings*, trans. and ed. Joseph A. Munitiz and Philip Endean (London: Penguin Books, 1996) 356. All further references to Ignatius in this essay will refer to this work, with the *Spiritual Exercises* cited by the standard numbered paragraphs.

hierarchical Church" (*Sp. Ex.* 353). Ignatius seems to presuppose in these words that the Church, like the late Cardinal Ottaviani, was *semper idem* (or, more properly, given the gender of "Church" in Latin, *semper eadem!*) In Rule 10, however, Ignatius distinguishes between the audiences before whom one might criticize aspects of the Church. "But just as harm can be done by speaking ill to simple people about those in authority in their absence, so it can do good to speak of their unworthy behavior to the actual people who can bring about a remedy" (*Sp. Ex.* 362).

How much can we Jesuits do to help the Catholic Church to think and feel about Islam? I know quite a few Jesuits who have exercised a good influence on how the Catholic Church thinks about Islam and about how I think about Islam. I will name only five deceased Jesuits who have exercised such influence: Paul Nwyia, Michel Allard, Louis Pouzet (all of whom worked at Université Saint-Joseph in Beirut), Robert Bütler (who worked in Pakistan) and, finally, a close friend of mine, Raymond Adams, who worked and studied in the Middle East but eventually died at the hands of a murderer in Ghana in 1989. There is a sixth Jesuit, who mainly worked in Syria, who probably died nearly two years ago, but we are not entirely sure: Paolo dall'Oglio. For all of them: *Inna l'illahi wa inna' ilayhi raji'un:* "Truly we belong to God and to God alone we will return" (Qur'an 2:156). *Rahimahum Allah:* May God grant them mercy. There are also many living Jesuits who continue to engage in dialogue with Muslims and who have taught the Catholic Church and have taught me a great deal about how we should be thinking and feeling about Islam. I don't want to take the risk of mentioning some and forgetting others, so I will leave them nameless. For all of them, my spiritual brothers in a double sense, *ad multos annos!*

Applying these rules of Saint Ignatius to the ecumenical task of thinking and feeling with the Churches, not just the Catholic Church, about Islam, I shall be pointing out to fellow churchmen, fellow Jesuits, some things that the Churches used to think about Islam in the past—symbolically, a hundred years ago, but actually for many centuries before that as well—and what the Churches think about

Islam today. Great changes have occurred over the past century, often for the better, but not always.

I will treat separately Catholic, Byzantine Orthodox and Protestant attitudes—and treat each of them through a few pivotal historical figures—with the caution that other Christian churches, especially the non-Chalcedonian churches of the East, also had their own thoughts and feelings about Islam then and now. In this forum, however, I will limit my attention to those three Christian ecclesial families, and particular historical figures within each of them, given the limitations of time and of my own expertise.

Let me reflect briefly on 1915 and 2015. We live at a time of harrowing memories: the centenary not only of the First World War but also of many tragic and consequential developments of that era. I single out for mention only four: (1) the carnage on many battle fronts, not only in Europe; (2) the Armenian genocide in the declining Ottoman Empire, a tragedy that still haunts Turkey today; (3) the secret Sykes-Picot treaty of 1916 between the British and the French, parceling out much of the Levantine Arab world between those two colonial masters at war's end, despite the lies told to the Arabs, knowingly or unknowingly, by T. E. Lawrence; (4) the stirring up of nationalist causes within what had once been the Ottoman, German, British, French, Austro-Hungarian and Italian Empires, with the effect not only of creating new nations but also of stranding ethnic or religious minorities in these new nations, for instance, Yugoslavia, Czechoslovakia, Hungary, Romania, and the United Kingdom of Great Britain and Northern Ireland, to name but five in Europe. Especially in the geographical area between the Bosporus and the Gulf of Aden, Christian communities, who had lived since the fall of Constantinople to the Ottomans in 1453 as minorities in that Empire, more or less tolerated at various times and in various locales, found themselves after the division of the Middle East following World War I distributed among several artificially created nations, very often in hostile situations.

How did the major Christian churches think about Islam a century ago? How do they think about Islam today?

Catholic Attitudes towards Islam, 1915–2015

The Catholic Church a hundred years ago inherited, along with Byzantine Orthodox Christians, Anglicans, and Protestants, a deep antipathy to Muslims and their faith. John of Damascus (d. 749) began that antipathetic tradition, and Ramon Llull (ca. 1315) and other medieval writers continued it in the Latin West. The adversaries Thomas Aquinas had in mind in his *Summa contra Gentiles* included both Jews and Muslims. The Crusades cemented that Latin Christian antipathy to Islam into a permanent element in the Western imagination.

In the 19th century, when some European and especially French politicians and intellectuals were recovering from Enlightenment-era hostility to Catholicism, Charles Martial Allemand Cardinal Lavigerie (1825–92), a French diocesan priest and church historian, became successively the Bishop of Annecy, the Archbishop of Algiers (and at his instigation) Archbishop of Carthage-Algiers. Lavigerie envisioned a grand scheme to revive the North African church of the second to the sixth centuries—the church of Perpetua and Felicity, Cyprian and Augustine—by converting North African Muslims (especially the Berbers of Kabylia, east of Algiers) to Catholicism. Lavigerie also sought to evangelize sub-Saharan Africa from the base of his see in North Africa, and for this purpose he hoped to abolish the slave trade, especially in Central and Eastern Africa. Originally a monarchist, like most of the French clergy of his time, Lavigerie gradually came to terms with Republican France, giving *"le Toast d'Alger"* to the French Republic in the presence of French military officers in Algiers on 12 November 1890. Catholic softening towards Republican France had become possible after Léon Gambetta (1838–82), a major political force at the beginning of the Third Republic in 1870, declared that anti-clericalism was not an item for export from metropolitan France. Even French secularists could appreciate that the *mission civilisatrice* of France could be accomplished more efficiently and cheaply by

French Catholic missionaries in parts of Asia, Africa, and the Arab world than it could by French military and colonial officers.[2]

As Archbishop of Carthage-Algiers, Lavigerie shepherded not only the French Catholics who had migrated to Algeria in large numbers after the French annexation of Algeria in 1830 but also the smaller numbers of Berber converts to Christianity. In 1868 he founded the *Société des Missionaires de Notre Dame d'Afrique* of Algiers (later simply the *Société des Missionaires d'Afrique*), a congregation of Catholic men in common life made up of priests and lay brothers; a year later he founded a parallel congregation of sisters charged, at first, with running orphanages for Algerian children. Lavigerie's male missionaries dressed in the North African fashion of the late nineteenth century: an enveloping white burnous (mantle) over a white gandoura (baggy cassock), a red tarboosh ("fez") and, around their necks, the Catholic version of the Muslim devotional *misbaha,* the rosary. This costume was created to make the missionaries look like *marabouts,* professional Muslim holy men who exercised much spiritual influence on the Berbers. Lavigerie soon sent "White Fathers" (so named unofficially because their original uniform differed so dramatically from the black soutanes worn by the diocesan clergy of Algiers) to sub-Saharan Africa where they experienced much more success than they did in Lavigerie's originally planned mission to peoples in North Africa. The comparative lack of success of that missionary venture in Algeria did not prevent Lavigerie from consecrating in 1872 an enormous basilica near Algiers in the suburb called Bologhnine. Dedicated to Notre-Dame d'Afrique, the basilica is called either Madame l'Afrique or Lalla Mariam ("Lady Mary") by local Muslims. In the apse over the main altar a prayer to the Virgin is set in the mosaic: *Notre Dame d'Afrique, priez pour nous et pour les musulmans.* Local Muslim wits sometimes add to that prayer a condition: *"si vous avez le temps."*

---

[2] On the involvement of Lavigerie in the French colonization of Tunisia, see J. Dean O'Donnell, Jr., *Lavigerie in Tunisia: The Interplay of Imperialist and Missionary* (Athens, GA: The University of Georgia Press, 1979).

A steadfast ally of Pius IX and the Ultramontanes at Vatican I,[3] Lavigerie welcomed to Algiers ex-Papal Zouaves (*Zuavi Pontifici*), military men from many Catholic nations (for instance, the Netherlands, Belgium, France, Ireland, French Canada). Their name came from the fact that they dressed in uniforms modeled on the dress of a North African Zenata Berber sub-group in Kabylia called Zwāwa (Zouaoua). These Papal Zouaves did not succeed in preventing the conquest of the Papal States in 1870 by the forces of the Kingdom of Italy. One of those unsuccessful Zouaves was a Frenchman, Léopold Louis Joubert (1847–1927), who after ten years of fighting for Pius IX, found new military employment assisting Lavigerie and the White Fathers to deal with "Arab" (Swahili and Omani) slavers in eastern Congo and other parts of what was once German East Africa (later Rwanda, Burundi and the originally Tanganyikan mainland of Tanzania) as well as in what are now Uganda and Kenya.

Lavigerie's military-missionary-colonial approach to Islam in North Africa, Central and Eastern Africa derives much of its imagery and rhetoric from the idealizing memory of the Crusades, a motif quite popular in 19th-century Europe. Traces of Crusader-related rhetoric can still be detected in Catholic official documents as late as 1925, when Pius XI issued the text of a prayer that was to be used on every Feast of Christ the King. The prayer, written with various secularizing forces in mind, especially in Europe, consecrated the whole of the human race to the Sacred Heart of Jesus. One short passage from that windy act of consecration betrays Crusader hostility to Islam: "Be Thou King of all those who are still involved in the darkness of idolatry or of Islamism, and refuse not to draw them all into the light and kingdom of God." The phrase, "the darkness of idolatry or of Islamism," sounds suspiciously like the medieval canard that Muslims worshipped an idol named Mahound, apparently a corruption of the name Muhammad. (Chesterton, in

---

[3] See Xavier de Montclos, *Lavigerie, le Saint-Siège et l'Église de l'avènement de Pie IX à l'avènement de Léon III, 1846-1878* (Paris: Éditions E. De Boccard, 1965) esp. 430–74.

the poem, *Lepanto*, says that "Mahound is in his paradise above the evening star.") The word, "Islamism," has been employed in recent years to denote the Wahhabi interpretation of Islam dominant in Saudi Arabia and among the Salafis of contemporary Egypt as well as similar rigorist Sunni Muslim groups. For Pius XI and his ghost writers, however, it simply designated Islam as a reprehensible form of faith.

The nostalgia felt by Lavigerie for North African Christianity still reappears, although in a very attenuated form, right down to modern times. Take, for example, a book partly authored in 2005 by Cardinal Joseph Ratzinger, shortly before he became Pope Benedict XVI, a work written in dialogue with a conservative Italian politician, Marcello Pera. Although a non-believer, Pera still wants to champion what he calls "Christian culture" in Europe, and especially in Italy. Ratzinger, discussing the origins of Europe with Pera, notes that Europe was at first considered to be "the Hellenistic states and the Roman Empire." Thus

> the lands facing the Mediterranean came to form a true continent by virtue of their cultural ties, trade routes, and common political system. It was not until the triumphal advances of Islam in the seventh and early eighth centuries that a border would be drawn across the Mediterranean, subdividing what had been a single continent into three: Asia, Africa, and Europe.

Ratzinger becomes more specific when he states that "the southern Mediterranean found itself cut off completely (in approximately A.D. 700) from what had been a cultural continent for centuries."[4] The term 'Europe,' according to Ratzinger, did not play a large role in European Christian thinking again until "the beginning of the modern era—as a means of self-identification, in response to the Turkish threat,"[5] by which the future Pope meant the Ottoman

---

[4] Joseph Ratzinger, later Pope Benedict XVI, and Marcello Pera, *Without Roots: the West, Relativism, Christianity, Islam*, trans. Michael F. Moore (New York: Basic Books, 2006) 52–53.

[5] Ratzinger and Pera, 54.

threat during the reign of Sulayman the Magnificent (1520–66). One can guess from these animadversions of Ratzinger why he opposed Turkey's admission to the European Union.

In the same book Ratzinger also mentions with some sympathy "a second, non-Western Europe. In Byzantium (which considered itself the true Rome), the Roman Empire had withstood the upheaval of migrations and the Islamic invasion." But in his evaluation of Eastern Christianity Ratzinger gives evidence of historical German episcopal hostility to the vernacular liturgical achievements of Saints Cyril and Methodius in the Slavic lands, where they introduced, in Ratzinger's words, "variants in the liturgy and in the ecclesiastical constitution, adopting a different script, and renouncing the use of Latin as the common language."[6]

These passages prepare us to understand the opinions expressed by Pope Benedict XVI in his lecture in September 2006 at the University of Regensburg, including his infelicitous quotation from the third-to-the-last Byzantine emperor, Manuel II Palaiologos (r. 1391–1425). Manuel had supposedly engaged in 'dialogue'—acrimonious debate would be the better characterization—with a nameless Persian scholar, perhaps during Manuel's brief period as a pawn of his father in the Ottoman court of Bayezid I (r. 1389–1403). Benedict in this lecture asserts that the emperor, without

> descending to details, such as the difference in treatment accorded to those who have the 'Book' and the 'infidels' . . . addresses his interlocutor with a startling brusqueness, a brusqueness that we find unacceptable, on the central question about the relationship between religion and violence in general, saying 'Show me just what Muhammad brought that was new, and there you will find things only evil and inhuman, such as the command to spread by the sword the faith he preached.'

---

[6] Ratzinger and Pera, 55. For a more positive evaluation of these vernacular developments, see Lamin Sanneh, *Translating the Message: The Missionary Impact on Culture*, 2nd ed. (Maryknoll, NY: Orbis Books, 2009), especially his treatment of Saints Cyril and Methodius, 81–92.

Descending to details should not be so easily dismissed or laid aside, and especially in a German university setting. Most people had never heard of Manuel II Palaiologos before Pope Benedict's address at Regensburg; furthermore, the emperor's understanding of Islam did not cry out to be included in a discussion of the relationship between faith and reason in a university setting. But the Pope did quote it, and the results are now famous or infamous, depending on one's point of view. In a footnote added subsequently to the definitive edition of the address, the Pope remarks apologetically that the brusque quotation from Manuel II "has unfortunately been taken as an expression of my own personal position, thus arousing considerable understandable indignation." He then goes on to write that "this sentence does not express my personal view of the Qur'an, for which I have the respect due to the holy book of a great religion."[7]

Despite this incautious misstep by Pope Benedict in 2006, the prevailing winds of Catholic relations with Muslims and comprehension of and sympathy with Islam as a form of faith had already taken a dramatic positive turn in the documents of the Second Vatican Council (1962–65), especially with the publication of the Council's Declaration on the Relationship of the Church to Non-Christian Religions (*Nostra aetate*) in 1965. The preparation for that document owes much to the intellectual career of several famous Catholic Islamicists, most notably the French scholar, Louis Massignon (1883–1962), and the Egyptian Dominican, Georges Anawati (1905–1994), the latter directly involved in the formulation of the paragraph on Islam in *Nostra aetate*.

I would like to comment fairly succinctly on that brief conciliar passage, sentence by sentence: "*The Church regards with esteem also the Moslems.*"[8] That may seem a bit bland for a starter, but we have come a long way from "the darkness of idolatry or of Islamism," to put it mildly. We have even gone ever so slightly beyond the text of the Second Vatican Council's Dogmatic Constitution on the Church,

---

[7] See note 3 to the address on the Vatican website: (w.w.w.vatican.va).

[8] I am using the English translation available at w.w.w.vatican.va; I am also using that site's translation for *Lumen gentium*.

Lumen gentium, promulgated a year earlier. This master document of the Council had declared:

> *The plan of salvation also includes those who acknowledge the Creator. In the first place amongst these there are the Moslems, who, professing to hold the faith of Abraham, along with us adore the one and merciful God, who on the last day will judge mankind (LG 16).*

The term 'Moslems' in this English rendering of Lumen gentium translates the Latin accusative plural *Musulmanos*, a word derived in Latin from the Italian, French and Spanish words for 'Muslims'; as such it reflects a Persian word for Muslims. ('Moslems' is the old *New York Times* spelling of what is usually rendered as 'Muslims' in English today). A year later, however, *Nostra aetate* refers in Latin to *Muslimos*, a new Latinism closer to the proper Arabic *Muslimun*, meaning those who have submitted themselves to God. The presence of Arabic-speaking Christians like Father Anawati among the *periti* had its effect.

The next sentence in *Nostra aetate* 3 is long and complicated:

> *They [the Muslims] adore the one God, living and subsisting in Himself; merciful and all-powerful, the Creator of heaven and earth, who has spoken to men; they take pains to submit wholeheartedly to even His inscrutable decrees, just as Abraham, with whom the faith of Islam takes pleasure in linking itself, submitted to God.*

That sentence was, like the entirety of this paragraph, originally written in Arabic by Catholic scholars deeply versed in Islam. Thus it reflects closely themes in the Qur'an, especially some of the key names of God. Note also how that sentence recognizes the centrality of Abraham to the Islamic tradition. The text hedges its bets a little, saying that the "the faith of Islam takes pleasure in linking itself" to Abraham. The Fathers of the Council were not quite ready to say that the Quranic version of Abraham is the same as the Biblical versions of Abraham in the Old Testament and the New Testament. (The Old Testament has several versions of Abraham and so too do the authors of the New Testament.) Very nicely, however, the conciliar text says that *"Abraham . . . submitted to God,"* a phrase which means, when translated into Arabic, that Abraham practiced *islam* in its root sense, the submission of oneself to God.

The Conciliar text distinguishes in the next sentence the portrayals of Jesus and Mary in the Qur'an from the accounts of them in the New Testament. *"Though they do not acknowledge Jesus as God, they revere Him as a prophet. They also honor Mary, His virgin Mother; at times they even call on her with devotion."* It is important to note the *caveat* there. The Quranic Jesus is a great prophet, but in no way the Son of God, even though his birth from the Virgin Mary is insisted upon, even more specifically than in the New Testament. But it is considered a miracle associated with the birth of the prophet Jesus and in no sense a sign of divine identity.

The eschatology of Muslims occupies the attention of the next sentence in *Nostra aetate.* *"In addition, they await the day of judgment when God will render their deserts to all those who have been raised up from the dead."* Once again, this hope for divine vindication on the day of the resurrection serves as a link between Catholic Christianity and Islamic teaching. Not mentioned in the text of the Council document is that Jesus is thought by Muslims not to have died on the Cross and his return is expected before the end of history.

Elements of what Muslims call the five pillars (*arkan*) of Islam are enumerated in the next sentence. *"Finally, they value the moral life and worship God especially through prayer, almsgiving and fasting."* The five pillars are (1) testifying to the oneness of God and the messenger-status of Muhammad; (2) the five-times daily practice of worship (*salat*); (3) payment of a precisely determined alms-tax (*zakat*) that is not the same thing as free-will charity; (4) fasting (*sawm*) annually for a lunar month, usually the month of Ramadan, but lost days in that month can be made up at other times; (5) the pilgrimage (*hajj*) to the holy places in Arabia associated with Abraham (not just Mecca), an obligation for the individual Muslim that is qualified for those unable to afford it or to make the *hajj* for good reasons.

Finally, and very realistically, the Council Fathers recognized the long history of tension between Christians and Muslims that dates back to the seventh century, but reached a climax in the era of the Crusades, a climax that is (alas!) only rivaled by the tensions in the post 9/11 world. Let the final words of the Council Fathers on Islam provide us with food for thought:

> *Since in the course of centuries not a few quarrels and hostilities have aris-*
> *en between Christians and Moslems, this sacred synod urges all to forget*
> *the past and to work sincerely for mutual understanding and to preserve as*
> *well as to promote together for the benefit of all mankind social justice and*
> *moral welfare, as well as peace and freedom.* (*Nostra aetate* 3)

Pope Paul VI, Pope John Paul II and even Pope Benedict, away from Regensburg, as well as Pope Francis have also had more positive things to say about Islam in the years since Vatican II; it would take too long in this context to detail these statements. A great deal has changed in Catholic official attitudes towards Islam in the hundred years that have passed since 1915. Nevertheless, professional Muslim-haters still thrive in the Catholic Church and in other Christian communities, and I find that such hatred is usually strongest in church personnel who live furthest from the realities of Christians surviving in majority-Muslim parts of the world.

The present situations of the Christian minorities in the Levantine Arab world (especially Syria and Iraq), as well as the Christian minorities in Egypt, Libya, Pakistan, Malaysia, northeastern Nigeria, the borders of Kenya and Somalia and elsewhere do not promise a great improvement of Christian-Muslim relations in those locales in the near future, to put it mildly. Hateful things are being shouted on all sides of these fraught situations. It is important, nevertheless, for Catholics, and especially for Catholic theologians, to keep in mind the commitments made at Vatican II to Christian-Muslim mutual understanding and the occasional beacons of light that sometimes still illumine the night-sky of the contemporary world.

Byzantine Orthodox Attitudes towards Islam, 1915–2015

Byzantine—and more general Eastern Christian—contact with Islam began during the lifetime of the Prophet Muhammad. The Qur'an itself, and especially the Medinan suras revealed after the year 622, are replete with references to Christians encountered by Muhammad and the first Muslims within Arabia. Sometimes those encounters were friendly, or at least friendlier than encounters with Jewish and pagan Arabs:

> You will find the most vehemently hostile to the faithful [Muslims] the Jews and those who associate [other gods with God]; and you will find the most loving to the faithful are those people who say "Yes, we are Christians *(Nasara)*." That is because there are among them priests and monks, people who do not vaunt themselves in pride. (Qur'an 5:82).

Friendly encounter with Christians deteriorated at a slower pace than friendly encounter with Jews and pagan Arabs in Muhammad's lifetime.

Not long after Muhammad's death in 632, the newly Islamized populations of Arabia joined forces with their fellow Arabs who had served for many years as military allies or mercenaries for both the Persians and the Byzantines in the lengthy war (602–628) that exhausted both empires. Within a few years of Muhammad's death in 632, most of Byzantine-ruled Syria, including Jerusalem, had fallen to the expansion of the caliphate based in Medina. It is said that Sophronius, the patriarch in Jerusalem, prevailed upon to give a tour of the holy sites in the ancient city to the caliph 'Umar (r. 634–644), confided to an aide in Greek that "In truth this is the Abomination of Desolation standing in the holy place as spoken of by Daniel the prophet."[9] Although, as mentioned earlier, John of Damascus (d. 749) began the Christian theological tradition of antipathy to Islam, it was precisely his location at the monastery of Mar Saba in Palestine, well within the territories of the Damascus-based Umayyad caliphate (which ruled between 661 and 750), that protected John from martyrdom at the hands of Leo the Isaurian (r. 717–741), the Byzantine emperor, who would have beheaded John for his defense of icons.

With the final surrender of the Byzantine Empire to the victorious Ottomans in 1453, many Byzantine Orthodox Christians

---

[9] Theophanes the Confessor, *Chronographia*, ed. Carolus de Boor (Leipzig: Teubner, 1885) I: 339.

joined their non-Chalcedonian fellow Christians in what we now call the Middle East as religious populations protected (*dhimmi*), for better or for worse, within the confines of their new political regime. Stymied in their ability to propagate Christianity in this new Islamic setting, Byzantine Orthodox Christians became one of several at least partly self-ruling *millets* (religio-political communities) among the many tolerated by the Ottoman rulers. Ottoman Muslim rule—the Ottoman Sultanate quite concretely from 1453 on and the consubstantial Ottoman Caliphate more theoretically after 1517—differed from the political arrangements in the new nations of the Middle East created after World War I in one central way. In the former regime each individual and each clan was ruled within a *millet*, not within a geographic locale, one or other governorate (*wilaya*). The inner politics of the Byzantine Greek Orthodox *millet* became extremely complex and unstable, especially when wealthy Byzantine lay people came to dominate the Patriarchate and willingly paid the Ottoman authorities the gratuity (*peshkesh*) associated with the investiture of a new Patriarch. Thus the Phanariots—these wealthy Greek lay people based in Constantinople/Istanbul operating in the vicinity of the Patriarchate (the Phanar)—manipulated the Patriarchal throne with moneyed ease. Andrew Sharp, a modern historian, sums up the situation: "From 1495 to 1595 CE there were 19 changes to the patriarchal throne, from 1595 to 1695 there were 61 changes involving 31 individuals (some being reappointed) and from 1696 to 1795 there were 31 appointments involving 23 individuals."[10] The intimate relationship between the Ottoman authorities and the Patriarch established in Constantinople/Istanbul as the head of the Byzantine Orthodox *millet* tended to exalt the Patriarch of Constantinople above his fellow Byzantine Orthodox Patriarchs, who lost both authority and influence.

> Though the centralization of Christian leadership in the patriarchate
> afforded a level of freedom to Christians in the empire, it also led

---

[10] Andrew Sharp, *Orthodox Christians and Islam in the Postmodern Age* (Leiden and Boston: Brill, 2012) 18.

to the rise of Greek hegemony within the Orthodox church. While, canonically speaking, the ancient patriarchates of Alexandria, Antioch and Jerusalem retained their independent status, in practice they had to defer to the patriarch of Constantinople in many situations, particularly since it was he who submitted names to the sultan for all patriarchal appointments.[11]

During the nineteenth century both the Christian minorities in the Ottoman Empire and the Muslim majority came more and more into contact with Europe and its ways—military, technical, ideological. Albert Hourani chronicles how various Ottoman Arabs came into contact with a whole range of new ideas after Napoleon's invasion of Egypt; those ideas took more than a century to penetrate the heart of the Ottoman Empire, but in the long run they led to the unravelling of Ottoman power and the dissolution of what remained of the Sunni caliphate.[12]

Throughout the late 18th century and the 19th century more and more of the dominantly Byzantine Orthodox territories within the Ottoman Empire (for instance, Serbia, Greece, Bulgaria, Romania) shook off Ottoman control. By 1915, Byzantine Orthodox Christians— ethnic Greeks and Arabs, especially—were increasingly minoritized in what remained of the once vast Ottoman Empire. The secularist "Young Turks" (the Committee for Union and Progress) after 1908 reduced the Sultan Abdul Hamid II to a constitutional monarch. When the Ottoman State, under Young Turk domination, allied itself with the German and Austro-Hungarian Empires against the French, British and Italian Empires in World War I, the stage was set for the birth of the new nations of the Middle East in which Christian minorities had decreasing power and influence.

In the Levantine Arab areas of the Ottoman Empire, Arab nationalists, Christian and Muslim, had begun to assert their shared secular identity as Arabs in the early 20th century, constructing

---

[11] Sharp, 17.
[12] Albert Hourani, *Arabic Thought in the Liberal Age 1798–1939* (Cambridge: Cambridge University Press, 1962, rev. ed. 1983).

something of an interreligious cultural mirage, Pan-Arabism, which continued to exercise considerable intellectual influence until the 1960s. Arab nationalist sentiment did manage to achieve the independence of countries like Syria, Lebanon, Jordan and Iraq from French and British rule. A typical Arab nationalist, the originally Byzantine Orthodox Michel Aflaq (1910–1989), co-founder of the Ba'th party within Syria, eventually died as an exile from Syria in Iraq, with Saddam Hussein himself claiming that Aflaq had converted to Islam before his death. For most of the Arab nationalists of the 20th century religion was a minor factor in their lives. The Islamization of politics in what was once the Ottoman Empire has largely developed over the past seven decades in tandem with the establishment and expansion of the Jewish State in Israel after 1948 and its backing by countries perceived by Muslims as dominantly Christian like the United States, the United Kingdom and the Federal Republic of Germany.

Turkish nationalists between 1915 and 1922 slaughtered 1.5 million Armenian Christians, a pogrom justified on the plea that Armenians had allied themselves with the Russians, Czarist and eventually Communist, against Turkey. In the aftermath of World War I ethnic Greek populations living in Turkey and ethnic Turkish populations living in Greece were moved out of their places of long residence and resettled in homelands they often hardly recognized. Not a few of the Greeks involved in this exchange of populations migrated to the United States and I have found over the years that it has colored Greek-American sentiment about Turks and Muslims more generally. The tensions between ethnic Turks and ethnic Greeks in Cyprus have only further exacerbated an already bad situation. Andrew Sharp sums this situation up succinctly: "The tragic events of this period have often overshadowed in the historical memory of Christians from the region the centuries of relatively peaceful coexistence between Christians and Muslims during the Ottoman years."[13] I know many Greek-Americans who would take umbrage at Sharp's positive judgment of those Ottoman years.

---

[13] Sharp, 32.

The Ecumenical Patriarchate remains in Istanbul to the present day despite the radical diminution of the number of Byzantine Christians in Turkey and the other dominantly Muslim countries in the region over the last few decades. Furthermore, long secular Turkey seems under the present administration of Recep Tayyip Erdoğan to be turning towards Islam, although his party's recent loss of its majority in the Turkish parliament may change all that. Turkish *laiklik* (a word derived from the French *laicité*) seems mainly to have been a phenomenon of Istanbul, Ankara and a few other urban centers.

In the late 1960s and early 1970s there was an increasing willingness on the part of several leading hierarchs of the Byzantine Orthodox tradition to engage in interreligious dialogue with their Muslim neighbors and fellow citizens. The exemplarity of Catholic engagement in dialogue with Muslims had struck a responsive chord in the intellectual leadership of the Byzantine Orthodox Churches. Much of that has changed more recently. The events in Syria and Iraq over the past five years, on top of the vivid memory of the Lebanese civil war (1975–90), have dampened enthusiasm for such dialogue considerably. The attacks on all Christians and other religious minorities (for instance, Yazidis, Isma'ilis, Mandaeans) in contemporary Syria and Iraq as well as the emigration of Christians from Israel and Palestine in recent decades, has considerably reduced the number of Christians in the Middle East, including the Byzantine Orthodox. In the earlier era of more openness to interreligious dialogue on the part of Byzantine Orthodox thinkers, two of the leading spokesmen for this trend were Anastasios Yannoulatos (1929–), now Byzantine Orthodox Archbishop of Albania, and Metropolitan Georges Khodr (1922–) of Lebanon. Both of these hierarchs are still alive, but quite elderly. Neither can be understood outside his historical and political context.

Archbishop Anastasios claims that his own views of other religions reflect the tradition of Christian openness to elements of Hellenistic and Roman religious traditions on the part of Christian authors in the first three centuries of Christian history. He contrasts this with the narrower theological attitudes that prevailed with the establishment of the Church in the Roman Empire after the era of Constantine or the even more reactionary theologies formulated by Christian writers after the rise of Islam. "In an eschatological perspective," Anastasios writes, "the appearance of Islam looked [to Byzantine Christians in the seventh century] like the beginning of the great final struggle as described by John the Evangelist in Revelation."[14] Recall the aside of Sophronius (see above, n. 9) when he served as Jerusalem tour guide for the caliph 'Umar.

Archbishop Anastasios in 1996 made much of the shared living situation of Byzantine Orthodox Christians and Muslims in the Middle East as a major factor predisposing the Orthodox towards a more positive evaluation of Islam.

> It is obvious that the cultural tradition and heritage of the Christians of the East bring them much closer to the Muslim world, with whom they have coexisted for many centuries. In spite of deep theological differences and our dramatic conflicts in the past, there is a move from many sides toward one common cultural ground.

That was written nineteen years ago; the situation of the Byzantine Orthodox in much of the Middle East today is very different, and coexistence with Muslims has become highly problematic.

Metropolitan Georges Khodr [Khidr] of Lebanon, the bishop of Mount Lebanon for the Orthodox Antiochian Church, likewise thinks that the attitudes of John of Damascus towards Islam do not provide a model for modern Orthodox theologians trying to make theological sense of the challenge posed by other religions, and especially by Islam. In 1971, a much more optimistic time in Lebanon than today, Khodr wrote: "What I should like to emphasize here is that this linear view of history is bound up with a monolithic ecclesiological approach . . . . It comes to this: contemporary theology must go beyond the notion of 'salvation history' in order to rediscover

---

[14] Yannoulatos as quoted in Sharp, 56.

the meaning of the *oikonomia*."[15] What did Khodr mean in 1971 by this reference to *oikonomia?* Andrew Sharp understands this word in terms of the separate processions of the Son and the Spirit from the Father in Byzantine Orthodox theology. For Metropolitan Georges Khodr this means that both the work of Christ and the work of the Spirit need to be recognized in evaluating non-Christian religious traditions, including Islam. He quotes Khodr's reflections written in 1980 on Clement of Alexandria's positive evaluation of non-Christian faith traditions. "In the thought of Clement of Alexandria, the divine Word speaks in the entire world, and God justifies mankind through numerous salvation paths. God is not only the God of Israel. He is also the savior of the world, and appears to be engaged throughout the world by means of multiple faces of his wisdom."[16] When it comes precisely to a Byzantine Orthodox evaluation of Islam, Khodr was very positive in an article he also wrote a long time ago (1969): "For those who believe in Jesus as God and Savior, the Abrahamic line is like a providential, mysterious path, going from the father of believers [Abraham] to the Arab prophet [Muhammad]." Khodr at that time even glossed over the vast differences between the New Testament and Quranic portrayals of Jesus, claiming that Muhammad is "one who brings forth [Jesus'] message."[17]

In the same year Metropolitan Georges made some statements that he may have thought irenic, but which Muslims would find the very opposite. In a moment of enthusiasm for Muslim-Christian mutual understanding that predates the Lebanese civil war by four years, Metropolitan Georges once wrote, "what really matters most for us [Orthodox Christians] is the search for the traces of Christ in the Koran [sic] as well as in the tradition of Islam, specifically within the Sufi [Islamic mystical] heritage . . . The Koran is Trinitarian rather than anti-Trinitarian."[18] Statements like these can end all possibility

---

[15] Khodr as quoted in Sharp, 58.
[16] Khodr as quoted in Sharp, 61.
[17] Khodr as quoted in Sharp, 73.
[18] Khodr as quoted in Sharp, 100.

of dialogue with Muslims, who do not want Christians to impose our ideas of Christ and the Trinity on the Qur'an or anything else Islamic.

Alas, the fairly general anti-mystical bias of most educated modern Muslims who live in the Muslim world today also finds reflections like these irenic words of Metropolitan Georges Khodr hard to swallow, although Muslims like the late Abdelwahab Meddeb (d. 2014), an intellectual based in Paris, found the Sufi tradition more acceptable as a presentation of Islam than the fulminations of Islamists like the late Sayyid Qutb (d. 1966) or the endlessly windy homilies of Sayyid Abu'l-A'la Mawdudi (d. 1979).[19] The writings of these two Muslim rigorists are entirely too available on the internet. The experience of the Lebanese civil war has cooled Metropolitan Georges' enthusiasm for such a meliorative approach to Islam and especially Islamic politics.

In a book published by the Center for Strategic Studies, Research and Documentation in Beirut in the mid-1990s, *Christian-Muslim Relations: an authoritative reading of history, the present and the future*, Metropolitan Georges Khodr makes it very clear that "free discussion between Christians and Muslims will not be possible until Islamic countries reach a degree of economic prosperity and intellectual creativity similar to that in the West." Metropolitan Georges also goes on to state quite clearly that

> he has no interest in discussing the elements of Islamic rule but he would like to be assured that there be no application of *hudud* punishments [caning, hand amputations, etc.] to non-Christians, no *jizyah* [taxes on non-Muslims] or the like, and that Islamists not arrive at power by violence. Nor does he accept arguments about *tahrif* [the Muslim charge that the Jewish and Christian scriptures have been distorted to hide the Islamic truth] and Christian belief because the Quran says so. The Muslims have to start applying textual criticism.[20]

---

[19] See Abdelwahab Meddeb, *Islam and the Challenge of Civilization*, trans. Jane Kuntz (New York: Fordham University Press, 2013) esp. 13–37.

[20] See John Donohue, S.J., "Dialogue in Lebanon," in *Muslim-Christian Relations: Dialogue in Lebanon* (Washington, DC: Georgetown University, Center for Muslim-Christian Understanding, 1996). Father Donohue made available to me an electronic copy of this article. The passages quoted, summarizing the

For all Christians, but especially for the Christians of the Middle East, Islam as a post-Christian religious development poses very different questions and calls for an evaluation very different from the way Christians may evaluate the religious traditions of Hindus, Buddhists and African Traditionalists. Some of the earlier cited words of Archbishop Anastasios and Metropolitan Georges sound very dated in view of the tragedies that have overwhelmed all the Christian communities in Iraq, Syria and Egypt in the last two years. The joint declaration issued by Ecumenical Patriarch Bartholomew and Pope Francis, at the end of the Pope's visit to the Phanar in Istanbul on November 30, 2014, deserves reflection here and now by all Christians:

> We express our common concern for the current situation in Iraq, Syria and the whole Middle East. We are united in the desire for peace and stability and in the will to promote the resolution of conflicts through dialogue and reconciliation. While recognizing the efforts already being made to offer assistance to the region, at the same time, we call on all those who bear responsibility for the destiny of peoples to deepen their commitment to suffering communities, and to enable them, including the Christian ones, to remain in their native land. We cannot resign ourselves to a Middle East without Christians, who have professed the name of Jesus there for two thousand years. Many of our brothers and sisters are being persecuted and have been forced violently from their homes. It even seems that the value of human life has been lost, that the human person no longer matters and may be sacrificed to other interests. And, tragically, all this is met by the indifference of many. As Saint Paul reminds us, "If one member suffers, all suffer together; if one member is honoured, all rejoice together" (1 *Cor* 12:26). This is the law of the Christian life, and in this sense we can say that there is also an ecumenism of suffering. Just as the blood of the martyrs was a seed of strength and fertility for the Church, so too the sharing of daily sufferings can become an effective instrument of unity. The terrible situation of Christians and all those who are suffering in the Middle East calls not only for our constant prayer, but also for an appropriate response on the part of the international community.

Arabic text of Khodr, are found on pages 9 and 10.

The grave challenges facing the world in the present situation require the solidarity of all people of good will, and so we also recognize the importance of promoting a constructive dialogue with Islam based on mutual respect and friendship. Inspired by common values and strengthened by genuine fraternal sentiments, Muslims and Christians are called to work together for the sake of justice, peace and respect for the dignity and rights of every person, especially in those regions where they once lived for centuries in peaceful coexistence and now tragically suffer together the horrors of war. Moreover, as Christian leaders, we call on all religious leaders to pursue and to strengthen interreligious dialogue and to make every effort to build a culture of peace and solidarity between persons and between peoples.[21]

On this melancholy note I conclude this section on Byzantine Orthodox thinking and feeling about Islam over the past century.

Protestant Attitudes towards Islam, 1915–2015

The first reality that must be kept in mind with regard to Protestant Christianity, at least in its sixteenth-century Lutheran and Calvinist beginnings, is that Protestants for the first two centuries of their history did not engage in missionary work outside the already Christian world. Kenneth Scott Latourette enumerates six causes for this phenomenon, which can be boiled down to five: (1) Protestants were busy staking claims to already Catholic areas of Europe and working out the differences between themselves and Catholics and between various groups of Protestants, sometimes in the theological forum and sometimes on the battle field; (2) Only the original Apostles, according to Luther, were commanded to preach the Gospel to every creature, and that had already been done; (3) Unlike the Spanish *Padronado* and the Portuguese *Padroado*, the Protestant monarchies of the sixteenth century showed no interest in spreading their own versions of Christianity beyond their home territories: *cujus regio ejus religio*; (4) Celibate religious men and

---

[21] Available online at www.vatican.va

women could more easily uproot themselves and travel over land and sea to foreign missions; the married Protestant clergy proved less mobile, given the rough nature of sea travel until the eighteenth century.[22] Furthermore, there was no central body like the papacy and its Sacred Congregation for the Propagation of the Faith (founded in 1622) for mandating such missions; (5) The neighbors of Protestant states in the sixteenth century were either other Protestant states or Catholic states; the expansionist Portuguese, Spanish and French states had reached the outer frontiers of Christendom and knew non-Christians as neighbors or even as enemies; the dramatic rise of the Dutch and the English as sea powers came later than the sixteenth century. Latourette does not mention it, but there were early Protestants who interpreted Romans 1:21–23[23] to mean that any people who "worshiped idols" or revered images (Catholics, Hindus, Jains, Native Americans, Africans, Buddhists) obviously had lapsed from the pure monotheism and Christianity the apostles had taught them and deserved no further evangelization.

Protestants began to take an interest in missionary endeavor when 17th-century Moravian Pietism, displaced to Germany from what is now the Czech Republic, began to affect Protestants in Germany, Denmark, and then more broadly. The greatest era of Protestant missionary work was the 19th century but continuing on through the early 20th century. During that time period, and especially towards the end of the 19th century, several Protestant attempts were made to evangelize Muslims or, at least, to preach the Gospel in Muslim settings. Nothing much came of these endeavors, at least as far as the

---

[22] Kenneth Scott Latourette, *A History of the Expansion of Christianity*, III: *Three Centruies of Advance A.D. 1500–A.D. 1800* (New York, Evanston and London: Harper & Row, 1939) 25–27.

[23] "Ever since the creation of the world his eternal power and divine nature, invisible though they are, have been understood and seen through the things he has made. So they are without excuse; [21]for though they knew God, they did not honor him as God or give thanks to him, but they became futile in their thinking, and their senseless minds were darkened. [22]Claiming to be wise, they became fools; [23]and they exchanged the glory of the immortal God for images resembling a mortal human being or birds or four-footed animals or reptiles."

Middle East was concerned. There are, however, not a few families in Nigeria's Middle Belt and the southwest of the country where the Christian descendants of Muslims still bear distinctly Muslim names, the result of Muslim conversions to Christianity, especially in the 20th century.

What is now the American University of Beirut (AUB) started its history in 1866 as the Syrian Protestant College; from the beginning it was not exactly an instrument for evangelizing Muslims or anyone else, even though its first president, Daniel Bliss, had originally come to what used to be called Greater Syria as a missionary. (The foundation that became the Jesuits' Université Saint-Joseph moved from a small town in Lebanon to Beirut a few years later, opening in 1875; competition with the Presbyterians seems to have played a role in that move.) The American University of Cairo (AUC) also owes its 1919 origins to Presbyterian missionaries who had come to Egypt in the mid-19th century and converted very few Muslims but did manage to persuade some Copts, Greek Orthodox, Armenians and other Middle East Christians to become Presbyterians. Some of the elite children of these Middle Eastern Protestant converts eventually converted to atheism, like the late Palestinian scholar Edward Said.

Perhaps the most famous American Protestant missionary to the Muslims of the Arab Middle East was Samuel Marinus Zwemer (1867–1952). The son of a Reformed Church pastor and the brother of four others, Zwemer went in 1890 without Reformed Church authorization to take up the cause of preaching Protestant Christianity to Muslims in the area of Basra (now in Iraq) and in Bahrein off the coast of the eastern Arabian peninsula; eventually the Reformed Church in America recognized his work and incorporated Zwemer and his few converts in 1894 into the Reformed Church of America. After 15 years in those central Arab lands, Zwemer returned to the United States, but in 1912 he went to Cairo where he spent another 17 years working under the sponsorship of the United Presbyterian Mission in Egypt, the missionary body that founded the American University in Cairo. Returning to the United States again in 1929, Zwemer became a professor of the history of religion and Christian missions at Princeton Theological Seminary, a post from which he retired in 1937. The founding editor of the journal now called *The Muslim World*, Zwemer published voluminously, always on the themes connected with the evangelization of the Muslim world. It is estimated, however, that he made less than a dozen converts from Islam to Christianity throughout all the years of his missionary career.[24]

Muslims today constantly return to the theme of the closeness of Christian missionary work in Muslim countries to colonial rule. (I know of one Nigerian Muslim who wrote in Arabic and always referred to missionaries in nineteenth-century Nigerian history as *salibiyyun*, "Crusaders," even when the missionaries involved were returned freedmen coming to Nigeria from Sierra Leone.[25]) Zwemer freely admitted the connection of Christian evangelization with colonialism. Speaking at a conference on Islam and missions held at Lucknow in India in 1911, but referring back to an earlier conference held in Cairo in 1905, Zwemer praised colonialism in the Muslim world as an example of God's providence:

> The statement was made at the Cairo Conference that the present political division of the Mohammedan world is a startling evidence of the finger of God in history and a challenge to faith because it indicates how many of the doors in Moslem lands are wide open. Three fourths of the Moslem world were then considered accessible to mission, and the late Dr. Jessup, speaking on this challenge of open doors, said, "It is a fact not to be ignored or lightly regarded that almost the only really open doors to reach Islam are in countries where Moslems are under Christian or non-Moslem rule. . ."[26]

[24] On the life and career of Zwemer, see Ruth A. Tucker, *From Jerusalem to Irian Jaya: A Biographical History of Christian Missions*, 2nd ed. (Grand Rapids, MI: Zondervan, 2004) 238–42.

[25] The Muslim involved was the late Adam 'Abd Allah al-Iluri (1917-92), writing in his book *Al-Islam fi-Naijiriya*, 2nd ed. (Beirut: Dar al-'Arabiyya, 1971) 148.

[26] Samuel M. Zwemer, "An Introductory Survey," in *Islam and the Missions: being papers read at the second Missionary conference on behalf of the Mohammedan world at Lucknow, January 23–28, 1911*, ed. Edward M. Wherry, Samuel M. Zwemer and Clarence G. Mylrea (New York: Fleming H. Revell Company, 1911) 22.

The founding president of American University of Cairo, Dr. Charles A. Watson, headed the institution for the first 27 years of its existence, 1919–1946. Two years after the opening of AUC—and still seven years before a first university degree would be granted—AUC opened its School of Oriental Studies. In 1958, twelve years after the completion of the presidency of Watson, and six years after the 23 July Egyptian Revolution led by the Free Officers (especially Naguib and Nasser), that School of Oriental Studies became the Center for Arabic Studies in AUC's Faculty of Arts. It has provided an excellent place for non-Arabs to learn Arabic in a fairly secularized setting, but in its origins it was much more oriented towards the linguistic training of Protestant missionaries for the Muslim world.

In the aftermath of World War I and the French and English colonization of Syria, Lebanon, Iraq and Jordan, some prominent Protestants started to think that the post-Ottoman Muslim communities in the Middle East were ripe for evangelization. In a 1920 volume that was a joint production of a group of Protestants called "The Committee on the War and the Religious Outlook," sentiments are expressed about the weakening of Islam as a result of the World War I defeat of the Ottoman Empire that can only serve to confirm the suspicions of Muslims in many parts of the world down to today that Christian missionaries are nothing but *Salibiyyun*, Crusaders. The book admits the fact that "followers of the ruthless Prophet of Arabia have, however, been found on both sides of the world conflict."[27] The Arabs organized by T. E. Lawrence to fight the Ottomans get at least that much recognition.

In Chapter XII of this book the authors gloat over the fact that the Germans did not succeed in their hope to "unite in one mass all the peoples of Islam and to use them as a decisive force."[28] They do recognize, however, that in Egypt "the movement which called itself nationalistic was much more Moslem than Egyptian. That was

---

[27] *The Missionary Outlook in the Light of the War* (New York: Association Press, 1920) 64.
[28] *Missionary Outlook* 139.

in great part caused by the opposition to the Christian overlordship of Great Britain. But the endeavor of Pan-Islamism, powerfully backed by German propaganda, was to stimulate again into political reality the old unified Islam. We all know how that failed."[29]

In a very brief review of this book in *The Jewish Tribune* (July 30, 1920) that I found pasted inside the front cover of the copy of this book I obtained by inter-library loan from Yeshiva University in New York City, a very apt judgment is made by the anonymous Jewish reviewer commenting on Protestant missionary medical work in the non-Christian world :

> Making the sick comfortable and at the same time endeavoring to convert them to a new religion spells a heartless benevolence. It does not mean help to the needy because they need it, but . . . utilizing their wretched situation for breaking their religious conscience and thus estranging them from their relatives and friends.

This post-World War I American-issued missionary volume was followed up in 1921 by a British volume giving an overview of the more general world to be evangelized; this volume, in an appendix on Islam by Duncan Black Macdonald, expresses a more learned and sympathetic view of the Muslim world, but still from a missionary perspective: The missionary to the Muslim world, Macdonald writes, must avoid becoming a "completely orientalized westerner" and yet "his success as a missionary will be largely in proportion as he solves the paradox of how to sink himself sympathetically in Muslim ideas and usages and yet retain the power of looking at them from the outside as an educated Christian of the twentieth century."[30]

The career of one prominent Protestant scholar of Islam in the twentieth century, who came to AUC in 1921 and left there in 1938 to become a professor at Columbia University in New York City, says

---

[29] *Missionary Outlook* 139.

[30] Duncan B. Macdonald, D.D., "Appendix V: The Study of Islam," in *An Introduction to Missionary Service*, ed. Georgina A. Gollock and Elizabeth G. K. Hewat, M.A., et al. (London: Humphrey Milford/Oxford University Press, 1921) 141.

a great deal about earlier Protestant ways of thinking and feeling about Islam. Arthur Jeffery, Australian-born (1892) and a Methodist minister and missionary with experience in the Solomon Islands and India, brought his extraordinary linguistic abilities with him from south India to AUC when he was 29 years of age. Previously he had pursued academic degrees in Australia and had been rejected for military service during World War I, apparently on health grounds. He worked for five years at Madras Christian College in what is now Chennai, the capital of Tamil Nadu State, India, and it is said that during those five years he mastered several Indian languages.

It was probably in Cairo after 1921 that Jeffery developed most of his expertise in Arabic. He was considered, from the time of his arrival at the newly founded School of Oriental Studies at AUC, the academic star of that School, precisely because of his extraordinary linguistic abilities.[31] In a 1960 tribute to Jeffery written after his death, John S. Badeau, a former colleague in Jeffery's last years at the American University of Cairo,[32] mentioned that Jeffery was originally reluctant to go Egypt in 1921 because, in Jeffrey's own estimation, he "was not yet a qualified Arabic scholar and had only a working knowledge of some half dozen languages."[33] Needless to say, Jeffery made up for whatever deficiencies once existed in his knowledge of Arabic over the next seventeen years. Badeau, himself an ordained Presbyterian minister and Arabist, underlines in his posthumous tribute the missionary side of Jeffery's work in Cairo; it seems mainly to have been of an academic nature:

> As a minister of the Methodist Church, he was devoted to the missionary enterprise and exemplified in his own life and interests

[31] See Lawrence R. Murphy, *The American University in Cairo: 1919–1987* (Cairo: American University of Cairo Press, 1987) 34.

[32] Badeau was a professor (1936–38), Dean of the Faculty (1938–45) and then President of the American University of Cairo (1945–53). The Kennedy administration appointed him to be the U.S. ambassador in Cairo (1961–64); subsequently he was director of the Middle East Institute at Columbia University (1964–71), and, after his retirement, a professorial lecturer at Georgetown (1971–74).

[33] See "Arthur Jeffery—A Tribute," *The Muslim World* 50 (January 1960) 49–51.

a deep Christian concern. His scholarship had a Christian purpose, for he believed that only by painstaking and exacting study of Islamic materials could the content of that faith be understood and a Christian contribution be made to those who followed it.[34]

Jeffery, after a one-semester visiting appointment at Columbia and Union Theological Seminary in the spring of 1937, resigned from his position in Cairo that fall and returned to Columbia to teach Arabic and Islamic Studies in February 1938. Badeau, in an oral history recorded when he was in his mid-seventies (later edited and published as a book in 1983) suggests that Jeffery wanted to leave Cairo in 1938 because his work on variant readings of the text of the Qur'an was provoking Muslim antagonism to him.[35] But it is at least as likely that his American wife, the gathering storm of war in Europe, the instability of the late years of the Egyptian monarchy and the prestige of an appointment at Columbia all contributed to Jeffery's academic move.

No one can mistake the fact that the scholarly writing on Islam by Arthur Jeffery emanates from the pen of a non-Muslim. His major original editorial work, *Materials for the History of the Text of the Qur'an*, is a study of some of the old codices of the Qur'an and the textual variants found therein. Some Muslims take this sort of scholarly work as an attack on the Qur'an, but scholarship of this sort simply recognizes, as not a few medieval and earlier Muslim scholars had always recognized, that there were variant readings of the text of the Qur'an (the *qirā'āt*), and that most of these variants are

---

[34] Ibid.

[35] John Badeau, *The Middle East Remembered* (Washington: Middle East Institute, 1983) 72–73. Later in the same memoir Badeau mentions that "Arthur Jeffery . . . a fine Islamicist . . . would fulminate against the modern Muslim—that isn't Islam at all he would say" (248). Murphy in his history of the American University of Cairo (note 31 above) notes that "Jeffery was criticized for examining Koran texts. As a result of these and other reports—some true, many exaggerated, others fabricated—a growing number of Egyptians no doubt became convinced that the American University of Cairo had attacked Islam" (65).

insignificant.[36] In *Materials* Jeffery works principally from the *Kitab al-masahif* of Ibn Abi Dawud al-Sijistani (d. 929)[37] but he also looks at variant readings in the works of other scholars that were not found in the text authorized by the caliph 'Uthman in the middle of the seventh century.

Materials begins with a preface in which Jeffery frankly admits that his scholarly work had offended Muslim collaborators. "The assistance of Muslim savants in this matter was not very helpful," he writes. "Invariably these savants took the position that the 'Uthmanic text is perfect and unchallengeable."[38] On the contrary, Jeffery insists that "the text which 'Uthman canonized was only one out of many rival texts" and "there is grave suspicion that 'Uthman may have seriously edited the text."[39] The hermeneutics of suspicion is not confined to Marx, Nietzsche and Freud, and some Shi'ite sources have harbored the same suspicions of 'Uthman's text. Nevertheless, Jeffery completes his Preface with acknowledgement of the cooperation of two Muslim scholars, quaintly called "Oriental savants": the first is a Tartar named Musa Jarullah Rostovdani of Kazan, and the second an Egyptian, Shaikh Sayyid Nawwar of Cairo. They had both read all the variant texts with him, Jeffery writes, "and taught me many things that a Christian can hardly learn for himself."[40]

Arthur Jeffery, dead since 1959, might be somewhat surprised, if he came back from the grave, to find out how his scholarly writing has fared on the internet over the past decade or so. Online Islam-haters have posted articles written by Jeffery nearly ninety years ago to support their high-decibel diatribes against Islam. At times the headlines labeling these articles have little or nothing to do with the

---

[36] See Rudi Paret, "Kira'a," *The Encyclopaedia of Islam (New Edition)* 5:127a–129a.

[37] *Materials for the History of the Text of the Qur'an*, ed. Arthur Jeffery (Leiden: Brill, 1937) 10–13.

[38] *Materials* viii–ix.

[39] *Materials* ix–x.

[40] *Materials* x.

attached writings of Jeffery.[41] Online Muslim apologists, on the other hand, have with equal vehemence leveled internet attacks on Jeffery's writings on the internet.[42] There is no doubt that much of Jeffery's Qur'an scholarship—not very different from certain types of textual and historical-critical Jewish and Christian scholarly work on biblical materials in his time—is difficult for devout Muslims to accept, and there is a definite edge to much of Jeffrey's scholarly writing that betrays some hostility to Islam. But there are Muslims like the late Algerian scholar, Muhammad Arkoun (d. 2010), who have called for an Islamic scripture scholarship parallel to the scripture scholarship done by Jews and Christians with the Hebrew Bible and the New Testament.[43] It may be expected that a new generation of Muslim scholars will eventually take up the challenge of textual and historical-critical Quranic studies, although the experience of Nasr Abu Zayd (d. 2010)[44] at Cairo University in the 1990s, together with the current political mood in Egypt and elsewhere in the Islamic world, does not bode well for such a development.

The World Council of Churches (WCC), founded in 1948, has been in dialogue with various interlocutors from the Muslim world since at least 1979 when it issued its "Guidelines on Dialogue with People of Living Faiths." A significant number of WCC statements have been issued on Islam over the years since then. A document entitled "Issues in Christian-Muslim Relations," published on 1 January 1992, has many sage and yet charitable things to say about

[41] See "Islam Is Repackaged Polytheism: Documentation," available at www.bible.ca/islam/library/Jeffery/historical_mhd.htm. The article that appears under this headline is a 1926 survey by Jeffery of biographies of Muhammad that has nothing to do with the repackaging of polytheism, although the article is very critical of what can be known historically about Muhammad.

[42] For example, see Sam Zaatari, "Rebuttal to Arthur Jeffreys's [sic] book: The foreign vocabulary of the Qur'an," available at www.answering-christianity.com

[43] *Rethinking Islam: Common Questions, Uncommon Answers*, trans. and ed. Robert D. Lee (Boulder, CO: Westview Press, 1994) 35–40.

[44] See Nasr Hamid Abu Zayd, with Esther R. Nelson, *Voices of an Exile: Reflections on Islam* (Westport, CT and London: Praeger, 2004). Of interest also is Abu Zayd's *Reformation of Islamic Thought: A Critical Historical Analysis* (Amsterdam: Amsterdam University Press, 2006) esp. 53–59.

Islam in past history and in the modern world. A short excerpt may serve to conclude this section on Protestant attitudes towards Islam, with the proviso understood that Protestant churches that do not subscribe to the WCC would not find these irenic but realistic words to their liking:

> There are many points of convergence between Christian and Islamic beliefs—both understand God as Creator and Sustainer, as Just and Merciful, as a God who reveals His word and who will call people to account for their stewardship over creation. Both communities of faith stress the centrality of prayer, and share common values and ideals such as the search for justice in society, providing for people in need, love for one's neighbour and living together in peace. Both Muslims and Christians often fail to recognize these points of convergence because they tend to see themselves in terms of the ideal and the other in terms of the actual.
>
> However, there are also real and substantial differences between Christian and Islamic teaching—many of which stem directly or indirectly from our respective scriptures. For example, Muslims often identify Christian belief in the Trinity with Tritheism. Muslims affirm that God does not beget and therefore condemn Christian belief in Jesus' divine Sonship. While the Qur'an represents Jesus as one of the greatest and, in some respects, unique among God's messengers, it denies his crucifixion and resurrection. Numerous passages warn against such teachings which are seen as compromising God's Unity (*tawhid*); many of these are in fact addressed to Arabian polytheists and pseudo-Christian sects. Conversely, since the gospel chronologically preceded the Qur'an, Christians have difficulty in dealing with Islam's claim to be a divinely revealed religion. While in Christian faith God has revealed himself definitively in Christ, in Islam God's complete and final revelation is given in the Qur'an. This can be problematical in the conduct of Christian-Muslim dialogue, especially since many Muslims hold that Christians altered their scripture in order to justify Trinitarian doctrine and Jesus' divine Sonship.
>
> Given these and other differences, it is essential for the continuing improvement of relations that both Christians and Muslims make greater efforts to learn more about each other's faith.
>
> It is worth recognizing that a number of churches and theological institutions have taken the initiative of promoting objective knowledge

about Islam. We also recognize that a number of similar efforts have recently been made in some Muslim institutions. We are aware of the difficulties but we call for greater efforts on both sides to ensure that each faith is presented on its own terms.[45]

A Concluding Reflection

I am a historian of religion rather than a theologian, strictly speaking, but I would like to end with a few animadversions that verge, however briefly, on a theology of religions. I find myself very uncomfortable with the stress made on Pneumatology rather than Christology by some Christian theologians wishing to take a more positive attitude towards Islam than has been taken by Christian theologians in times past. Whatever some Christian theologians with an interest in Islam have been saying about the distinct and separate processions of the Son and the Spirit from the Father, the unity of God is too central a theme in both Christianity and Islam for either faith tradition to ignore or minimize.

The Christology of Islam hardly seems adequate to mainstream Christians, even if there have been some theologians who have suggested otherwise, such as the late John Hick (1922–2012). A former member of the United Reformed Church in Great Britain who died a Quaker, Hick came for a visit to the University of Ghana in 1977 while I was teaching there. He gave a presentation before an assembly made up largely of African Protestants involved in Christian-Muslim dialogue and encounter throughout the continent. Hick maintained, in his keynote lecture at that conference, that we Christians could get on much better with Muslims if we only lowered our Christological claims. His lecture sounded like an advertisement for the book he had just edited and published in 1977, *The Myth of God Incarnate.*

[45] This lengthy WCC statement is available online in its full form at www.oikoumene.org/en/resources/documents/wcc-programmes/interreligious-dialogue

Some people in Hick's audience thought otherwise. One very tall Sudanese Lutheran at the conference raised his long arm to ask Hick, in view of the fact that Muslims already accuse Christians of corrupting (*tahrif*) the Scriptures to make Jesus divine, whether we will now have to change the Scriptures again to make Jesus non-divine so that we can get along better with Muslims. Hick smiled vacantly at what he obviously thought the theological naiveté of the Sudanese Lutheran.

As the conversation continued I gradually began to realize that Hick was only slightly acquainted with the Qur'an. He was under the mistaken impression, for instance, that Jesus, among all the prophets, was mentioned the most in the Qur'an. Moses, in fact, is mentioned by name more often and many more verses concern Abraham, a former idol-maker turned idol-smasher. According to the Qur'an Abraham sacrificed Hagar like a scapegoat and was also willing to sacrifice his first son, not named in the Qur'an but understood by all Muslims to be Ishmael. Abraham's two sacrifices are central to the highpoint of Muslim ritual life, the annual *hajj,* where both the plight of Hagar and the near sacrifice of Ishmael are commemorated.

I am not surprised that John Hick died a Quaker. Silence about Christ and God might be the only solution for one whose Christian faith was so shaken. I remember with particular poignancy a luncheon for him and his wife, Hazel (something of a Marxist), that I hosted one afternoon at the University of Ghana that summer of 1977. While we were dining, the son of John and Hazel Hick arrived to join us. He had just spent much of the morning visiting Pentecostal churches in Accra, about which he gave a most enthusiastic report. The son's personal Pentecostal spirituality and the theology that underlay it obviously made his parents uncomfortable, but it was so much better than the drugs the youth had abused for some years that his parents listened appreciatively to his report.

I liked and felt great sympathy for John and Hazel Hick as devoted parents of a disturbed young man possibly on the road to recovery through a simple faith, and I remember that afternoon fondly. Hazel died in 1996 and John in 2012. May they rest in peace.

Patrick J. Ryan, S.J., the Laurence J. McGinley Professor of Religion and Society at Fordham University, previously lived and worked in Nigeria and Ghana for 26 years. His Ph.D. is from Harvard in the comparative history of religion, specializing in Arabic and Islamic Studies.

List of Participants

1. AMBROS, Pavel   (BOH)
2. ANTONIO, Natnael Samson   (AOR)
3. AUGUSTYNIAK, Krzysztof   (PMA)
4. DALY, Robert   (UNE)
5. FARRUGIA, Edward   (MAL)
6. GAMBERINI, Paolo   (ITA)
7. HEIDING, Fredrik   (GER)
8. HOWELL, Patrick   (ORE)
9. KUNNAPPALLY, Sunny Th.   (KER)
10. LLYWELYN, Dorian   (CFN)
11. MECHERRY, Antony   (KER)
12. PRAKASH, Cedric   (GUJ)
13. RABESON, Jocelyn   (MDG)
14. RAUSCH, Thomas   (CFN)
15. RYAN, Patrick   (UNE)
16. SACHS, Randy   (UNE)
17. SAJGÓ, Scabolcs   (HUN)
18. SCHMIDT, Markus   (ASR)
19. SEXTON, Peter   (HIB)
20. SICKING, Thom   (PRO)
21. SORENG, Xavier   (RAN)
22. STUYT, Jan   (NER)
23. XALXO, Pius   (RAN)